THE PEDAGOGY OF THE HOLY SPIRIT ACCORDING TO EARLY CHRISTIAN TRADITION

Jackie David Johns

PROLOG

This volume contains a doctoral dissertation completed at the Southern Baptist Theological Seminary in Louisville, Kentucky in 1987. Other than this Prolog and the Epilog, this edition of the dissertation reproduces the original without alterations except for changes in formatting and corrections of typographical errors.

TABLE OF CONTENTS

TABLE OF ABBREVIATIONS

ACW   Ancient Christian Writers

ANF   Ante-Nicene Fathers

LXX   Septuagint

NAS   New American Standard

NIDNTT   New International Dictionary of New Testament Theology

TDNT   Theological Dictionary of the New Testament

ZPEB   The Zondervan Pictorial Encyclopedia of the Bible

PREFACE

The completion of a dissertation requires the focused efforts of an individual who has benefited from the expertise and insights of many others. The inspiration and motivation to pursue the specific areas of study reflected in this project were largely the products of the modeling of the quest for the foundations of Christian education by others. Professors Martin Baldree of Lee College, Lois LeBar (retired) of the Graduate School of Wheaton College, and Findley B. Edge (retired) of The Southern Baptist Theological Seminary were especially significant. Recognition must also be given to the Committee of Instruction which provided the needed oversight of this project. Professor William Rogers, who served as chairman of the committee, provided exemplary support and guidance. Professor R. Alan Culpepper and Professor Daniel Aleshire graciously served on the committee and contributed insightful suggestions from their respective fields of scholarship. The committee's guidance was especially meaningful because the entire project was completed in absentia which placed an added burden on the process.

The contributions by my wife, Cheryl, to the development of this project were beyond measure. Ours has been a shared journey. In the midst of her own research and writing of a dissertation, she has been a friend, a wife, a helper, a peer, and a guide. She has spent many hours listening to me share new insights and frustrations. My oldest daughter, Alethea, has been a gracious young lady who empathetically understood the pressures and gently encouraged and prodded me in times of despair. My other daughter, Karisa, was born during the research stage of this project and reintroduced me to the joys and challenges of life while modeling a determined spirit. Nelda George, who typed my dissertation, has been efficient, compassionate, and understanding, proving herself to be a true friend. Lastly, recognition must be given to Janice Hood, a partner in ministry, who has assisted greatly in my professional responsibilities during the time of this project.

Chapter 1

INTRODUCTION

Early Christian literature reveals that the church perceived its teaching ministry, indeed its entire existence, as being under the close supervision of the Holy Spirit.[1] According to the Johannine tradition Jesus instructed his disciples that the Spirit would be their post-ascension teacher. The Lukan and Pauline traditions also point to a common belief in an active, pedagogical presence of the Spirit of God in the life of the church. Further, an instructional imagery continued to be applied to the Spirit throughout the patristic period.[2]

However, within the field of Christian education little attention has been given to the role of the Holy Spirit in church pedagogy. Only two works have been dedicated to that purpose.[3] The methods and scopes of those works granted only limited consideration to early Christian understandings of the place of the Spirit in Christian instruction. The purpose of this dissertation is to set forth a descriptive study of the pedagogy of the Holy Spirit according to early Christian tradition and to construct a paradigm for Christian education based upon that study.

STATEMENT OF THE PROBLEM

The problem addressed by this study is the need for a comprehensive attempt from within the field of Christian education to understand and draw implications from early Christianity's perception of the Holy Spirit as an

---

[1] "No more certain statement can be made about the Christians of the first generation than this: they believed themselves to be living under the immediate government of the Spirit of God." Charles Kingsley Barrett, *The Holy Spirit and the Gospel Tradition* (London: S.P.C.K., 1966), p. 1.

[2] Examples of the Johannine, Lukan, Pauline, and patristic use of pedagogical imagery for the Holy Spirit will be cited in this chapter. The nature of those and other references will constitute the bulk of this project.

[3] Rachel Henderlite, *The Holy Spirit in Christian Education* (Philadelphia: Westminster Press, 1964); Roy B. Zuck, *The Holy Spirit in Your Teaching* (Chicago: Scripture Press, 1963).

agent of pedagogy. The need for this study can be viewed from two perspectives. First, from the perspective of early Christian literature, a tradition of pedagogical imagery for the Holy Spirit clearly existed among Christians of the first centuries which has been largely unexplored by modern scholarship. Second, from the perspective of Christian education as a field of study, representatives of the field have long established the need to link Christian education theory and practice to historical and theological foundations but have given only limited consideration to the role of the Holy Spirit in Christian education.

THE PERSPECTIVE OF EARLY CHRISTIAN LITERATURE

Early Christian literature contains numerous references to the Holy Spirit which have explicit pedagogical imagery. In the writings of the New Testament a pedagogical image of the Holy Spirit was clearly projected in the Johannine corpus and the Pauline and Lukan material. The imagery continued in Christian writings throughout the patristic period. A survey of some of the more explicit references is offered here.

Johannine Literature. The Upper Room discourses of John's Gospel record Jesus's assurances to his followers that after his departure he would send them another Paraclete, the Holy Spirit (John 14:16-26, 15:26, 16:7-16). This new "Comforter" would teach them all things (John 14:26), remind them of everything Jesus had said to them (John 14:26), and guide them into all the truth (John 16:13). He would speak what he was to hear from the Father and Son. He would tell of things yet to come and he would bring glory to Christ by taking from what is Christ's and making it known to the disciples (John 16:13-14). This new teacher would be sent by the Father in the name of Jesus to be with the disciples forever (John 14:26). They already knew him for he had been with them. In his new role he would be in them. Further, the world would not be able to receive him because it does not see him nor know him (John 14:17).

The first epistle of John continued the imagery when it encouraged believers to test the spirits (1 John 4:1-6). The Spirit of God can be distinguished from other spirits in that it is he who acknowledges that Jesus has come in the flesh. Believers know they live in Christ and Christ lives in them because they have received his Spirit. The Spirit testifies to them of Jesus Christ because the Spirit is the truth. Thus, in the Johannine tradition the Holy Spirit acted to teach, remind, guide, speak, and inform about the future. He acknowledged, confirmed, and testified. Clearly, he was perceived as having pedagogical functions within the church.

Lukan literature. The writings attributed to Luke also cast the Spirit into pedagogical functions. Jesus prepared his disciples for the time when they would be brought before the authorities by assuring them that the Holy Spirit would teach them in that hour what they were to say (Luke 12:12). In the Acts of the Apostles the Spirit was portrayed as fulfilling these words of Jesus when Peter was brought before the Sadducees and High Priests (Acts 4:8) and when Stephen was brought before the Sanhedrin (Acts 6:10). Elsewhere in Acts, the Spirit revealed future events (Acts 11:28, 21:11) and guided the church in decisions (Acts 13:2, 15:28).[4]

Pauline literature. The Pauline corpus further portrayed the Spirit as instructor of the church. Within the Corinthian correspondence Paul stated it was the Spirit who had revealed to the believers the hidden wisdom of God (1 Cor. 2:10-13). The Spirit searches all things, even the deep things of God. Just as it is only the spirit of the individual which knows the inner thoughts of that person, only the Spirit of God knows the thoughts of God. Thus, believers have received the Spirit who is from God in order that they may understand what God has freely given to them. Those who are without the Spirit cannot understand the things which come from the Spirit of God. Conversely, those who are spiritual have through the Spirit the very mind of Christ.

Later, Paul sought to instruct the Corinthian church about "things spiritual," that is, the gifts of the Holy Spirit (1 Cor. 12:1-31). Like John, he asserted that it is only by the Holy Spirit that Jesus is confessed as Lord. In the list of gifts he included words of wisdom, words of knowledge, prophecy, the ability to speak in different kinds of tongues, and the ability to interpret tongues. Hence, the Spirit was portrayed as a divine agent of communication and instruction within the church.

Patristic literature. Similar examples are to be found in the writings of the ante-Nicene fathers. Clement of Rome associated the Spirit with the Wisdom of God and reminded the Christians that through the Spirit and Wisdom God had promised to teach his speech.[5] Ignatius reminded the Ephesians that their fidelity (that is, submission to the bishop) was the product of their having been instructed by the Spirit.[6] He further admonished them that they could be taught by the Holy Spirit in the same manner that the

---

[4] The prophet Agabus twice spoke "by the Spirit" to reveal the future. He warned the believers of a coming famine (Acts 11:27-30) and he warned Paul of his imprisonment at Jerusalem (Acts 21:10-12). The Spirit also gave directions to the church at Antioch to send Paul and *Barnabas* as missionaries (Acts 13:2) and the Spirit is said to have shared in the decision of the Jerusalem Council (Acts 15:28).

[5] Clement of Rome, *First Clement*, XXVII, *The Ante-Nicene Fathers*, ed. Alexander Roberts and James Donaldson (Grand Rapids: Wm. B. Eerdmans, 1956), I, 20.

[6] Ignatius, *Epistle to the Ephesians*, IV, ANF, I, 50.

apostle Paul had been.[7] Hermas wrote that he was transported by the Spirit to a place of instruction,[8] and he further affirmed that prophets were still speaking to the church by the Holy Spirit in his era.[9] Justin asserted that the Holy Spirit teaches through the Scriptures.[10] Tertullian described the Spirit as functioning to give direction in discipline, reveal the Scriptures, and reform the intellect.[11] Tatian proposed that the Spirit teaches the just by combining with their souls to make known the hidden things of God.[12] Irenaeus understood the Spirit as being the one who inspired the writings of the Apostles concerning Jesus and the one who continued to inspire understanding in those who heard the preaching of the Gospel so that they could distinguish truth from error. In fact, the Spirit was teaching the things of God even to those who could not read or write.[13] Clement of Alexandria understood the Spirit to be the one who brought illumination to converts by the training of faith within them.[14] Origen proposed that the Scriptures were clear on all necessary points but that the gifts of the Holy Spirit were required to understand their foundational meanings.[15]

Conclusions. It may be concluded that there existed a strong tradition of pedagogical imagery for the Holy Spirit throughout the early centuries of the church and that a descriptive study of the tradition is warranted. It will be helpful however to address first the need for such a study from the perspective of the field of Christian education.

THE PERSPECTIVE OF CHRISTIAN EDUCATION THEORISTS

Christian education is an interdisciplinary field which draws from the resources of the theological and pedagogical sciences. The manner in which the field of Christian education is to be informed by those sciences has been a matter of extended debate since 1940.[16] In the early part of this century the religious education movement accepted liberal theology and progressive

---

[7] Ibid. XV, ANF, I, 28.

[8] *Shepherd of Hermas*, I.1.1, ANF, II, 9-11.

[9] Ibid., ANF, II, 28.

[10] Justin, *First Apology*, XLIV, ANF, I, 177.

[11] Tertullian, *On the Veiling of Virgins*, I, ANF, IV, 28.

[12] Tatian, *Address to the Greeks*, XIII, ANF, II, 70-71.

[13] Irenaeus, *Against Heresies*, III.4.2, ANF, I, 417.

[14] Clement of Alexandria, *Instructor*, I.6, ANF, II, 217.

[15] Origen, *De Principiis*, "Preface" 3 & 8, ANF, IV, 239, 241.

[16] Kendig Brubaker Cully, *The Search for a Christian Education Since 1940* (Philadelphia: Westminster Press, 1965), pp. 13-16.

education as inseparable expressions of a common cause. Pragmatism was considered the approach to life ordained by God and democracy was thought to be the highest form of social interaction. Thus, the kingdom of God was considered to be emerging as the "democracy of God."[17]

The Elliott-Smith Debate. The liberal-progressive dream of a democratic world order was severely challenged by the social dilemmas of the 1930's. A new theology arose in Europe which called for a more orthodox understanding of how God works in the world. Harrison Elliott responded to the threat of this new movement by raising the question "Can Religious Education Be Christian?" in a book by that title published in 1940. He identified three schools of religious educational thought which offered answers to this question. The first school centered its theoretical concerns around the effective communication of the traditions and practices of the church. The second school identified with the religious education movement with its focus on social and cultural development. The third school was the one emerging out of the neo-orthodox theological interpretation of the Christian religion.[18]

Elliott's own response to the question arose from the second school and served as an apology for the religious education movement and a defense of the liberal understanding of Christianity. According to Elliott religious education can be Christian only if a liberal definition of what it means to be Christian is accepted.[19]

H. Sheldon Smith was already at work developing a response to the religious education movement when Elliott's book was published. Smith accepted the validity of the emerging challenge from Europe and saw the central questions of Christian education to be those of "Faith and Nurture." His book by that title was published in 1941. Smith carefully demonstrated how the writers in religious education who had denied the significance of theology had themselves held to a definite theology which was drawn more from secular philosophical positions than from biblical or historical roots. He issued a call for an approach to Christian education which took seriously the

---

[17] George Albert Coe was one of the organizers of the Religious Education Association in 1903. He remained a leading spokesperson for the liberal-progressive religious education movement throughout the early decades of the century. His *A Social Theory of Religious Education* (New York: Charles Scribner's Sons, 1917) is the most authoritative source for understanding the philosophy behind the movement. On the "democracy of God" concept see especially pp. 54-57.

[18] Harrison S. Elliott, *Can Religious Education Be Christian?* (New York: Macmillan Company, 1940), pp. 1-11.

[19] Ibid., pp. 307-321.

newer theological currents and their concern for the historical basis for the Christian faith.[20]

The search for solutions. In the period following the Elliott-Smith "debate" a variety of solutions have been offered for the problem of the relationship between theology and pedagogy. Kendig Cully identified eight approaches to the problem which emerged during the two ensuing decades. Each approach represented a theological perspective and its corresponding value and belief systems.[21] Others have adopted classifications of Christian education theories similar to Elliott's triad of schools.[22] William Burgess grouped modern theories according to Elliott's triad but added a fourth school, the social-science theoretical approach. This latter approach he saw as the unique contribution of James Michael Lee.[23] Thus, Cully and Burgess have both demonstrated the concern among Christian education theorists for historical and theological foundations for their theories.

The diversity of the approaches may be demonstrated by a review of specific examples of leading theorists. Randolph Crump Miller suggested that the "clue" to Christian education is "the rediscovery of a relevant theology which will bridge the gap between content and method."[24] Theology must be the guiding principle for Christian education.[25] Lewis Joseph Sherrill suggested that the key to church education is an understanding of revelation as personal encounter with God which comes through the redemptive Self-disclosure of God within the Christian community.[26] James Smart proposed

---

[20] H. Sheldon Smith, *Faith and Nurture* (New York: Charles Scribner's Sons, 1941), pp. vi-ix.

[21] K. Cully, *Search*, pp. 26-182.

[22] Among these are James D. Smart, The *Teaching Ministry of the Church: An Examination of the Basic Principles of Christian Education* (Philadelphia: Westminster, 1954), and James Michael Lee, *The Flow of Religious Instruction* (Birmingham, Alabama: Religious Education Press, 1975), p. 15.

[23] Harold William Burgess, *An Invitation to Religious Education* (Birmingham, Alabama: Religious Education Press, 1975), p. 15.

[24] Randolf Crump Miller, *The Clue to Christian Education* (New York: Charles Scribner & Son, 1950), p. 15.

[25] Miller did not presuppose a given theology but rather that each educator had to have a theology. Theology being defined as "truth-about-God-in-relation-to-man." Theology was the background guide for the process. In the foreground was to be the human response to God and God's response to humans. See his "Theology in the Background," in *Religious Education and Theology*, ed. Norma H. Thompson (Birmingham, Alabama: Religious Education Press, 1982), pp. 17-26.

[26] "Strictly speaking, then, this education is not God-centered, nor is it man-centered. It is bi-polar; that is, it is concerned with the meeting between God and the human creature, and with the tension which rises within the encounter, calling for human response to God and for divine response to man.

It is distinctive, still again, because of the nature of the results which take place within the encounter. It leads primarily not to knowledge about the self, but to self-knowledge. It leads

to establish a "comprehensive" theological basis for Christian education arguing that the practical considerations of the church "are as thoroughly theological as those that arise in the Biblical, systematic, and historical departments of theology,"[27] but that the practical can be understood only if it is traced back to biblical and theological roots.[28] Iris V. Cully also sought to draw implications for the church's teaching task from classical theological understandings of the church.[29] Lois LeBar applied inductive methods of study to the Scriptures and concluded that the living Christ must be kept at the center of church education by following the pattern of Jesus as revealed in the Scriptures.[30] Thomas Groome applied the taxonomy of story and vision from narrative theology to the process of Christian catechesis.[31]

So thorough was the return to linking theology and education that Howard Grimes wrote in 1966, "The struggle for the recognition of the crucial nature of theology in relation to Christian teaching has probably been won."[32] New challenges have, however, since arisen. The chief defiance came from James Michael Lee who proposed a social-science theory of religious instruction through which he attempted to free education from the subservient role of water-boy to theology.[33] The final influence of the social science approach is yet to be determined, but history indicates that Sara Little was correct in her assessment that whatever the future shape of Christian

---

primarily not to knowledge about God, but to knowledge of God." Lewis Joseph Sherrill, *The Gift of Power* (New York: Macmillan Company, 1955), p. 90. Refer also to pp. xi-xii, 44-52, and 65-79.

[27] Smart, *Teaching Ministry*, p. 38.

[28] Ibid.

[29] Iris V. Cully, *The Dynamics of Christian Education* (Philadelphia: Westminster Press, 1958), p. 10.

[30] Lois E. LeBar, *Education That is Christian* (Old Tappan, New Jersey: Revell, 1958), pp. 49-118.

[31] Thomas H. Groome, *Christian Religious Education: Sharing Our Story and Vision* (San Francisco: Harper & Row, 1980), pp. 31-51.

[32] Howard Grimes, "Theological Foundations for Christian Education," in *An Introduction to Christian Education*, ed. Marvin J. Taylor (Nashville: Abingdon Press, 1966), p. 39.

[33] Lee wrote *The Shape* to "present the overall rationale and foundation for the social science approach as contrasted to the theological approach." See James Michael Lee, "To Change Fundamental Theory and Practice," in *Modern Masters of Religious Education*, ed. Marlene Mayr (Birmingham, Alabama: Religious Education Press, 1983), p. 301.

For a more "concise" statement of Lee's understanding of the relationship between religious instruction and theology refer to James Michael Lee, "The Authentic Source of Religious Instruction," in *Religious Education and Theology*, ed. Norma H. Thompson (Birmingham, Alabama: Religious Education Press, 1982), pp. 100-197.

education theories, the "health" of Christian education "is intertwined with that in theology."[34]

Tradition and the Spirit Considered. Of the theorists considered above, Cully, Smart, LeBar, and Groome have each dialogued with early Christian tradition in their efforts to formulate approaches to Christian education. Cully and Smart interacted with C. H. Dodd's theoretical distinctions between kerygma and didache in early Christianity to suggest contemporary approaches to the communication of the Word of God.[35] LeBar drew from Scripture a model for allowing the Living Word (Jesus) to make the Written Word (Scripture) relevant for the learner.[36] More recently Groome interacted with early Christian concepts of knowing in his quest for an epistemological basis for Christian religious education.[37]

Many theorists have also alluded to the significance of the Holy Spirit in Christian education, but without extensive clarification. Representatives of the contemporary theological approach "usually believe that God through the Holy Spirit is revelationally present and actively involved in making the religion teaching process effective."[38] Their focus was upon the Spirit as the divine presence within the church which makes knowledge of God a corporate reality. Evangelical theorists, like LeBar, have emphasized the individual's subjective relationship with the Holy Spirit as a basis for Christian education. The teacher must be led by the Spirit and the learner must be directly taught by Him.[39] Lee rejected all such notions of the Spirit's personal involvement. He asserted that "The Spirit-as-variable fallacy represents a flat

---

[34] Sarah Little, "Theology and Religious Education," in *Foundations for Christian Education in an Era of Change*, ed. Marvin J. Taylor (Nashville: Abingdon Press, 1976), p. 39.

[35] Cully found in Dodd's treatment of kerygma a theological support for an existential methodology; Cully, Dynamic, pp. 114-120, 157-177. On the other hand, Smart rejected Dodd's distinctions between kerygma and *Didache* . For Smart kerygma penetrated *Didache* and thereby prohibited moralistic teaching; Smart, *Teaching Ministry*, pp. 19-23.

[36] LeBar, *Education*, pp. 203-207.

[37] Groome, *Christian*, pp. 141-145.

[38] Burgess, *Invitation*, p. 113. Miller articulated this position in an article first printed in 1962. He asserted that education becomes Christian when all the data taught serves to help the student discover God at work in history, in the Bible and in his world. The Bible speaks to the issues of life when there is an atmosphere in which grace flourishes. The worshipping community supports this process of discovering grace. The Holy Spirit works to illumine and persuade the learner, to forgive the learner, and to restore the learner to genuine fellowship with God and others. The church is the community in which the Holy Spirit works. The church plants and waters; God, by his Spirit, provides the growth. Randolf Crump Miller, "The Holy Spirit in Christian Education," *Religious Education*, 57 (1962), 178-184, 237-238.

[39] K. Cully, *Search*, p. 101.

rejection of the natural law in any form, and ultimately reduces all human activity including religious instruction to a nihilistic and spooky affair."[40]

The histories of Christian education have given little attention to early Christian tradition and practices. The pattern followed by Clarence Benson,[41] C. B. Eavey,[42] and Kenneth Gangel and Warren Benson[43] was to offer an analysis of Jesus as a model teacher and then to shift the focus to biographical sketches of major educators and the development of educational institutions.[44] Sherrill offered an exception to this pattern in *The Rise of Christian Education*. In that work he attempted to understand the belief systems which produced educational activities among Christians but he gave little attention to the pedagogical processes involved.[45]

Sherrill also made extensive allusion to the role of the Holy Spirit in Christian education during the period of primitive Christianity.[46] Two other works of lesser prominence have been devoted entirely to clarifying the role of the Holy Spirit in Christian education: *The Holy Spirit in Your Teaching* by Roy B. Zuck[47] and *The Holy Spirit in Christian Education* by Rachel Henderlite.[48] Neither author interacted extensively with early Christian traditions on the subject. However, they have provided definite approaches to the role of the Holy Spirit in Christian education which offer needed points of dialogue for this study.

Summary. In summary, this survey of significant theoretical and historical literature from the field of Christian education reveals a concern for the relationship between theology and pedagogy, but it also reveals an absence of any serious attempt to understand early Christianity's perception of the Holy Spirit as a divine agent of pedagogy. The major works which

---

[40] Lee, "Authentic," p. 101.

[41] Clarence H. Benson, *A Popular History of Christian Education* (Chicago: Moody Press, 1943), pp. 30-49.

[42] C. B. Eavey, *History of Christian Education* (Chicago: Moody Press, 1964), pp. 75-99.

[43] Kenneth O. Gangel and Warren S. Benson, *Christian Education: Its History and Philosophy* (Chicago: Moody Press, 1983), pp. 51-94.

[44] Gangel and Benson argued that "it is readily apparent that education was of paramount importance in the New Testament." Ibid., p. 67. On the other hand, O. C. Edwards argued that "the reason that we do not have a history of Christian Education for the first century and a half of our era is that explicit evidence is lacking for the construction of such a history." O. C. Edwards and John H. Westerhoff, eds. *A Faithful Church: Issues in the History of Catechesis* (Wilton, Connecticut: Morehouse-Barlow, 1980), p. 11.

[45] Lewis Joseph Sherrill, *The Rise of Christian Education* (New York: Macmillan Company, 1944), p. 2.

[46] Ibid., pp. 137-207.

[47] Roy B. Zuck, *The Holy Spirit in Your Teaching* (Chicago: Scripture Press, 1963).

[48] Rachel Henderlite, *The Holy Spirit in Christian Education* (Philadelphia: Westminster Press, 1964).

attempted to establish a theoretical basis for church education either neglected early Christian tradition all together or failed to investigate the role of the Holy Spirit. The histories of Christian education (with the exception of Sherrill) which reviewed this early period also neglected this repeated tradition. Finally, the two works which have addressed the role of the Spirit in church education failed to draw from the record of early Christian tradition.

REVIEW OF THE LITERATURE

As has been stated above, Zuck and Henderlite have written the only two works devoted entirely to the role of the Holy Spirit in Christian education. However, Sherrill's history has provided the most extensive treatment to date of Christian education in the early church and gave prominence to the role of the Holy Spirit during the period of primitive Christianity. These three works differ in method and scope, and therefore offer three separate paradigms of Christian instruction.

LEWIS JOSEPH SHERRILL ON THE HOLY SPIRIT IN PRIMITIVE CHRISTIAN EDUCATION

Lewis Joseph Sherrill taught Christian education at Louisville Presbyterian Seminary from 1925 to 1950 and also served as dean of that institution from 1930 to 1950. In 1950 he became Skinner and McAlpin Professor of Applied Theology at Union Theological Seminary in New York. During that time-frame Sherrill wrote extensively in the field of Christian education.[49]

The Scope and Method of Inquiry. *The Rise of Christian Education* was the first volume of an intended series of texts on the history of Christian education. It covered the period of pre-Christian Hebrew education down to the beginning of the fifteenth century.[50] Subsequent volumes were never completed. Of significance to this study were three chapters on Jesus and primitive Christianity.

The method of study utilized by Sherrill was to apply four foundational questions to various periods of ecclesiastical history. First, what were the convictions held regarding the nature of the Supreme Being? Second, how was the Supreme Being thought to manifest his or herself most significantly?

---

[49] Wayne R. Rood, *Understanding Christian Education* (Nashville: Abingdon Press, 1970), pp. 241-245.

[50] Sherrill, *The Rise*, pp. vii-viii.

Third, how was the will of the Supreme Being for humankind to be known? Finally, what were the supreme values of existence and how were they to be secured? For Sherrill these questions constituted four perennial efforts of all religious persons which provide a basis for classifying and studying the beliefs and practices of Christianity.[51]

The Pattern of Jesus. After considering responses to those quests in the periods of Hebrew and Jewish education, Sherrill turned his attention to the life and teachings of Jesus. As for the nature of the Supreme Being, God is both King and Father in the teachings of Jesus. He manifests himself most significantly in the person of Jesus. The supreme values of existence are persons. His will is summed up in the two great commandments of love toward God and toward the neighbor. Thus, the whole concept of Christian education was seen to move in the realm of personality and relationships between personalities.[52]

When applied to the church, the mission and message of Jesus constitutes a charter of liberty for the human soul. The individual by accepting the sovereignty of God as revealed by Christ may attain that autonomy which consists in self-rulership under God. This liberty and autonomy for the individual calls forth a society of persons over whom God is admittedly the final Sovereign. The future of that society is shaped by its members' comprehension and use of the mission and message of Jesus. Thus, if it is to maintain continuity with the purposes of its founder, it must be guided into the future by the Spirit of Christ.[53]

The Pattern of Primitive Christianity. Sherrill contended that for the church the time immediately after Christ was characterized by the experience of the Spirit in its corporate life. Education in the period of primitive Christianity was an extension of the mission of Jesus through the power of the Holy Spirit. Within and through the Christian society the Spirit acted to make known both God and his will. By the Holy Spirit individual liberty which was formulated in Jesus came to be actualized in the church. Preaching and teaching, the instructional activities of the church, were done in the power of the Spirit. And the person of the teacher was divinely appointed through the reception of a spiritual gift, or charisma, of spiritual knowledge.[54]

In primitive Christian churches the Supreme Being was the God and Father of the Lord Jesus Christ, with the double meaning that God is the God of whom Jesus taught and the God of whom he is Son. Jesus was the supreme manifestation of God but through the experience of the Spirit that

---

[51] Ibid., pp. 1-3.
[52] Ibid., pp. 133-134.
[53] Ibid., pp. 135-136.
[54] Ibid., pp. 136-139.

manifestation was not localized in time or space. The manifestation of God through Jesus Christ was as it were extended into the present through the experience of the Spirit.[55]

In the experience of the Spirit the Christian society discovered the will of God for them day by day. As with Jesus himself, the supreme values of existence were personalities; to which was added the discovery of the equality of persons before God. People enter this estate of equal personalities living under the guidance of the Spirit by means of faith in Jesus Christ; faith not in a creed but in a living person.[56]

The idea embodied in the early Christian meetings was that the Spirit was within the Christian community and that it was the Spirit who brought knowledge of God. Within the meeting the Spirit taught through spontaneous prayers, hymns, or prophesies. Apostolic letters and the Hebrew Scriptures were read on occasion but "the uppermost idea was the fresh and direct communication of the Spirit then and there."[57] Teaching was a ministry of the Spirit via an inspired address or interpretation of the Hebrew Scriptures or reiteration of the Christian traditions concerning faith and conduct. While a revelation might come to any member of the congregation, it was subject to the criticism of other believers as it was through and within the community that the Spirit operated.[58]

Sherrill concluded that the Christian communities soon lost the experience of the Spirit. Early in the second century creedal confessions, incipient in the faith, became the focus of the faith. The church began to replace the Holy Spirit in the Christian experience. The devolution was so complete that the items concerning the Spirit in the later creeds took on the appearance of an undeveloped vestige.[59]

An Inferred Paradigm. Sherrill did not construct a paradigm of Christian instruction based upon his treatment of primitive Christianity, but his interpretations were paradigmatic. Should earliest Christian education as he described it serve as a model, the implications are clear. First, Christian education must understand the Supreme Being to be the God of the Judeo-Christian heritage, the King and Father of all, the one of whom Jesus is Only Begotten Son. Second, God is made manifest to persons through Jesus Christ who by the experience of the Spirit is a living personality. Third, the Spirit should be making the will of God known to the church on a day by day basis through charismatic teachers in pneumatic gatherings. Finally, the supreme

---

55 Ibid., pp. 163-164.
56 Ibid., p. 164.
57 Ibid., p. 154.
58 Ibid., pp. 153-157.
59 Ibid., p. 208.

values of the church should be freedom for individuals through the guidance of the Holy Spirit which is achieved through a faith encounter with the person of Jesus.

ROY B. ZUCK ON THE HOLY SPIRIT
IN CHRISTIAN TEACHING

Almost two decades after Sherrill wrote *The Rise of Christian Education*, Roy B. Zuck completed his doctoral dissertation at Dallas Theological Seminary. In 1963 that dissertation was published in book form under the title *The Holy Spirit in Your Teaching*. Zuck's objective was to provide a practical guide for teachers and other Christian education workers in local churches. His purpose was two-fold. First, he wanted to demonstrate the need for the ministry of the Holy Spirit in Christian education. Second, he sought to discuss how the Spirit works in the various phases of the teaching-learning process.[60]

The Method and Scope of Inquiry. The method used by Zuck was to address four questions concerning the Holy Spirit in Christian education. First, what is the biblical doctrine of the Holy Spirit as a teacher? Second, what is the relationship between human teachers and the Holy Spirit as divine teacher? Third, what is the relationship between the Holy Spirit and the Bible? Fourth, how does the Spirit relate to the teaching-learning process? These four questions were discussed sequentially to form the four major sections of the book. A fifth section offered a brief survey of historical references to the Holy Spirit in teaching.[61]

The scope of the work was limited to selected biblical passages as interpreted by twentieth century evangelical scholars and the application of those interpretations to three major elements of the pedagogical enterprise, that is, the teacher, the content, and the teaching-learning process. In essence, Zuck applied a doctrine of the Holy Spirit to selected "laws" of teaching and learning.

A Biblical Basis. Following an introductory chapter, Zuck offered in the first division of the book a biblical understanding of the Holy Spirit as teacher. First, he identified the biblical titles of the Spirit as teacher. These were listed with textual references and brief comments as: a) Spirit of wisdom, b) Spirit of wisdom and understanding, c) Spirit of counsel and

---

[60] Zuck, *Holy Spirit*, pp. xi-xii.

[61] Zuck did not describe his method of study. The four primary questions were stated in the introductions to their respective divisions of the book; ibid., pp. 15, 51, 85, 113.

might, d) Spirit of knowledge and of the fear of Jehovah, e) Spirit of truth, f) Paraclete, and g) Spirit of wisdom and revelation.[62]

Second, he discussed five teaching ministries or activities of the Holy Spirit as revealed in the Bible. Referring primarily to John 14:26, 16:12-15, and 1 Corinthians 2:10-13, Zuck concluded that the Spirit: a) instructs, b) reminds, c) guides, d) declares, and e) reveals.[63]

In the final chapter of this division Zuck discussed four ministries of the Spirit which are related to teaching: a) inspiration, b) conviction, c) indwelling, and d) illumination. Inspiration is "that supernatural work of the Holy Spirit whereby He so guided and superintended the writers of Scripture that what they wrote is the Word of God, inerrant as originally written (2 Peter 1:21)."[64] This doctrine was for Zuck the cornerstone for understanding the Holy Spirit in teaching. Inspiration has precedence over teaching. While all believers may receive the Spirit's teaching, only the writers of the Scriptures were involved in the Spirit's work of inspiration. Inspiration was an historical act once for all completed with the sixty-six books of the Bible. Inspiration differs from revelation in that revelation is the Spirit's disclosure of divine truth, whereas inspiration is the Spirit's superintending process of the recording of revelation. Divine teaching follows inspiration in that "divine teaching is the work of the Spirit enabling man to understand and appropriate personally this recorded revelation."[65]

Conviction and indwelling are also acts of the Spirit related to teaching. Conviction is the act of the Spirit whereby the sinner is convinced of his or her sin and made to understand certain truths requisite to an appropriation of salvation by faith in Jesus Christ. Indwelling is the once-for-all act occurring at the moment of salvation whereby the Spirit takes up his permanent residence in the heart of the believer positioning Himself to teach God's truth.[66]

Illumination is that supernatural work of the Spirit whereby he enables the individual to apprehend the already revealed truth of God. Illumination of the Spirit always relates to the Word of God, the Bible. It is the work of the Spirit on the mind and heart enabling the individual to apprehend the truth of God revealed. Apprehension of the truth requires reception and appropriation, not mere perception.[67]

---

[62] Ibid., pp. 17-24.

[63] Ibid., pp. 25-34.

[64] Ibid., p. 35.

[65] Ibid., p. 37.

[66] Ibid., pp. 38-44.

[67] Ibid., pp. 45-48.

The Two Teachers. In the second division of the book Zuck addressed four aspects of the relationship between the human teacher and the Spirit as divine teacher. First, he denounced four false views of the relationship: a) the Holy Spirit, because he is God, excludes human teachers as unnecessary, b) the Holy Spirit is a substitute for human effort, making preparation unnecessary, c) the Holy Spirit adds a spiritual addendum to teaching which is otherwise secular or natural, and d) the Holy Spirit is totally unnecessary since teaching and learning are natural processes.[68]

He further sought to define the spiritual gift of teaching. Spiritual gifts, including teaching, "are divinely bestowed endowments of grace empowering believers to minister to the edifying of the church."[69] The gift of teaching is a Spirit-endowed ability to expound the truth of God revealed in the Scriptures through systematic instruction and application of the doctrines of God's Word. This endowment is to persons and not occasions and may be the supernatural enhancement of natural abilities or the supernatural addition of new abilities following conversion. Only those persons who have the gift of teaching should teach in the church.[70]

Next, the distinctive ministries of the divine and human teachers were clarified. While the Spirit dispenses the gift of teaching, it is the human teacher who must utilize it. The human teacher is cooperating with the divine teacher when he or she discovers and utilizes the natural laws of teaching and learning which were, after all, created by God. The role of the human teacher, then, is to seek to be an informed and spiritually sensitive channel through which the Spirit can operate. The human teacher must endeavor to proclaim and portray in character the Word of God in a manner that manipulates factors outside of the pupils enabling the Spirit to do his work of molding their inner beings.[71]

The Bible as Content. In the third division of the book Zuck addressed the issue of the Holy Spirit and the Bible in Christian education. Zuck's understanding came out of his earlier treatment of inspiration and revelation. The Bible is the authority of all of living and is therefore the authoritative source for concepts of Christian education. The Bible is also the essential content of Christian education. Because the Bible brings persons into direct contact with the living God, Christian education must be transmissive of that content. Illumination of the Word by the Holy Spirit is

---

[68] Ibid., pp. 53-59.

[69] Ibid., p. 64.

[70] Ibid., pp. 62-74.

[71] Ibid., pp. 75-80.

the basis for personal Biblical interpretation but it is subject to objective verification by others.[72]

The Teaching-learning Process. The fourth division of *The Holy Spirit in Your Teaching* reflects Zuck's attempt to clarify how the Holy Spirit wishes to operate in the teaching-learning process. Four aspects of the process were considered: the goal of Christian teaching, the nature of learning, the laws of effective learning and teaching, and the use of methods and materials. The goal of Christian teaching is for the Holy Spirit to make the truths of God relevant to the life needs of the pupils. Learning is best achieved when the Holy Spirit enables the teacher to apply the four principles, or laws, of learning. These are the principle of motivation, the principle of relevance, the principle of activity, and the principle of readiness.

Effective teaching is enhanced by the Holy Spirit's assistance in the application of the three principles, or laws, of teaching. These are the principle of teacher preparation, the principle of pupil understanding, and the principle of communication. Concerning the selection and utilization of proper methods and materials, the teacher and congregation must seek the Spirit's guidance in order to identify those methods and materials which conform to the laws of effective Christian education.[73]

RACHEL HENDERLITE ON THE HOLY SPIRIT IN CHRISTIAN EDUCATION

Rachel Henderlite began her work on the Holy Spirit in Christian education about the same time as Zuck. Her quest began in response to a conference on Christian education at Drew University in 1959. In 1963 and 1964 she developed and delivered a series of lectures on the subject. Her book, *The Holy Spirit in Christian Education*, was published in 1964.[74]

The Method and Scope of Inquiry. Henderlite wrote from the reformed tradition and was representative of the contemporary theological school of Christian education theorists. She proposed to discover what the church has known of the Holy Spirit through its own experience as opposed to speculative theology. The resulting method of her study was to consider three aspects of the church's experience of the Holy Spirit which she viewed as having significant bearing on Christian education. The three aspects were

---

[72] Ibid., pp. 87-112.

[73] Ibid., pp. 113-141.

[74] Henderlite, *Holy Spirit*, pp. 9-10.

the Holy Spirit and faith, the Holy Spirit and the Scriptures, and the Holy Spirit and the church.[75]

Her procedure was to ask a theological and an educational question of each aspect of the church's experience of the Holy Spirit. Concerning the Holy Spirit and faith she asked "How does the Holy Spirit act on the human heart to bring men to God?" and "How does this doctrine of the work of the Holy Spirit to call forth faith affect our method of working in Christian education?" From the answers to these questions she proposed to offer a theory of learning in Christian education.[76]

Concerning the Holy Spirit and the Scriptures she asked "How does the Holy Spirit act in and through Scripture to bring men to God?" and "How does this doctrine of the work of the Holy Spirit in Scripture affect our use of the Bible in Christian education?" Answers to these questions were intended to guide the use of basic content or subject matter in Christian education.[77]

Finally, she addressed two questions to the role of the Holy Spirit in the church: "How does the Holy Spirit act in and through the church to bring men to God?" and "How does this doctrine of the work of the Holy Spirit in and through the church affect the work of Christian education?" The context and means of Christian education were to be described by answering these questions.[78]

The Holy Spirit and Faith. On the Holy Spirit and faith she concluded that the Spirit's work is to bring Christ into the present and make him real. Christians of every generation should know Jesus the same way that Peter and Paul knew him--face to face. That kind of encounter with Christ is made manifest through a transformation of the individual which results in a personal expression of the essential moral nature of Christ.[79]

A corresponding task of Christian education is to bear responsible witness to Jesus Christ. The Christian educator with the whole church is responsible to teach the data of the faith. The Spirit may then use the data to point to Christ. A second task of the Christian educator is to confront each person with the necessity for decision, leaving the individual free to decide as he or she is able.[80]

The Holy Spirit and the Scriptures. On the Holy Spirit and the Scriptures she addressed the issues of illumination, revelation, and inspiration. Of illumination she asserted that the Holy Spirit acts in a three-

---

[75] Ibid., p. 31.

[76] Ibid., pp. 31-32.

[77] Ibid., p. 32.

[78] Ibid.

[79] Ibid., pp. 39-46.

[80] Ibid., pp. 57-65.

fold manner. He acts to convince persons that the Bible is the word of God. He uses the Scriptures as a witness to his work in Jesus Christ. Thirdly, he acts to make the events of the Scriptures contemporary and personal. However, individual interpretation must be tested against the judgment of the church.[81]

As an agent of revelation, the Holy Spirit has acted in historical events and given interpretation of those events as recorded in the Bible. The Scriptures tell the story of the Spirit of God moving in the hearts of persons to draw them into the kingdom of God and now uses that story to draw more persons into the kingdom. Thus, illumination and revelation are essential to the Christian faith.[82]

Inspiration, for Henderlite, was a secondary doctrine in origin and function. The doctrine arose out of the experience of the church in possessing the Scriptures through which God spoke. It was deduced from that experience that if God speaks through the Scriptures he must have breathed their words. Functionally, the doctrine is also secondary in that redemption does not depend upon acceptance of the dogma.[83]

Four applications to Christian education were drawn from this analysis of the Holy Spirit and the Scriptures. First, it is imperative that a literalistic use of the Bible be avoided as a distortion of its true nature and hindrance to the Spirit's use of the Scriptures to speak to human hearts today. Second, because the Bible is God's book, Christian education should be based upon it without anxiety about its authority. The authority of the Bible is immediately apparent to faith by the power of the Holy Spirit. Third, because the church is called to be interpreter of the Scriptures, Christian education must give itself to serious study. Finally, the method of Bible study must ensure the openness of the student to confrontation by the Spirit and the willingness of the student to wrestle with the Spirit until he or she is overcome.[84]

She gave four steps to an appropriate method of Bible study. The student must hear the story of what God has done. The student must identify his or herself with the story. The student must explore the meaning of the story. Finally, the student must pledge obedience to the commands inherent in the message of the story.[85]

The Holy Spirit and the Church. On the Holy Spirit and the church, Henderlite addressed the problem of the Spirit's proper relationship to the church. She concluded that the Spirit, because he is the Spirit of the risen

---

[81] Ibid., pp. 57-65.

[82] Ibid., pp. 66-69.

[83] Ibid., pp. 69-74.

[84] Ibid., pp. 75-81.

[85] Ibid., pp. 81-83.

Jesus Christ, is the Lord of the church. He is a person who calls the church to obedience to Christ.[86]

The Christian educator must take into account two aspects of the Spirit's working in and through the church. First, the Spirit intends to bring persons to a new life in Christ Jesus. Second, the Spirit intends to use the church's own life as a means of pointing the world to Christ. Therefore, the Christian educator must include in the teaching program as much as possible of the church's rich heritage of stories, hymns, prayers, and confessions "for these have been expressions of the church's experience of Jesus Christ and may again lead to him."[87] Likewise, the sacraments must be fully incorporated.[88]

However, his presence does not automatically confer authority upon the church. Authority rests in the risen Lord. The presence of the Spirit in the church attests to the church's confession of Christ as Lord and calls the church to the holiness required of it by its Lord.[89]

Henderlite concluded with three suggestions for Christian education. First, the Christian educator must never separate the Spirit from Christ, but must make available to the Spirit the heritage of the church as a source for the ongoing work of Christ. Second, because the Spirit is seeking to work through the church, the Christian educator must recognize that the church's educational program can be nothing other than education for mission. Third, because of the Holy Spirit's desired involvement with the church, all aspects of the life of the church must be subject to the Spirit to be used for the nurture of its members.[90]

SUMMARY

The works of Sherrill, Zuck, and Henderlite reveal diverse understandings of the role of the Holy Spirit in Christian education. This diversity is made clear by comparing their positions from the perspective of six categories of pedagogical inquiry: the role of the teacher, the goals of education, the content of education, the role of the learner, the environment for learning, and the methods of instruction. However, it will be helpful to first review the methods of inquiry and scopes of research used by the three scholars.

---

86 Ibid., p. 89.
87 Ibid., p. 96.
88 Ibid., pp. 89-92.
89 Ibid., pp. 92-93.
90 Ibid., pp. 94-114.

Methods and Scopes of Inquiry. The three authors utilized three unique methods of inquiry. Sherrill's method was designed to surface the major educational issues of any religious society. His focus was on the belief system which produces educational activity, not the actual activities. On this point O. C. Edwards criticized him for having confused content with method, suggesting that his work "sounds more like New Testament theology rather than a history of Christian pedagogy."[91] While Edwards's criticism was based on a narrow understanding of pedagogy, the point was well made that Sherrill's four methodological questions do not address the practical issues of Christian pedagogy.

Zuck was concerned with the practical. His method was rooted in deductive logic. If the Holy Spirit has certain pedagogical functions within the church, and God has ordained certain laws of teaching and learning, then the Christian teacher must learn to work with both the Spirit and the laws of God.

Henderlite's method shared Sherrill's concern for the larger theological issues and Zuck's commitment to the practical. However, her method held the two in tension throughout the study placing theology and education in constant dialogue.

The scopes of research for these three works reveal further disparagement. *The Rise of Christian Education* was a historical work which spanned two millenniums. Sherrill addressed the pedagogy of the Holy Spirit only as a consequence of his inquiry into one period of church history, primitive Christianity prior to A.D. 125. Zuck considered the Bible to be the primary source for understanding the role of the Spirit in Christian teaching. The Scriptures were interpreted literalistically from the perspective of twentieth century evangelical scholarship. Henderlite considered experience to be the source for understanding the role of the Holy Spirit in the educational work of the church. The experience of the church held precedence over "speculative theology" causing a scope which was limited to contemporary interpretations of three aspects of the life of the church: faith, Scripture, and community life.

Three Paradigms. In the absence of a paradigm offered by Sherrill, certain inferences were made from his chapter on primitive Christianity. The role of the teacher was that of an instrument for the Holy Spirit. The Spirit himself taught through gifts to the church. The goal of education was to attain liberty and autonomy as persons under the sovereignty of a personal God. The content of Christian education centered on direct revelations by the Holy Spirit but was inclusive of inspired interpretations of Hebrew Scriptures, Christian writings, and Christian traditions. The role of the learner

---

[91] Edwards, *Faithful Church*, p. 10.

was that of an active participant as all members of the community were givers and receivers of the Spirit's gifts. The environment for learning was that of a pneumatic gathering of believers and the methods of instruction were spontaneous exercises of prayer, prophecy, exhortation, and songs all of which were believed to be direct revelations from God.

Zuck offered a much more reserved version of the pedagogy of the Holy Spirit. There are two teachers: the Spirit and the human teacher. The Spirit is the true teacher being the only one who can actualize change within the learner. The human teacher is a necessary element of the learning process but operates in the realm of factors outside of the learner. The human teacher's role is to cooperate with the Spirit by serving as a model and utilizing the God-given laws of pedagogy. The goal of education is for the Spirit to make the truths of God as revealed in the Scriptures relevant to the life needs of pupils. The essential content of Christian education is the Bible. The learner is in need of illumination, which is the product of the human teacher's application of the laws of learning and the work of the Holy Spirit within his or her heart and mind. The environment for learning is especially important as it is the realm within which the human teacher applies the laws of teaching and learning by effectively manipulating factors outside the learner. Finally, the methods of instruction are transmissive but consistent with the laws of teaching and learning. The operative concept is the effective transmission of Bible content.

Henderlite provided a contrasting paradigm of pedagogy for the Holy Spirit. Like Zuck there are two teachers -- the Spirit and the human educator. The role of the human teacher is to confront the learner with the data of the Christian faith and to confront the learner with the necessity of decision while leaving the individual free to decide. The Spirit serves to make the faith and the person behind the faith, Jesus Christ, a living reality for the learner. The goal of Christian education is for Christians of every generation to know Jesus as the apostles knew him, face to face, as evidenced by a transformation which produces the essential moral nature of Christ within the believer. The content of Christian education is the story of how the Holy Spirit has acted in history to move in the hearts of persons to draw them into the kingdom of God. The Bible contains a record of many of those events and contains interpretations by the Spirit on some of those events but the Bible is not salvific and should not be used in a literalistic manner. The learner is called on to respond to the story in a most active way. He or she is challenged to wrestle with the Spirit until he or she can identify with the story and pledge obedience to the commands inherent in its message. The environment of Christian education is the church which by its obedience to Christ serves as model, pointing the world to Christ. All aspects of the life of the church must be used for the nurture of its members. Thus, the methods of Christian education are the methods of the life of the church; whatever means the church uses to confront and challenge its members and the world with the story of the Spirit's involvement in the world.

Summary. Sherrill, Zuck, and Henderlite have offered separate and often opposing understandings of the role of the Holy Spirit in Christian education. Their differences are rooted in varying methods and scopes of research, and touch upon all aspects of the pedagogical endeavor. The diversity of their thought indicates the need for another reference point, that is, early Christian tradition on the Holy Spirit.

METHOD AND SCOPE OF STUDY

The method of study followed in this inquiry is that of an inter-disciplinary descriptive analysis of early Christian literary references to the Holy Spirit's pedagogical presence within the church. The disciplines which give direction to the research are those of historical theology and pedagogy. The process involves asking a series of questions from the perspectives of both disciplines. Theological questions and pedagogical questions are linked as a means of probing into the historical record of early Christian references to a pedagogical presence of the Holy Spirit within the church.

Three historical-theological questions are considered. First, among Christians of the first three centuries what was the perceived identity of the Spirit, especially as related to the teaching ministry of the church? Second, what was the perceived relationship between the Holy Spirit and the church? Third, what was the perceived role of the Holy Spirit in the process of Christian formation? Each of these questions is linked to one or more related pedagogical questions.

The pedagogical questions are those already applied to the comparisons of the works of Sherrill, Zuck, and Henderlite. What was the role of the teacher associated with the Spirit? What were the educational aims associated with the Spirit. What was the environment for instruction associated with the Spirit? What was the role of the learner associated with the Spirit? What was the content of Christian education associated with the Spirit? And what were the methods of instruction associated with the Spirit?

The linking of the two sets of questions constitutes the substance of this project. The perceived identity of the Holy Spirit is related to the pedagogical question of the role of the teacher in order to describe the functions of the Spirit as teacher. The Holy Spirit's role in the life of the church is associated with the pedagogical issues of aims, environment for learning, and role of the human teacher. The Holy Spirit's function in the process of Christian formation is linked to the pedagogical issues of the role of the learner, the content and the methods of instruction.

From these inquiries into the perceived pedagogy of the Holy Spirit a paradigm for Christian education is constructed. The paradigm follows the pattern of research in terms of issues considered. The role of the teacher (both divine and human), the central aims of Christian education, the environment for learning, the role of the learner, the use of content, and the methods of instruction are described.

The scope of this research project is limited to Christian literature of the first three centuries of the Church. References from that period are representative of a broad spectrum of church life and are sufficient to document and critique the early tradition of pedagogical imagery for the Holy Spirit. The writings of this period reflect the Church's experience of the Spirit as opposed to the later "speculative" theologies which focused on the doctrine of the Spirit. Also three major conflicts over the experience of the Spirit were confronted during this period; Gnosticism, Montanism and Monarchianism challenged the church to clarify the place of the Spirit in its midst. Thus, the literature of the first three centuries provides an adequate field of reference for determining the pedagogy of the Holy Spirit according to early Christian tradition.

Chapter 2

PERCEPTIONS OF THE HOLY SPIRIT IN THE ROLE OF TEACHER

The purpose of this chapter is to clarify the early church's perception of the Holy Spirit as teacher. The historical-theological issue considered is that of the identity of the Spirit among Christians of the first three centuries. The pedagogical concern is that of the role of the teacher. The central question being, in light of who, or what, the Spirit was thought to be, how was he perceived to function as teacher?

THE PERCEIVED IDENTITY OF THE SPIRIT

In basic understanding the Holy Spirit was thought of by Christians of the first three centuries as the Old Testament Spirit of the Lord which was again at work in the lives of the people of God. The Christian experience of the Spirit was interpreted as fulfillment of Old Testament themes related to the Spirit. Early Christian references to the Spirit thus reflected background meanings of "spirit" and expanded on existing theological identifications for the Holy Spirit. Three dominant and interrelated themes were the Spirit as the power of God, the Spirit as the agent of prophecy, and the Spirit as the source of eschatological renewal for the people of God. However, Christian images of the Spirit broke with those of Judaism with the development of a personal identity for the Spirit.

BACKGROUND MEANINGS OF "SPIRIT"

There were two probable sources for the early Christian understanding of the word "spirit," Greek and Jewish conceptions of spirit. The Greek word for spirit in the New Testament was *pneuma*. Classical Greek usage of *pneuma* differed from that of its Jewish counterparts, *neshama* and *ruah*.

"spirit" in Classical Greek Usage. In classical Greek usage the primary meaning of *pneuma* was that of "wind" or "breath." As such, it was an

25

unseen material which carried the idea of a special substance with an underlying stress on its inherent power.[1]

Through association it came to denote life, and even the soul. In poetic literature *pneuma* sometimes took on a meaning which transferred the physical concepts of blowing or breathing to corresponding mental or spiritual realities, for example, a breath or spirit which blows in interpersonal relations of ill- or goodwill, or which blows from the invisible world of the divine. Later, especially in Manticism, *pneuma* took on a special meaning as a breath which inspires, stirs, enthuses, and fills. In the religious philosophy of Stoicism *pneuma* became a cosmic and universal power or substance which was used linguistically for the being and manifestation of deity itself.[2] But in Greek understanding *pneuma* could only figuratively break loose from its etymology. It was essentially tied to the natural sense-phenomenon of wind or breath.[3]

"spirit" in the Old Testament. The Hebrew words for breath and wind were *neshama* and *ruah*. *Neshama* was closely associated with life, both in God and people. In reference to God *neshama* could be creative or destructive. On one hand it was the breath of God whereby "man became a living soul" (Gen. 2:7). On the other, it was a breath of judgment which comes like a mighty wind out of the nostrils of God (2 Sam. 22:16; Ps. 18:15; Isa. 30:33).[4] However, *neshama* was not the word usually associated with the concept of spirit.

The Hebrew word most closely associated with spirit was *ruah*. In the LXX *ruah* was usually translated as *pneuma* (264 of 377 instances in the Masoretic Text). The basic meaning of *ruah* in the Old Testament was that of "blowing" or "wind." Roughly one third of the instances of *ruah* in the Old Testament referred to the wind. However, the idea behind *ruah* was the fact that something as intangible as air should move. It was not so much the movement which drew attention as the energy manifested in the movement. Thus, *ruah* was essentially wind which emanated from an unseen force, God.[5]

A second use of *ruah* in the Old Testament was that of "breath," both of humans and beasts. In that context *ruah* was the life-force which flows from God and returns to him at the death of the individual. It was never used of

---

[1] Eberhard Kamlah, "Spirit, Holy Spirit." *The New International Dictionary of New Testament Theology*, ed. Colin Brown (Grand Rapids: Zondervan Publishing House, 1979), III, p. 689.

[2] Herman Kleinknecht, "Pneuma." *Theological Dictionary of the New Testament*, ed. Gerhard Kittle and trans. Geoffrey W. Bromily (Grand Rapids: Wm. B. Eerdmans Publishing Company, 1964), Vol. II, pp. 334-339.

[3] Ibid., p. 359.

[4] Dale Moody, *Spirit of the Living God: The Biblical Concepts Interpreted in Context*, (Philadelphia: The Westminster Press, 1968), p. 11.

[5] Kamlah, "Spirit," p. 690.

that higher quality of humanity which distinguishes humans from the beasts.[6] But it was used to connote the seat of the emotions, the intellectual functions, and the attitude of will.[7]

A third use of *ruah* was as a special force associated with the presence of God. The Spirit of God, or Spirit of the Lord, was frequently portrayed as effective divine power, especially God's creative power.[8] Robert Koch suggested it was "that mysterious force which proceeds from God and takes powerful effect in the history of the covenant people."[9] In the writing prophets that power was associated with moral and eschatological purpose. The Spirit of God was morally defined power; it was the power which worked out God's personal will especially as expressed toward religious and moral ends.[10] Thus, the Spirit was seen in judgment and corresponding salvation (Isa. 35:15-20). A chief example being the future salvation of Israel which was to come through the offspring of David who was to be ordained by the Spirit of God (Isa. 11:1-8). That offspring was to bring special blessings to Israel, one of which was to be the irrevocable gift of God's Spirit (Isa. 42:1-4; 49:1-6).[11]

The nature of the Spirit of God in the Old Testament was not that of a person. Personifications of the Spirit were present (Ex. 28:3; Isa. 11:2) and provoked images of personal characteristics, but they did not imply personal identity. According to Koch the Holy Spirit was "conceived of not yet as a person but merely as a force, as a physical reality, as a kind of extremely fine matter."[12]

"spirit" in Intertestamental Judaism. Intertestamental Judaism, expanded on the Old Testament images of spirit. First, as a life force within creation, spirit was refined in understanding so as to carefully distinguish it from the Creator. The spirit which was the breath of life was a vital force which was breathed into the living and formed a distinct part of the personal being; a part not distinguished from the soul. Palestinian Judaism was especially careful not to construe the body as the prison of the heavenly spirit or as a seducer into sin. Similarly, spirit was not a divine substance but rather something divinely created.[13]

---

[6] Ibid., pp. 690-691.

[7] Friedrich Baumgartel, "Pneuma." TDNT, II, pp. 360-362.

[8] Ibid., pp. 362-363.

[9] Robert Koch, "Spirit." Bauer *Encyclopedia of Biblical Theology*, ed. Johannes B. Bauer (London: Sheed and Ward, 1970), III, p. 873.

[10] Baumgartel, "Pneuma," p. 365.

[11] Kamlah, "Spirit," p. 692.

[12] Koch, "Spirit," pp. 875-876.

[13] Hellenistic Judaism was more inclined to borrow from the Greek images of *spirit* and less concerned with preserving the distinctive nature of the Creator God. For the distinctions

Second, Judaism developed a concept of good and evil spirits. Evil spirits, or demons, were associated with Satan, God's chief adversary who tempted persons to sin. Rabbinic literature portrayed evil spirits as having power to bring harm to health or even to threaten life. Good spirits were angels which contributed to the health and wellbeing of God's people.[14]

Intertestamental Judaism also expanded on the Old Testament concept of the Spirit of God. The Spirit of God became a more distinguished entity which stood outside of the human spirit and came to the individual from God under special circumstances. With increasing force Old Testament references to influences outside of the individual which affected the human spirit were thought of as acts of the Spirit of God.[15] Thus, Judaism developed a special identity for the entity which suggested a surprising level of autonomy. In Rabbinic writings the Spirit was often spoken of in personal categories. However, the Spirit was not regarded as a *hypostasis* or personal angelic being. As Erik Sjoberg has written,

> The personal categories used to describe the activity of the Spirit are not designed to present Him as a special heavenly being but rather to bring out the fact that He is an objective divine reality which encounters and claims man. . . . The decisive thing is that man stands here before a reality which comes from God, which in some sense represents the presence of God, and yet which is not identical with God.[16]

From a functional perspective the Spirit of God was for Palestinian Judaism primarily the Spirit of prophecy which had acted in Israel's past. In particular, the Spirit had spoken in the Hebrew Scriptures. Hence, sayings in the Law might be thought of as a word of the Torah or a word of the Holy Spirit. Presently the Spirit was thought to be prophetically inactive except to confirm the Torah by serving as a special presence with those who lived righteous lives conforming to the Law. It was believed that one day the Spirit would again be the active voice of God by bringing eschatological renewal to Israel. At that time Israel would experience the words of God through the Spirit just as Moses had before them.[17]

---

between *spirit* in Palestinian and Hellenistic Judaism see Erik Sjoberg, "Pneuma." TDNT, II, pp. 367-389.

[14] Kamlah, "Spirit," p. 693.

[15] Sjorberg, "Pneuma," p. 381.

[16] Ibid., pp. 387-388.

[17] Ibid., pp. 387-388.

THE HOLY SPIRIT IN EARLY
CHRISTIAN THOUGHT

Early Christian understandings of the Holy Spirit were established in the New Testament portrayal of the Spirit. That portrait of the Holy Spirit may be seen in the use of *pneuma* for the Spirit, the functional identifications of the Spirit which were rooted in Jewish thought and the development of a personal identity for the Spirit.

"spirit" in the New Testament. The New Testament usage of *pneuma* built off of the Hebrew understanding of spirit. James D. G. Dunn suggested that like *ruah* in Jewish thought, *pneuma* denoted "that power which man experiences as relating him to the spiritual realm, the realm of reality which lies beyond ordinary observation and human control."[18] The most frequent use of *pneuma* in the New Testament was as the Spirit of God, but it was also used in the Hebraic sense of wind, the human spirit, and good and evil spirits.[19]

While roughly one third of the Old Testament references to *ruah* were to wind, *pneuma* was used in that sense only twice in the New Testament (John 3:8; Heb. 1:7). In reference to the human spirit, *pneuma* denoted human existence insofar as it belongs to the spiritual realm and interacts with the spiritual realm.[20] In that context "spirit" continued in the pattern of Hebrew thought as the life-force which comes from God and returns to him at the death of the individual (Matt. 27:50; Luke 8:55; Jas. 2:26). It was the seat of perceptions and feelings (Luke 1:47; John 11:33; 13:21), the seat of thought (Mark 2:8; 8:12), and the seat of decision making (Matt. 26:41; Acts 20:22). *Pneuma* was further used to depict a state of mind or attitude within people (Luke 1:17; Matt. 5:3; John 4:23; Rom. 12:11).[21]

The human spirit was in some way possessed by the individual (Rom. 8:16; 1 Cor. 2:11; 5:5; 16:18; 1 Thess. 5:23), but the ancient Hebraic idea of spirit as the breath of God persisted and the imagery was merely a way of speaking about the belongingness of humanity to the spiritual realm. Thus, the human spirit was that aspect of human existence through which God was most immediately encountered (Rom. 8:16; 2 Cor. 2-10-16; Gal. 6:18; Phil. 4:23).[22]

In the New Testament evil and good spirits followed the pattern set in Palestinian Judaism. Mysterious powers that afflicted people were thought of as evil or unclean spirits. The power of evil in the world was focused in a

---

[18] James D. G. Dunn, "Spirit, Holy Spirit." NIDNTT, III, p. 693.

[19] Ibid.

[20] Ibid.

[21] Koch, "Spirit," pp. 877-878.

[22] Dunn, "Spirit," pp. 693-695.

particular spirit, Satan (Matt. 12:22-26; 1 Cor. 2:12; 2 Cor. 2:11; Eph. 2:2). Forces which aided persons in their lives were thought of as good spirits, or angels (2 Cor. 11:14-15; Heb. 1:7; 12:9). Good spirits received far less attention than evil ones, but Christians were admonished to distinguish between the two (1 Cor. 12:10; 2 Cor. 11:4; 1 John 4:1-6).[23]

As with intertestamental Judaism, the most significant development in the New Testament concerning spirit was in the concept of the Spirit of God. Within the New Testament, the dominant use of *pneuma* was for the Spirit of God (335 of 375 instances). Henry P. Van Dusen has analyzed the New Testament references to the Spirit and pointed out that 220 of the 335 references were simply to "Spirit" or "the Spirit." Only 19 references were made to "the Spirit of the Lord," "the Spirit of God," or "the Spirit of the Father." On the other hand, "Holy Spirit," which occurred only twice in the Old Testament, was found 91 times in the New Testament. There were five additional references to "the Spirit of Christ."[24] These shifts in nomenclature for the Spirit were indicative of deeper changes in the conceptualization of the essential nature of the Spirit, changes which were not readily apparent due to the adoption of Jewish themes for the Spirit.

The Spirit of Power. One Jewish theme incorporated into Christian thought was the image of the Spirit of Power. The Hebrew concept of the Spirit as the power of God was utilized in the Gospels of Matthew and Mark, and was further portrayed in Acts. The Ante-Nicene witness maintained the theme but gradually shifted the focus of the power of the Spirit away from cosmology toward ecclesiology, especially the church's power to forgive sins.

In essentials Matthew and Mark understood the Holy Spirit in a manner consistent with the Old Testament sense of the power to perform special acts, especially the power to create and to bring eschatological renewal. In the birth narrative of Jesus, Matthew recorded the role of the Holy Spirit in the virgin birth and thereby portrayed the Spirit in the Old Testament pattern of the creative power of God (Matt. 1:18-20).[25] However, there are no Jewish parallels to this form of life-giving, creative power by the Holy Spirit. C. K. Barrett has pointed out that in the Old Testament *ruah* acted creatively only in primal creation and in relation to the redemption of the people of God (with the possible exception of Psalm 104:30 which Barrett understood as breath rather than Spirit).[26] Barrett concluded that the part played by the Holy Spirit in the birth narrative must be seen as "the fulfillment of God's

---

[23] Ibid.

[24] Henry P. Van Dusen, *Spirit, Son, and Father: Christian Faith in the Light of the Holy Spirit*, (New York: Charles Scribner's Sons, 1958), p. 52.

[25] Schweizer, "Pneuma," p. 402.

[26] C. K. Barrett, *The Holy Spirit and the Gospel Tradition*, (London: S.P.C.K., 1966), pp. 18-20.

promised redemption in the new act of creation, comparable with that of Genesis 1."[27]

All of the Gospels are clear that at his baptism Jesus was anointed with the Spirit and thus entered into his messianic role (Matt. 3:17; Mark 1:11; Luke 3:22; John 1:33).[28] Here again the Spirit was acting as a creative power, calling forth the new creation and the conditions of the messianic era.[29]

After his baptism, Matthew and Mark portrayed Jesus as being under the guidance of the Spirit as he was led into the wilderness to be tempted (Matt. 4:1; Mark 1:12). Mark's strong idea of the Spirit driving Jesus into the wilderness was toned down to a leading in Matthew. But the imagery of power over Satan was increased in Matthew by the details of the three temptations and the inclusion of the triumphant rebuke "Begone, Satan!" (Matt. 4:10).[30]

It was by the Spirit that Jesus had power over the demons and he understood that power to be the sign of the eschatological kingdom (Matt. 12:28). Further, it was blasphemy against the Holy Spirit to attribute those exorcisms to the power of the devil rather than to the power of God (Mark 3:28-30). To deny the power of the Spirit of God was to deny the Kingdom which had come, for which there was no forgiveness.[31]

Matthew and Mark both included the idea of David's inspiration by the Spirit (Matt. 22:43; Mark 12:36). Both also recorded the assurance of Jesus that the disciples would be inspired during times of trial (Matt. 10:19-21; Mark 13:11). The latter reference reiterates the theme of the power of the Spirit overcoming the powers of the world and in the context of divine inspiration for the members of the new kingdom.

The theme of power was further associated with the Spirit in Acts. Jesus promised his followers that they would receive power after the Holy Spirit came upon them (Acts 1:8). The gift of the Spirit was a transforming power in the lives of individuals. Pentecost changed the band of timid disciples into a dynamic religious movement.[32]

Among the Ante-Nicene writers the Spirit was the power of God in creation. Hermas (ca. 160) spoke of the Holy Spirit as having created all

---

[27] Ibid., p. 24.

[28] Dunn, "Spirit," p. 697.

[29] Barrett, *Holy Spirit*, p. 45.

[30] Moody, *Spirit*, p. 43.

[31] James D. G. Dunn, *Jesus and the Spirit: A Study of the Religious and Charismatic Experience of Jesus and the First Christians as Reflected in the New Testament*, (Philadelphia: The Westminster Press, 1975), pp. 48-49.

[32] Henry P. Van Dusen, *Spirit, Son, and Father: Christian Faith in Light of the Holy Spirit*, (New York: Charles Scribner's Sons, 1958), pp. 58-59.

creation.[33] Theophilus (ca. 180), writing in the second century, identified the Spirit with the wisdom of God by which (along with the Word of God) all things were made.[34] The Spirit was that vitalizing power which was active in creation[35] and continued to embrace creation.[36] Irenaeus (c. 130- 202) repeated this tradition of the Word and Wisdom, Jesus and the Spirit, constructing all things.[37] Further, the Spirit was the life-giving force within the church causing its youth to be continually renewed.[38] With Tertullian (c. 160-220) the focus of the power of the Spirit shifted to the preservation of sound teaching through the true church,[39] the transformation and perfection of believers within the church,[40] the sealing of believers,[41] and the granting of indulgence to fornicators.[42] Hippolytus (c. 170-235) connected the power of the Spirit with ordination into church office whereby the bishop obtained the ability to remit sin and "loose every bond."[43] Cyprian (d. 258) linked even more closely the power of the Spirit with the church's power to forgive sins.[44] By the third century the pattern of thought was to tie the power of the Spirit to the functions of the church.

The Spirit of Prophecy. A second Jewish theme incorporated into Christian thought was the identification of the Holy Spirit with prophecy. The return of the Spirit of Prophecy was a theme of Luke's Gospel and the Book of Acts but also permeated virtually all of the Ante-Nicene writings. True prophecy came through the Holy Spirit, pointed to the central figure of Jesus Christ, and was a sign that the renewal of the people of God was through the church.

Luke portrayed a deep and distinct interest in the Holy Spirit. There were three times as many references to the Spirit in Luke as in Mark, and the first twelve chapters of Acts contained the highest concentration of references to the Spirit in the Scriptures.[45] Luke adopted the typically Jewish idea that the Holy Spirit was the Spirit of Prophecy. Insight into the will of

---

[33] Hermas, *Similitude*, 5.6, ANF, II, 35-36.

[34] Theophilus, *To Autolycus*, i.7, ANF, II, 91; ii.18, ANF, II, 101.

[35] Ibid., ii.13, ANF, II, 99-100.

[36] Ibid., i.5, ANF, II, 99.

[37] Irenaeus, *Against Heresies*, iv 20.3, 4; ANF, I, 488; ii.30.9, ANF, I, 406.

[38] Ibid., III 24.1, ANF, I, 458.

[39] Tertullian, *On Prescription Against Heretic*, Chap. 22, ANF, III, 253.

[40] Tertullian, *On Veiling Virgins*, Chap. 1, ANF, IV, 27-28.

[41] Tertullian, *On Modesty* , Chap. 21, ANF, IV, 98-100.

[42] Ibid.

[43] Hippolytus, *The Apostolic Tradition*, Chap. 1, trans. B. S. Easton (Ann Arbor: Archon Books, 1962), p. 34.

[44] *Epistle 73: To Bishop Jubaianus*, 6-11, ANF, V, 381-382.

[45] Schweizer, "Pneuma," p. 404.

God especially as it led to concrete actions was strongly emphasized as a chief work of the Spirit.[46]

The Lukan infancy narratives (chs. 1; 2) introduced the Gospel with a theme that the Spirit of Prophecy had returned. The Prologue to the Gospel (1:1-4) was followed by the annunciation of Gabriel that Zechariah would become the father of a great prophet, one specifically compared to Elijah but also having parallels with Samson. This new prophet in Israel would be filled with the Holy Spirit "even from his mother's womb" (1:15). Later, at Mary's arrival, Elizabeth was "filled with the Holy Spirit" and cried out a prophetic blessing upon Mary (1:39-45). At the naming of John, Zechariah's tongue was loosed and he was "filled with the Holy Spirit and prophesied" (1:67). As Jesus was being presented in the temple the Holy Spirit "was upon" Simeon who came "in the Spirit" into the temple having had it revealed to him "by the Holy Spirit" that he would see the Lord's Christ before he died (2:25-35). Inspiration was also depicted in the thanksgiving of Hannah (2:36-38).[47]

Luke's treatment of the baptism and temptation of Jesus emphasized the abiding of the Spirit on Jesus. Prayer and prophetic inspiration were linked as Luke alone recorded that Jesus was praying when the Spirit descended (3:21-22). A double reference to the Spirit introduced the temptation events; Jesus was "full of the Holy Spirit" and was "led about in the Holy Spirit into the wilderness" (4:1-2). After the temptation he returned to Galilee "in the power of the Spirit" (4:14).[48] The connection between the ministry of Jesus and the abiding presence of the Spirit was reiterated in Luke with the account of Jesus' return to his hometown where he read from Isaiah's prophecy, "The Spirit of the Lord is upon me" (Luke 4:18).[49]

The Lukan travel narrative (9:51-18:14) included one passage with clear reference to the Holy Spirit as the source of prophetic experience. At the return of the Seventy, Jesus was said to have rejoiced greatly in the Holy Spirit (10:21). The cause of his jubilation was the disciples' joyful realization of the power of the name of Jesus over demons (10:17). Associated with the event was Jesus' testimony of a vision of Satan falling from heaven while the Seventy were out exercising authority over demons (10:18). A prophetic oracle was also given by Jesus (10:21-22). Thus, he was a visionary in the pattern of the Old Testament prophets and his message was one of a new relationship with God, a relationship with a heavenly Father. Dale Moody has summarized the significance of his event:

---

[46] Ibid., p. 407. However, while miracles were significant in Luke's narratives, they were never ascribed by him to the Holy Spirit.

[47] Moody, *Spirit*, pp. 49-53.

[48] Ibid., pp. 53-54.

[49] Schweizer, "Pneuma," p. 405.

> The portrait of Jesus as one full of the Spirit, speaking and acting in the power of the Spirit, is a pneumatic Jesus, a charismatic Christ, who has authority and power, *exousia* and *dynamis*. His words are God's words, and his deeds are God's deeds. Ecstatic power and prophecy have come to perfection in the person of this Son of the Most High God who addresses him as "Abba." All three of the Synoptic Gospels report the Voice from heaven that declared this intimate relationship; . . . but this Q oracle relates it in a unique way to the ecstatic experience inspired by the Holy Spirit.[50]

The theme of the Spirit of Prophecy found in the Gospel of Luke was repeated in the Acts of the Apostles but with stress on the reality of the Spirit in the life of the church. The Spirit infused the church almost as a tangible prophetic force, visible in its effects, if not in itself (Acts 2:1-4; 4:31; 8:39).[51]

He was the Spirit who had inspired the prophets and other writers of the Old Testament (1:16; 4:25; 28:25). He was now fulfilling the ancient hope of Moses that all would prophesy and the words of Joel concerning prophecy, dreams, and visions in the last days (Num. 11:29; Joel 2:28-30; Acts 2:16-21). The personal experience of the Spirit was an experience of individual revelation and inspiration resulting in prophetic utterances.[52] Persons prophesied at the time of their initial infilling with the Spirit (Acts 2:4; 10:44-46; 19:6) and when refilled during times of crises (4:8, 31; 13:9-12). The Spirit also served as a power to enable effective testimony and teaching (5:32; 6:10; 8:29-38). There arose a class of prophets, both resident and wandering, who in some way possessed a distinct ministry of prophecy within the larger community of persons who prophesied (11:27-28; 13:1; 15:32; 21:9, 10-11).

The Spirit of Prophecy made known the will of God and gave direction to the church. It was the Spirit who guided the church personally and collectively through its mission. The three-fold geographic outreach of the church based upon Acts 1:8 ("you shall be my witnesses both in Jerusalem, and in all Judea and Samaria, and even to the remotest part of the earth" NAS) set the tone for much of the church's relationship with the Spirit.[53] In Jerusalem the Spirit was portrayed as giving direction to the preaching of the whole congregation (2:1-13; 4:31), but with a special emphasis upon the early leadership (2:14; 5:1-11, 12; 6:1-7). With the death of Stephen the Spirit became more clearly the director of the church's mission, guiding the

---

50 Moody, *Spirit*, pp. 55-56.

51 Dunn, "Spirit," p. 698.

52 Van Dusen, *Spirit*, p. 59.

53 Moody, *Spirit*, p. 59.

evangelists into new opportunities of ministry throughout Judea and Samaria (8:29; 10:19; 11:12).[54] With the expansion of the church into the rest of the world the Spirit was depicted as guiding the church through institutional structures. The Spirit spoke to the church at Antioch and *they* laid hands on Paul and Barnabas and sent them away (13:1-4). The Jerusalem Council's decision seemed good to the Holy Spirit and to the participants (15:28). And the Holy Spirit appointed overseers for the Churches (20:28). However, the Spirit continued to give personal direction in mission (16:6, 7; 20:23). Thus, the Spirit of Prophecy made certain the will of God in the life of the church.

In the mind of the early post-apostolic church the Holy Spirit was most characteristically the Spirit of Prophecy. Predominantly, the thought was applied to the inspiration of the Old Testament. The Law and the Prophets were the only canonical scriptures until the middle of the second century. They were the most conspicuous monument of the Spirit's handiwork. Through them he had beforehand witnessed to the truth of the Gospel. In the second century the New Testament canon was established and equated with the Old Testament. The evangelists spoke by the same Spirit as the prophets. Furthermore, prophetic inspiration was not regarded as having ceased with the Apostles. The Spirit of Prophecy continued to speak throughout the Ante-Nicene period. Hermas, the writer of the *Didache*, Irenaeus, and even anti-Montanist writers presented prophecy as an ongoing gift of the Spirit within the church.[55]

The Spirit of the New Age. The most comprehensive Jewish theme related to the Holy Spirit adopted by Christians was the identification of the Spirit with the arrival of the eschatological new age. The return of prophecy and manifestations of the power of God were but integral aspects of the renewal of the people of God. The Spirit's role in the new aeon was most fully developed in the Pauline corpus.

Paul fundamentally associated the Holy Spirit with the arrival of the new age through Jesus Christ. The Spirit of Christ was ushering in the new aeon through the proclamation of the Gospel, the transformation of believers into citizens of the kingdom of God, and the up-building of the church as the body of Christ.

One way in which the believers experienced the Spirit was as the inspiration for the apostolic preaching of the new age. Paul understood the impact of his own proclamation of the Gospel as being rooted in a presentation of the Gospel which was not in word only but also in the power and demonstration of the Holy Spirit (Rom. 15:l9; 1 Cor. 2:4; 2 Cor. 6:6-7; 1

---

[54] Dunn, "Spirit," p. 700.

[55] Henry Barclay Swete, *The Holy Spirit in the Ancient Church: A Study of Christian Teaching in the Age of the Fathers*, (Grand Rapids, Michigan: Baker Book House, 1966), pp. 381-385.

Thess. 1:5). The result was a faith built upon the power of God rather than human wisdom, a knowledge of God rooted in the personal revelation of the cross (1 Cor. 2:1-5). Thus, the Spirit determined both the content and the form of true apostolic preaching.[56]

A second aspect of the Spirit's eschatological work for Paul was in the transformation of the believer into a citizen of the new age. To live in the new time was to live by the Spirit. The most frequent references to the Holy Spirit in Paul's writings were in relationship to the spirit of the believer.[57] The Holy Spirit working through the human spirit was establishing the dominion of God. The Spirit was the power of the new age bringing the light of God into the lives of persons surrounded by a world of spiritual darkness.

As the power of the new age, the Spirit was transforming believers into citizens of the kingdom of Christ (1 Cor. 6:9-11). The internal change of the believer by the Spirit

resulted in justification and sanctification (1 Cor. 6:11; 1 Thess. 4:3-8). The transformation was into the glorious image of Christ (2 Cor. 3:18) which was bringing forth personal characteristics suitable to the kingdom (Gal. 5:22-24). Paul especially associated the Spirit with the dispositions of love, joy, peace, and hope (Gal. 5:22; Rom. 4:17; 15:13; 1 Thess. 1:6).[58]

The transforming work of the Spirit in the life of the believer was linked to the Spirit's function of bringing the knowledge of God to the individual (1 Cor. 2:6-16). It was that knowledge which was producing the sweet aroma of Christ in the lives of the believers (2 Cor. 1:14-16). In form, Paul's thought paralleled that of Gnosticism: the Spirit had searched the depths of God and revealed the thoughts of God to natural beings (1 Cor. 2:10, 14-15),[59] but in terms of content a clear distinction was present. The knowledge communicated by the Spirit was tied to the historical event of the cross, the event which was already dividing the new creation from the old (1 Cor. 2:8).[60]

The knowledge which the Spirit brought was a certainty of relationship with God, an awareness that one was a child of God through Jesus Christ (Rom. 8:14-17). The Spirit further gave a certainty of the future redemption of the body (Rom. 8:23) and an assurance of eternal life (Gal. 6:8). Conversely, knowledge and confession of Jesus was the evidence of the Spirit's presence in the believer (1 Cor. 12:3). Thus, the Spirit both called persons to the knowledge of God in Jesus Christ and effected that knowledge

---

[56] Schweizer, "Pneuma," p. 425.

[57] P. K. Jewett, "Holy Spirit," p. 187.

[58] Moody, *Spirit*, pp. 108-117.

[59] Schweizer, "Pneuma,", p. 427.

[60] Ibid., pp. 427-428.

within them; he produced the gift of faith within believers (1 Cor. 12:9) and was the gift of God to believers in response to faith (Gal. 3:1-5, 14).[61]

However, life in the Spirit was not uncontested. The spiritual walk of the faithful was depicted as a tension, or a warfare, between the powers of the old age and those of the new. The struggle was most characteristically described as a conflict between flesh and the Spirit (Rom. 7:14-25; 8:10-13; Ga. 4:23-29; Philip. 3:3). The mind-set of the flesh was death and hostility, but the mind-set of the Spirit was life and peace (Rom. 8:5-8).[62] The tension was also described as between the Law and the Spirit (Rom. 2:29; 7:6; 2 Cor. 3:6). The Law was spiritual but served only to identify sin and therefore catered to the flesh. The Spirit delivered from the flesh and therefore made the written code obsolete (Gal. 5:1, 16). For the believer the battle will end when the individual becomes a "spiritual body," wholly belonging to the new age, and completely under the Spirit's direction (Rom. 8:11, 23; 1 Cor. 15:44-49; 2 Cor. 5:1-5; Eph. 1:14).[63] In the present the Spirit served as the "first fruits" of the end time (Rom. 8:23), the first installment of the believer's inheritance in God's kingdom (Rom. 8:15- 17; Gal. 4:6-7; Eph. 1:13-14), and the down payment and guarantee that God will complete the work begun in Christ (2 Cor. 1:20-22; 5:5).

A third aspect of the Spirit's eschatological work was depicted by Paul in the edification of the church. He offered several figurative descriptions of the church which associated the Spirit with the up-building of the end-time community of God. The church was the "household of God" made up of those who have access to the Father through the Spirit (Eph. 2:19, 18; 4:6). It was the new Israel receiving the blessing of Abraham through the promise of the Spirit (Gal. 3:14). The church was the body of Christ, (Eph. 1:22-23; Col. 1:18), and membership in the body was by the Spirit (1 Cor. 12:13). The church was also for Paul the temple of God being constructed, dwelt in and held together by the Holy Spirit (1 Cor. 3:16; Eph. 2:19-22).[64]

The Spirit as Personal Divine Being. The Christian concept of the Holy Spirit broke with Jewish thought with the development of a personal identity for the Spirit. The Christian experience of God through the Spirit compelled a definition of him as a "self" within the Godhead. Jewish monotheism had to be reinterpreted to make room for the realities of grace and truth made flesh in Christ and actualized in the communion effected by the Holy Spirit.[65] The Old Testament themes associated with the Spirit were

---

[61] Schweizer, "Pneuma," p. 427.

[62] Moody, *Spirit*, p. 119.

[63] Dunn, "Spirit," p. 702.

[64] Lothar Coenan, "Church," NIDNTT, I, 300.

[65] George Johnston, "The Doctrine of the Holy Spirit in the New Testament," *Scottish Journal of Theology*, 1 (1948), 53-54.

now fulfilled in conjunction with the life and mission of Jesus. The identification of the Spirit as a person was reflected in the Pauline concept of the Spirit of Christ, the Johannine portrait of the other Paraclete, the association of the Spirit with angels and the development of the doctrine of the Trinity.

For Paul the Holy Spirit was characteristically the Spirit of Christ. James D. G. Dunn summarized the Pauline relationship between the Spirit and the resurrected Jesus:

> Most significant of all, the Spirit for Paul has been constitutively stamped with the character of Christ. Christ by his resurrection entered wholly upon the realm of the Spirit (Rom. 1:4; cf. 8:11). Indeed, Paul can say that Christ by his resurrection "became life-giving Spirit" (1 Cor. 15:45). That is to say, the exalted Christ is now experienced in, through, and as Spirit. Christ now cannot be experienced apart from the Spirit: the Spirit is the medium of union between Christ and the believer (1 Cor. 6:17); only those belong to Christ, are "in Christ," who have the Spirit and in so far as they have the Spirit (Rom. 8:9, 14). Conversely, the Spirit is now experienced as the power of the risen Christ--the Spirit now cannot be experienced apart from Christ.[66]

Paul did not make the Spirit and the risen Christ the same entity, however.[67] The Spirit was the source of the Christian knowledge of God and created within the believer an awareness of relationship with both God as Father and Jesus as Lord (Rom. 8:15-17; 1 Cor. 12:3). Thus, the Spirit could not be thought of as synonymous with either and a Trinitarian element was reflected from the believer's experience. Paul further made use of a Trinitarian imagery (1 Cor. 12:4-6; 2 Cor. 13:14). Jesus and the Spirit were distinct persons but inseparably one in Paul's interpretation of the Christian encounter with God.[68]

In the Gospel of John the Spirit was carefully distinguished from Jesus and his ministry in a fashion that suggested intentional comparisons of the two divine persons. Only three references were made to the Spirit outside of the final discourse.[69] But in that unit Jesus spoke freely of the Spirit as another

---

[66] Dunn, "Spirit," p. 703.

[67] C. F. D. Moule, *The Holy Spirit*, (Grand Rapids: William B. Eerdmans Publishing Company, 1978), p. 26.

[68] Dunn, *Jesus and the Spirit*, p. 326.

[69] Two references were parallel passages in which Jesus spoke of the Spirit as the antithesis of the "flesh." "That which is born of the flesh is flesh; and that which is born of the Spirit is spirit" (3:6). "It is the Spirit who gives life and the flesh profits nothing" (6:63). In the third

Paraclete, the Spirit of Truth. A personal identity for the Spirit was suggested by the use of the personal title, Paraclete, the use of personal pronouns for the Spirit, and the functions ascribed to the Spirit.[70] But the personhood of the Spirit was most strongly implied by the personal similarities between Jesus and the Spirit.

Parallels between the Paraclete and Jesus are unmistakable. Jesus has come from the Father into the world (5:43; 16:28; 18:37); the Paraclete will come from the Father (15:26; 16:7, 8, 13). The Father gave the Son (3:16); the Father will give the Spirit (14:16). Jesus was sent by the Father (3:17); the Father will send the Spirit (14:26). Jesus came in the name of his Father (5:43); he will send the Spirit from the Father (15:26; 16:7). Jesus is the truth (14:6); the other Paraclete is the Spirit of Truth (14:17; 15:26; 16:13). Jesus is the Holy One of God (6:69); the Paraclete is the Holy Spirit (14:26). Raymond Brown has concluded from this type of comparison that the Spirit was thought of as another Jesus who was considered the presence of Jesus when Jesus was absent. The Spirit was for the church what Jesus would be if bodily present. For John, the Spirit was a person sent to take the place of the ascended Jesus.[71]

One post-Apostolic association of the Spirit with Jesus as personal beings was the adoption of the Jewish doctrine of angels for the two divine beings. Hermas wrote of seven angels, one glorious angel and six others. The glorious angel was the God, Christ, who was synonymous with the angel Michael.[72] In the *Ascension of Isaiah* Gabriel was called the Angel of the Holy Spirit who rests upon Isaiah to speak through him and the other prophets.[73] Later Origin cited a Hebrew source for his view that the two Seraphim of Isaiah 6 were the Son and the Holy Spirit.[74] According to Hippolytus, a Jewish Christian gnostic, Elkesai, had a vision of two great angels, one male (the Son of God), the other female (the Holy Spirit).[75] In the *Testaments of the Twelve Patriarchs* the Holy Spirit was identified as the Angel of the Temple who

---

passage John vividly portrayed Jesus' consciousness of the Spirit's relationship to him when he breathed on his disciples and said, "receive the Holy Spirit" (20:22).

[70] Moody, *Spirit*, p. 164. Moody concluded, "It is in the Paraclete sayings that the personality of the Spirit is most pronounced, and the pattern of a Holy Trinity is highly developed."

[71] Raymond E. Brown, "The Paraclete in the Fourth Gospel," *New Testament Studies*, 13 (1967), p. 124.

[72] Jean Danielou, *The Theology of Jewish Christianity*, trans. John A. Baker (Philadelphia: Westminster Press, 1977), pp. 119-124.

[73] *Ascension of Isaiah*, IX.27-36; XI.32-35 in Danielou, *Jewish Christianity*, p. 129.

[74] Origen, *De Principiis* I.3.4, ANF, IV, 253.

[75] Hippolytus, *Refutation of All Heresies* IX.8, ANF, V, 131-132.

abandoned it at the crucifixion of Christ (thereby rending the veil) to spread himself like fire over the nations.[76] Jean Danielou has concluded,

> In fact the word angel has an essentially concrete force; it connotes a supernatural being manifesting itself. . . . the word represents the Semitic form of the designation of the Word and the Spirit as spiritual substances, as 'persons,' though the latter terminology was not to be introduced into theology until a good deal later. 'Angel' is the old-fashioned equivalent.[77]

Thus, the association of the Word and Spirit with angels pointed to personal identities and constituted an early form of the theology of the Trinity.

The Trinity. The personal identity of the Spirit reached ultimate formulation in the various articulations of the doctrine of the Trinity. From the earliest Christian times the Spirit belonged to the sphere of the divine in so far as he was the object of faith and adoration. Early baptismal creeds professed faith in Father, Son, and Holy Spirit. Doxologies and hymns glorified the Spirit along with the Father and the Son.[78]

Athenagoras was the first to elaborate on a philosophical explanation of the relationship of the Father, Son and Spirit.[79] Irenaeus depicted an "economic" Trinity with Jesus and the Spirit serving as the two hands of God.[80] The term "Trinity" was introduced into Christian literature by the end of the second century but it was not until the Monarchian heresy of the third century that the church focused its attention on the philosophical clarification of the three divine persons. Tertullian was the first to explicitly describe a trinity of Divine Persons and to set forth an extensive theological explanation of the situation of the persons to each other.[81]

Against the backdrop of Monarchianism, Origin subordinated the Spirit to the Father and Son insisting that the Spirit was generated by the Son. On the other hand, he insisted Catholic Christianity held to one God existing in three persons (*hypostases*), Specifically, the Spirit was not to be considered a divine force as he was a personal existence.[82] In a later work Origin taught

---

[76] The Testaments of the Twelve Patriarchs, XII.9, ANF, VIII, 37. A similar theme of the Spirit forsaking the temple is found in the work of Tertullian; *An Answer to the Jews*, ANF, III, 170.

[77] Danielou, *Jewish Christianity*, p. 118.

[78] Swete, *The Holy Spirit in the Ancient Church*, p. 359.

[79] Clyde L. Manschreck, *A History of Christianity from Persecution to Uncertainty* (Englewood Cliffs, NJ: Prentice-Hall, Inc., 1974), p. 52.

[80] Justo L. Gonzalez, *A History of Christian Thought, Vol. 1, From the Beginnings to the Council of Chalcedon in A. D. 451*, (Nashville: Abingdon Press, 1970), pp. 164-165.

[81] Ibid., pp. 182-186.

[82] Origen, *Commentary on John*, II.6, ANF, X, 328.

that the Son and Spirit were of equal honor being equally far above criticism.[83]

Hippolytus followed the subordinationism of Origin in his defense of the Trinity against the Modalism of Noetus and Sabellius.[84] A similar view was espoused by Novatian in *On the Trinity*, his attempt to refute Sabellianism.[85] It was not until the Arian controversy of the fourth century that the orthodox doctrine of the Trinity was firmly established. The Council of Nicea affirmed the deity of Christ as being of the same substance (*homoousian*) as God the Father while existing as separate persons (*hypostasis*). But the Council only said of the Spirit, "We believe also in one Holy Spirit."[86]

The battle over Arianism was finally won at the Alexandrine synod of A.D. 363 where the doctrine of the Holy Spirit played a dominant role and the divinity of the Spirit was established.[87] At Constantinople in A.D. 381 the Nicene formula was amplified to read, "I believe in the Holy Ghost, the Lord, the Giver of Life, who proceedeth from the Father, who with the Father and the Son together is worshipped and glorified, who spake by the prophets."[88] The intent was to make it clear that the Holy Spirit was a separate person (*hypostasis*) but of the same substance (*homoousian*) as God the Father and God the Son.[89] With the Nicene Creed the personhood of the Spirit intimated in the New Testament writings and the experience of the church became explicit in the doctrinal statement of the church.

In conclusion, very early in Christian thought the Holy Spirit transcended the Jewish imagery of a God-given prophetic force or impetus by taking on personal features. John brought the personality of the Spirit to the fore by giving the Spirit masculine titles, by referring to the Paraclete/Spirit with masculine personal pronouns, and by presenting the Spirit as another Jesus. A personal identity for the Spirit was also implied by the Pauline corpus and post-apostolic association of the Spirit with angels. The formulation of the doctrine of the Trinity gave a final affirmation of the personal being of the divine Spirit.

---

[83] Origen, *On First Principles*, I.3, ANF, IV, 251-256; II.7, ANF, IV, 284-286.

[84] Gonzales, *Christian Thought*, pp. 238-240.

[85] Ibid., pp. 242-243.

[86] Kenneth Scott Latourette, A *History of Christianity, Vol. I, Beginnings to 1500*, (New York: Harper and Row, 1975), p. 155.

[87] Gonzales, *Christian Thought*, pp. 291-293.

[88] Quoted from Latourette, *A History of Christianity*, p. 164.

[89] Ibid.

42

THE HOLY SPIRIT AS TEACHER

The intent of this section is to clarify early Christianity's perception of the Holy Spirit's role as a teacher. The Paraclete sayings of John serve as the fountainhead of the church's imagery of the Spirit as teacher. Contained in the Final Discourse of Jesus between the last supper and the crucifixion, those sayings vividly portrayed the Spirit as a successor to the teaching ministry of Christ. The attributes of the Spirit as teacher set forth there were consistent with earlier Christian writings and were expanded upon by those which followed.

ANOTHER TEACHER

The Paraclete sayings of the Gospel of John are located during the period between the last supper (ch. 13) and the arrest of Jesus (ch. 18). There were five sayings (14:16-17; 14:25-26; 15:26-27; 16:7-11; 16:12-15) each of which could be isolated as literary units but also fit within the larger text as a homogenous and coherent unit.[90] An understanding of the Johannine portrait of the Paraclete requires a review of the meaning of "paraclete": and an analysis of the five Paraclete sayings.

THE MEANING OF "PARACLETE." A great variety of backgrounds have been postulated as the source of meaning for the Johannine "Paraclete." The most common theory relates the Paraclete of John to those of ancient Greece who served as legal advocates or defense attorneys. The *paracletos* was literally one called alongside to help.[91] But the functions attributed to the Spirit-Paraclete were predominantly non-forensic and those which were legal in nature did not follow the Greek pattern. He was a witness (John 15:26), not a counselor; a prosecutor (John 16:8-11) not an advocate.[92] A more general Greek understanding of a paraclete was that of any intercessor, mediator, or spokesperson. But the Paraclete of John speaks to and through the believers, not for them[93] J. G. Davies argued for the authorized translation of "comforter" on the basis of the LXX usage of the verb *parakalein* as the

---

[90] Eskil Franck, *Revelation Taught: The Paraclete in the Gospel of John*, (Gleerup: CWK, 1985), p. 13.

[91] W. Bauer, "Paracletos," *A Greek-English Lexicon of the New Testament and Other Early Christian Literature*, trans. and ed. by W. F. Arndt and F. W. Gingrich, (Chicago: University Press, 1957), p.d 624.

[92] George Johnston, *The Spirit-Paraclete in the Gospel of John*, (Cambridge: University Press, 1970), p. 85.

[93] Brown, "Paraclete, " p. 117.

dominant translation of the Hebrew concept of counseling.[94] But the Johannine usage does not suggest the role of a consoler. Rather, he was one sent from God to be an active helper.[95] Eskil Franck suggested the answer rests in the consideration of the macrostructure and microstructure within which the term was used. When looking at the whole there is a legal structure which runs throughout the Gospel of John. The forensic background of *paraclete* thus served to tie the Paraclete sayings to the macrostructure of the book. When looking at the immediate context *paraclete* must be defined by the function it fills. In the microstructure Paraclete is what the Paraclete does.[96]

Raymond Brown also argued for an understanding of the Paraclete based on literary use. He suggested Jesus and the Paraclete in John fell within an established pattern of tandem relationships in Jewish history such as Moses and Joshua, Elijah and Elisha. The transference of spirit was a noted element of those cases. Thus, Jesus and the Paraclete represent a tandem relationship of two salvific figures.[97] The Paraclete was, as it were, a second Jesus. Through him Jesus was experienced in the life of the church and the later Christian, as for understanding, was no further removed from the ministry of Jesus than the first generation of believers.[98] Inasmuch as the Johannine portrait of Jesus was that of a rabbi, or teacher,[99] it follows that the Paraclete would assume the role of a teacher.

Another possible solution to understanding the meaning of *paracletos* rests in the New Testament usage of its possible cognate forms. If *paracletos* was understood as a verbal adjective used as a noun then the way is open to the semantic field made up by the verb *parakalein*. Davies used this process to find the meaning of "consoling" in the LXX. But in the LXX the semantic field of the verb embraced comfort, encourage, reprove, exhort, teach, and preach.[100] In the New Testament it also embraced several meanings: call, invite, ask for help, plead, make an inquiry, comfort, exhort, reprove, etc..[101] In certain passages the verb was clearly connected with the concept of preaching-teaching (Acts 13:15; Hebrews 13:22; 1 Thess. 2:3; 1 Tim. 4:13)

---

[94] J. G. Davies, "The Primary Meaning of Paracletos," *Journal of Theological Studies* 4 (1953) pp. 35-38.

[95] Bauer, "Paracletos," p. 624.

[96] Franck, *Revelation Taught*, p. 21.

[97] Brown, "Paraclete, " pp. 120-123.

[98] Ibid., p. 129.

[99] Jesus was referred to as rabbi five times in John 1:38, 49: 3:2, 26; 6:25. It should be noted that the references were in the opening section of the Gospel where Jesus was being introduced as the one sent from God and the parallelisms between Jesus and the Paraclete were being set.

[100] Kenneth Grayston, "A Problem of Translation: The Meaning of Parakaleo, Paraklesis in the New Testament," *Scripture Bulletin*, 11 (1979), pp. 27-31.

[101] Bauer, "Paracletos," p. 624.

and elsewhere with prophecy (Acts 2:40; 15:32; 1 Cor. 14:3, 22, 31).[102] It follows that *paracletos* may well have been understood as both a forensic and didactic term by the early readers of John. The precise meaning rests in the functions of the Paraclete in the context of the five sayings.

The Five Paraclete Sayings. Jesus made five references to the Paraclete. All five references contained pedagogical overtones and two of the five cast the Paraclete into the specific role of a teacher. Each passage portrayed the Spirit as responding to the needs of the disciples of Jesus as an extension of Christ's own relationship with them and thereby unveiled aspects of the early Christian perception of the role of the Spirit as teacher.

The first Paraclete saying (14:15-17) was given against the background of the disciples' pending loneliness (14:18). The basic concept of another Paraclete was introduced. Jesus was the first Paraclete who was about to leave the disciples to go where they could not presently go (13:33, 36). The second Paraclete was to be given by the Father to be with them forever (14:17). He was a person and a power. He was the Spirit of Truth (14:17).[103] He was "another" in the sense of "the same kind" as Jesus.[104] The difference between the two was to be their locations. Jesus would be with the Father (14:2- 4, 28) while the Spirit would be in the disciples (14:17).

The second Paraclete saying (14:25-27) addressed the need of the disciples for a deepened knowledge of the teachings of Christ. The primary function of the Paraclete was set forth; he will teach.[105] The identification of the Paraclete with the Spirit was repeated as was the Spirit's role in continuing the ministry of Jesus. The Paraclete will be sent in the name of Jesus and will teach "all things" and "remind" the disciples of everything Jesus had said. These two clauses were parallel thoughts, that is, the reminder of everything Jesus had said was synonymous to the teaching of all things.[106] Also, the "all things" which the Spirit will teach (vs. 26) serve in contrast to "these things" which Jesus has already taught (vs. 25) so that the role of the Spirit as teacher will be to add to what Jesus has taught. Jesus as teacher in human flesh had

---

[102] Franck, *Revelation Taught*, pp. 30-35.

[103] Georg Brauman, "Advocate, Paraclete, Helper," NIDNTT, I, 90.

[104] Moody, *Spirit*, p. 165.

[105] The etymological root of "to teach," *didasko*, meant to repeatedly extend the hand as if to give or receive something. Hence, the primary meaning was to pass from one person to another. Knowledge, opinions, facts, and skills could be transferred from the teacher to the pupil through repeated activity on the part of both. In the LXX the word meant chiefly instruction in how to live, the subject matter being the will of God especially as expressed in moral and practical terms. In the NT the meaning is almost always to teach or instruct in the patter of the OT. Klaus Wegenast, "Teach," NIDNTT, III, 759-765.

[106] Raymond E. Brown, *The Anchor Bible: The Gospel According to John* (xiii-xxi), (Garden City, NY: Doubleday & Company, Inc., 1970), pp. 650-651.

been limited to the time of his "abiding with" the disciples but the Spirit will not be limited.[107]

But what was the intended extent of "all things" (vs. 26)? What would the Spirit add to what Jesus had taught? Would the Spirit teach quantitatively more than Jesus, literally all things? Since the teaching of all things was synonymous with the reminding of everything Jesus had said then the answer is no. Rather, the function of the Spirit-teacher would be to interpret the sayings of Christ so as to enable the disciples to see the full meaning of Jesus' words.[108] His reminding would be re-presentation in a living manner; the words of Jesus would through the Spirit be freshly applied to the lives of the disciples.[109] "All things" refers to their level of understanding. The Paraclete would bring the words of Jesus to bear in a meaningful way on all the situations of life.

The third Paraclete passage (John 15:26-27) addressed the needs of the disciples as persons exposed to the hatred of the world (15:18-26) and projected the Spirit into the role of a witness. The Paraclete was to be sent by Jesus from the Father as a witness of him. This saying has been generally interpreted as forensic in nature. Either Jesus in on trial before the world and the Spirit-Paraclete is the chief witness in his behalf, or conversely the world is on trial before Jesus and the Spirit is the chief witness against it.[110] However, Franck argued convincingly from John's other uses of "witness" (*marturiu*) that the primary meaning is didactic in nature. The objective of Johannine witnessing is to create knowledge and thereby increase faith. Thus, instruction is the objective of the Paraclete's witness while judgment lies as a consequence in the background. In the absence of Jesus the task of the Spirit is to reveal "an actual, living, and authoritative knowledge about Jesus, which provokes a response in people."[111] The disciples will also be witnesses of Christ. However, their witness will not be in addition to that of the Spirit. It will be because of the witness of the Spirit. As Raymond Brown has stated, "the disciples' witness is simply the exteriorization of the Spirit's witness. . .".[112] Together they witness of the supreme revelation of God to men, Jesus Christ.

The fourth Paraclete passage (16:4-11) is given against the backdrop of the disciples' sorrow over the removal of Jesus. The Paraclete is presented as one who confronts the world. When he comes he will "convict" the world of sin, righteousness, and judgment. The intent of this saying is difficult to

---

[107] Moody, *Spirit*, p. 166.

[108] Brown, *Anchor Bible*, p. 650.

[109] Brown, "Paraclete, " p. 129.

[110] Brown, *Anchor Bible*, p. 699.

[111] Franck, *Revelation Taught*, p. 56.

[112] Brown, *Anchor Bible*, p. 690.

ascertain.[113] The Greek word *elenchein*, translated "convict," means "to expose"[114] with the sense of proving wrong.[115] Dale Moody associated the phrase with the work of the Roman judge in cross-examining three times the one charged.[116] The idea being to expose the guilt within. Barrett suggested that the Paraclete was promised here to help the disciples by intensifying the work of the conscience of the world.[117] R. E. Brown argues for the meaning of "to prove wrong" but concluded from the grammar that the disciples are the object of the convincing.[118] That is, the Paraclete will help the disciples by convincing them of the guilt of the world. In either case the Paraclete will function to clarify the presence of wrong in terms of sin, righteousness, and judgment. Thus, the forensic function has at its core the teaching function.[119]

The final Paraclete passage (John 16:12-15) addressed the disciples inability to instantly embrace the full revelation of Christ and produced the most extensive pedagogical imagery of the Spirit. The role of the Spirit as teacher which had been set forth in the second passage was in this passage expanded.[120] Jesus repeated a statement on his inability due to time to teach the disciples everything they needed to know and he also repeated his promise that the Spirit of truth will come to them to complete their instruction.

The two primary functions of the Spirit in this passage were to guide into all truth and to bring glory to Christ. He will guide into all truth by speaking what he hears and proclaiming what is yet to come. He will glorify Christ by proclaiming that which belongs to Christ.[121]

To guide (*hadagasei*) is to lead in the sense of showing the way.[122] Textual differences allow for either "in" or "into" all truth. The difference in meaning is slight and the context suggests that whichever the reading the disciples will by the Spirit come to exist in the whole sphere of truth.[123] Their existence within the truth will be actualized by the Paraclete's speaking what he hears

---

[113] D. A. Carson, "The Function of the Paraclete in John 16:7-11," *Journal of Biblical Literature* 98 (1979), pp. 547-566. Carson gave a concise review of the major interpretations of this passage and the problems encountered by each.

[114] C. K. Barrett, *The Gospel According to St. John, An Introduction with Commentary and Notes on the Greek Text*, (London: S.P.C.K., 1960), p. 405.

[115] Carson, "The Function of the Paraclete," pp. 549-551.

[116] Moody, *Spirit*, pp. 172-173.

[117] Barrett, *The Gospel According to St. John*, p. 405.

[118] Carson, "The Function of the Paraclete, " pp. 551-553.

[119] Franck, *Revelation Taught*, pp. 58-65.

[120] C. H. Dodd, *The Interpretation of the Fourth Gospel*, (Cambridge: University Press, 1968), p. 415.

[121] Franck, *Revelation Taught*, p. 66.

[122] Brown, *Anchor Bible*, p. 707.

[123] Barrett, *The Gospel According to St. John*, p. 407.

from the Father and the Son. Jesus has many things to tell (*legein*) the disciples. The Spirit will speak (*lelein*) only what he hears. The speaking function of Jesus focuses on the content of what has been said. The speaking function of the Spirit focuses on the vocal and speech-function itself. The implication is that the Paraclete will guide by serving as a mouthpiece of the absent Jesus.[124] Likewise, to proclaim (*anagelei*) what is yet to come focuses on the task of repeating an announcement or delivering a message.[125] One task of the Paraclete will be to declare to the disciples a message from Jesus concerning future events. The message will contain new information and will not be limited to recalling the words of the historical Jesus. The Paraclete will extend the message of God in Christ to cover details of the future.[126]

The Spirit will glorify Christ by receiving that which belongs to Christ and proclaiming it to the disciples. To receive (*lambanei*) is to take up which implies the Spirit will function as a messenger whose delivery is from Christ to the disciples. His method of delivery will be the same as when he reveals what is to come; that is, he will proclaim (*anagelei*) in the sense of announcing that which belongs to Christ.

That which the Paraclete receives of Christ is also of the Father. He thus serves to instruct the disciples in the divine relationship between Jesus and the Father.[127] The Spirit was to bring the mission and being of Christ into the present reality of the church.[128] The good news of the incarnation would find fulfillment in the return of the resurrected Christ to the Father from whence he would by the Spirit direct his followers to their ultimate end.

Summation. In summary, the Johannine Paraclete was the Spirit-teacher who was to be sent by Jesus and the Father in order to continue the mission of Christ by serving as a helping-presence within the disciples. The Paraclete would serve as another Jesus, doing what Christ would do if bodily present. In fact, the presence of the Spirit meant the presence of Jesus as well.

The primary function of the Paraclete would be to serve as a teacher continuing the instruction begun by Christ while on earth. The didactic activities of the Spirit were to include reminding, witnessing, exposing, guiding, speaking and proclaiming. The reminding activity of the Paraclete would involve the interpretation and re-presentation of the words of Jesus in a fresh and living manner. As a witness the Spirit would reveal an actual, living and authoritative knowledge of Jesus which would provoke a response

---

124 Franck, *Revelation Taught*, p. 67.

125 Barrett, *The Gospel According to St. John*, p. 408

126 Dunn, *Jesus and the Spirit*, p. 352.

127 Johnston, *Spirit-Paraclete*, pp. 86-87.

128 Barrett, *The Gospel According to St. John*, pp. 408-409.

in people. This witness would be a direct action of the Paraclete but would also be actualized through the witness of the disciples. The Spirit was to teach by exposing wrong in a manner that created a consciousness of sin, righteousness, and judgment. The act of guiding within the sphere of all truth would be accomplished through revelations of the continued mission of Christ. Jesus would be glorified by the Spirit serving as his mouthpiece whereby he would continue to speak of that which he shares with the Father. Likewise the Paraclete was to proclaim the message of Christ concerning things which were yet to come. His task was to receive and reveal.

Conclusions. The Paraclete sayings of John reveal a well-defined understanding of the role of the Holy Spirit as teacher in the life of the early church. The Paraclete's status as teacher was based upon his intimate, tandem, and ongoing relationship with Jesus. He was of the same nature as Jesus being sent by Jesus and the Father to help the disciples in their needs. His primary teaching function was to speak after Jesus. This task was fulfilled through the living interpretation of the words of Christ and the announcement of things yet to come in the ongoing revelation of Christ.

SPIRIT-TEACHER THEMES

Five themes emerged from the Final Discourse concerning the role of the Holy Spirit as teacher. First, the Spirit teaches by bringing experiential knowledge of God. God is known by direct encounter through the Spirit. Second, the Spirit teaches by serving as an internal witness to the standards of life in Christ. The Spirit will cause the commandments of Christ to remain fresh within the believer. Third, the Spirit teaches by directing disciples in their confrontation of the world. Fourth, the Spirit teaches by causing the disciples to have a heightened understanding of the Word of God. Finally, the Spirit teaches through prophetic proclamation. These five themes for the Spirit appeared throughout the Anti-Nicene period with varying points of adaptation.

The Knowledge of God. Jesus taught that to know him was to know the Father (John 14:7) and that when the Paraclete comes the disciples will know that Christ is in the Father, they are in Christ, and Christ is in them (John 14:20).[129] Thus, the indwelling of the Paraclete will actualize the indwelling of the Father and Son and fulfill the prayer of Christ (John 17:21). The role of the Spirit is to cause believers to know the Lord God in the sense

---

[129] Some have interpreted this knowledge as coming with the final return of Christ. However, "on that day" (14:20) refers to the return of Christ (14:18) through the ministry of the Paraclete (14:16-17). See Dodd, *The Fourth Gospel*, pp. 404-405.

of knowing by encounter.[130] Rudolf Bultmann clarified the differences in the Greek approach to knowledge and that of the Hebrews. The Greek word for "know" was *ginoskein* which had as its dominant meaning "an intellectual looking at" and strongly connoted objectivity. The object of knowledge was externalized and contemplated from a distance. The Hebrew word for "know" was *yada* which connoted knowledge as an experience of an object in relation to the subject. As a consequence, "knowledge was not thought of in terms of a possession of information. it was possessed only in its exercise or actualization."[131] Accordingly, for the Hebrew to know God was to experience and respond to him in his works and words. For John, to know God was to have union with God; a union which transformed the believer from death to life (John 17:2-3).[132]

Earliest Christian literature presented the Spirit as the agent of the believer's transformation into a familial relationship with God. The Spirit was the source of the individual's fellowship (*koinonia*) with both the Father (1 John 3:19-24; 4:13-16) and the Son (1 John 4:1- 6; 5:6-12).[133] And it was the Spirit who caused believers to know they had fellowship with God (1 John 3:24; 4:13).[134] It was the Spirit who enabled believers to cry out "Abba! Father" (Rom. 8:15-16; Gal. 4:6) and caused them to be members of his household (Eph. 2:18-19). This knowledge of God was not the product of intellectual pursuit but was rather the result of divine action which by the Spirit united the believer with God.[135] Such knowledge was impossible without the Spirit for the Spirit knew the Father and Son directly and revealed them to whomever he willed.[136]

In a related fashion the early church thought of the Holy Spirit as the source of visionary encounters with God. The Spirit was depicted as having removed the veil from the faces of the people that they might behold God face-to-face (2 Cor. 3:16-18) and as having rent the veil of the temple opening up access to the throne of God.[137] He was the ladder whereby

---

[130] For a portrait of the Johannine understanding of the knowing of God, see Dodd, *The Fourth Gospel*, pp. 151-169.

[131] Rudolph Bultmann, "Ginoksо," TDNT, I, 697.

[132] Dodd, *The Fourth Gospel*, pp. 187-200.

[133] Moody, *Spirit*, pp. 175-181. Origin, *De Principiis*, 1.3.5 ANF, IV, 253.

[134] Irenaeus, *Against Heresies*, 3.17.2 ANF, I, 444-445; 3.24.1 ANF, I, 458.

[135] Ignatius, *Epistle to the Ephesians*, 90 ANF, I, 53. Irenaeus, *Against Heresies*, 3.17.2 ANF, I, 444-445. Tatian, *To the Greeks*, 16 ANF, II, 71.

[136] Origen, *De Principiis* 1.3.4 to 1.3.5 ANF 4, p. 253.

[137] *Testament of the Twelve Patriarchs*, XII.9 ANF, VIII, 37. Origen reflected a similar thought, "But if we turn to the Lord, when also is the Word of God, and when the Holy Spirit reveals spiritual knowledge, then the veil is taken away, and with unveiled face we shall behold the glory of the Lord in the Holy Scriptures. *De Principiis* 1.1.2 ANF, IV, 242.

believers ascended to God[138] and an angel who carried saints into the highest heaven to meet with the Father.[139] All of this was possible because humans who bore the Spirit could see God and live.[140] The prophets had promised this for all through Christ so that the believers might be fashioned into the very likeness of God (2 Cor. 3:18).[141]

An Internal Witness. A second teaching function of the Spirit was to serve as an internal witness to the new commandments of Christ. As the helper who is within he will remind in a living fashion the disciples of everything Jesus had said and commanded. In the discourses the teachings of Jesus were refined into the central command to love each other (13:34; 15:9, 10, 12, 17). Love was to be the essential characteristic of a disciple of Jesus and the motivational force behind obedience to him (14:15, 21, 23; 15:13). For Jesus love as expressed in obedience was the disciples' means of communion with the Father (14:21, 23; 16:27). The relationship of Jesus to the Father was also described in terms of love (14:31; 15:10). The witness of the disciples before the world was dependent upon their love for each other (13:35; 14:31). As these were also the functions of the Paraclete, it followed that the Spirit would serve to actualize within the disciples this new standard of living.

The Final Discourse gave two other commands of Jesus which called forth the internalization of his very character. The disciples were to receive within themselves his joy (15:11; 16:20-22) and peace (14:27; 16:33). While these were not directly attributed to the Spirit, they were gifts from Jesus tied to the reception of his words (15:11; 16:33) and his presence with them (16:22, 33). Since it was the Paraclete who brought the presence of Jesus and the living reminder of his words, the Spirit was clearly associated with the joy and peace of Christ.

Love, joy and peace were common themes associated with the Spirit in early Christian literature. It was by the Spirit that believers knew that Christ lived within and fulfilled his command that they love one another (1 John 3:23-24). Love was the focal point of the gifts of the Spirit and set the eternal

---

138 Irenaeus, *Against Heresies*, 3.24.1 ANF, I, 438.

139 *The Shepherd of Hermas*, ANF, I, 9-58. Also, Tatian wrote of the soul, "if it enters into union with the Divine Spirit, it is no longer helpless, but ascends to the regions whether the Spirit guides it . . ." *To the Greek*, 13, ANF, II, 70-71.

140 Irenaeus, *Against Heresies*, 4.20.6 ANF, I, 489. Also, Clement of Alexandria worte, "We who are baptized have the eye of the Spirit, by which alone we can see God, free from obstruction and bright, the Holy Spirit flowing in upon us from heaven." *The Instructor*, 1.6, ANF, II, 215-216.

141 Irenaeus, *Against Heresies*, 4.20.6, ANF, I, 489.

standard of Christian living (1 Cor. 12-14).[142] Love, joy and peace along with other graces were thought of as fruit produced by the Spirit within the believer and were contrasted with the evil deeds of the flesh (Gal. 5:16-25).[143]

The Spirit was also depicted as serving as the internalized standard of God's righteousness.[144] In fulfillment of Jeremiah 31 he was writing the law of God upon the hearts of people.[145] He was the power of God who enabled believers to discipline themselves against the works of darkness.[146] The Spirit brought the standards of life which fulfilled the shadowy standards of the law of Moses.[147]

Direction in Confrontation. The large picture out of which the final discourse was drawn contained in its background the realities of a church in confrontation with the world. Jesus gave special attention to the preparation of the disciples for that confrontation (John 15:18-27) and gave the promise of the Paraclete as their leader in the confrontation (John 15:26-27; 16:7-11). A common and dominant theme for the Spirit in early Christian literature was that he served as a guide to the believers in their encounters with the world.

The manner in which the Spirit gave direction and guidance took many forms. He provided the words with which to refute the opposition.[148] He guided the actions of the believers so as to avoid certain dangers.[149] In his

---

[142] For Clement of Alexandria the "true gnostic" strives to be spiritual and "is united to the Spirit through the love that knows no bounds." *The Instructor*, 2.2.20, ANF, II, 242.

[143] According to Irenaeus the Spirit overcame the weakness of the flesh by absorbing that weakness into his power. The flesh then made manifest the power of the Spirit through a pure life, *Against Heresies*, V.9.2, ANF, I, 472.

[144] For Novation it was the Spirit who checked insatiable desires, broke unbridled lusts, quenched illicit passions, overcame fiery assaults and resisted evil while binding believers together in love, strengthening their good affections, and explaining the Rule of Truth, *Treatise Concerning the Trinity* , XXIX, ANF, V, 640-641. Clement of Rome said the Spirit provided an "insatiable desire for doing good," when fully outpoured on believers; *First Clement*, ANF, I, 5.

[145] Irenaeus offered this interpretation, believers "have salvation written in their hearts without paper and ink by the Spirit," *Against Heresies*, III.4.2, ANF, I, 417.

[146] Tertullian, *On Modesty* , XXI, ANF, IV, 98.

[147] Hermas described the Spirit as producing a proper character in true prophets, a character marked by gentleness, quietness, humility, and refraining from worthless desires; *The Shepherd of Hermas* II.11, ANF, II, 22-28.

[148] When some within the church had tried to mislead Ignatius, the Spirit would not allow it. He made an announcement to Ignatius which included the well-known line, "Do nothing without the bishop." Ignatius, *Epistle to the Philadelphians*, vii, ANF, I, 83.

[149] Tertullian appealed to imprisoned believers not to grieve the Holy Spirit who had entered prison with them. Having kept them he would lead them out "to the Lord." Indeed, they are in prison by the Spirit to trample upon the devil in his own house. To the Martyrs I.1, ANF, III, 693. Cyprian was warned of a coming struggle by the Holy Spirit, *Epistles of Cyprian*, LIII.5, ANF, 338.

most powerful manifestation he gave believers the grace of martyrdom so that they might follow in the footsteps of Jesus and Stephen.[150]

Understanding the Word. The central focus of the didactic function in the Paraclete sayings was that the Spirit will communicate the words of Jesus. In the second Paraclete saying the teaching and reminding functions of the Spirit centered on the historic teachings of Jesus. But the task of the Spirit would be to bring the fulness of those teachings to the consciousness of the disciples. He would add to their understanding, not to the message of God revealed in Christ.

In the final Paraclete saying the Spirit was to speak after Christ his ongoing message to the church. The content of the ongoing message would be consonant with the historic life and teachings of Christ but would not be limited to them. The Spirit would bring new information, information they would need to continue to exist in the sphere of all truth. Their understanding of the words of Jesus would be heightened by hearing through the Spirit the other things which Jesus had to tell them. For John, the Spirit brought a heightened understanding of Jesus who was the Word of God.

The early church understood that it was by the Spirit that the Apostles recorded and interpreted the life and teachings of Jesus. Very early the Gospels were recognized as being marked by the same divine inspiration that had guided the Old Testament prophets. Similarly, the epistles were thought of as products of the Spirit's instruction.[151] The Spirit was believed to have given to the apostles a perfect understanding of God's revelation in Christ. Therefore, not only their writings, but the traditions of instruction associated with the apostles were also considered inspired by the Spirit.[152]

---

[150] The Lukan narrative of Stephen is permeated with the presence of the Spirit. This early master was three times referred to as being full of the Spirit (Acts 6:3, 5; 7:55). The Jewish opposition was unable to overcome the wisdom of the Spirit with which he spoke (6:8-10). Irenaeus taught the strength of the Spirit was able to absorb the weakness of human flesh enabling the martyrs to bear witness and despise death, following the readiness of the Spirit rather than the weakness of the flesh; *Against Heresies*, V.9.2, ANF, I, 535. In The *Martyrdom of Polycarp* the flames could not kill him. When pierced by a sword there came out of him as dove, the symbol of Spirit, XVI, ANF, I, 42. The Montanist Perpetua was said to have been so completely under the power of the Spirit that she felt no pain during torture; In *Passion of Perpetua and Felicitas* VI.3, ANF, III, 705.

[151] P.R. Ackroyd and C.F. Evans (eds.), *The Cambridge History of the Bible*, Vol. 1, From the Beginnings to Jerome, (Cambridge: Cambridge University Press, 1970), pp. 284-297. Tertullian considered Paul so inspired he placed him in juxtaposition to the Holy Spirit as if the two could not be separated, *To His Wife* II.2, ANF, IV, 45.

[152] Irenaeus, *Against Heresies*, III.1.1, ANF, I, 414; 3.4.1, ANF, I, 417. Tertullian doubted the mental state of anyone who thought the apostles were ignorant of anything. They were ignorant of nothing because Christ had fulfilled his promise of the Spirit of Truth to lead them into all truth; *On Prescription Against Heretics* XXII, ANF, III, 253. Ignatius admonished the

This interpreting work of the Spirit was not thought to be limited to the apostles. They may have possessed it in perfect measure but all true believers were described as having been enlightened by the Spirit. Because of the work of the Spirit even the poor, ignorant, and illiterate possessed divine understanding of the doctrines of Christ. And by the Spirit the traditions of the apostles were carefully preserved and recognized.[153]

Prophetic Proclamation. The speaking functions of the Holy Spirit recorded in the final Paraclete saying cast the Spirit into a role consistent with the Old Testament prophets. He announces the message of another. He speaks not his own words but those of Christ. Included in his proclamations are revelations of things to come. This function of the Spirit requires the participation of others within the community of disciples. In order for him to be a mouthpiece he must have a mouthpiece.

Throughout the ante-Nicene period the Spirit was experienced as teaching the church through prophetic utterances. In some settings the Spirit freely moved upon numbers of individuals to give prophetic exhortations and predictions. Some individuals were especially recognized as instruments through whom the Spirit spoke. Itinerate prophets traveled from church to church and were considered teachers of the Spirit. Resident prophets were eventually institutionalized and brought under the control of the church hierarchy but there remained throughout the early centuries a belief in the prophetic work of the Spirit within the church.[154]

Magnesians to "be established in the doctrine of the Lord and the apostles," *To the Magnesians* XIII, ANF, I, 64.

[153] Ignatius exhorted the Ephesians to "let the Holy Spirit teach us to speak the things of Christ in like manner as he (Paul) did." Ignatius, *To The Ephesians* IV, ANF, I, 56. Tertullian declared the Holy Spirit the Vicar of Christ because of his role as teacher, preserving sound doctrine and the traditions of the true church. *On Prescription Against Heretics* XXVIII, ANF, III, 256. Also *On Veiling Virgins* I, ANF, IV, 27-28, where, as a Montanist, Tertullian used this Paraclete concept to defend a more ascetic way of life; the Spirit was leading the true church into deeper understanding of sexual purity. The same argument is related to monogamy, *On Monogamy II*, ANF, IV, 60, and the refusal to forgive post-baptismal sins, *On Modesty* XXI, ANF, IV, 98-100. Clement of Alexandria stressed that the illumination associated with baptism was the work of the Spirit and takes place when the Spirit chooses, with or without baptism. Clement of Alexandria, *The Pedagogue* I.6, ANF, II, 217. Also, Irenaeus, *Against Heresies* III.4.2, ANF, I, 417. Clement, *First Clement II*, ANF, I, 5. Origen, *De Principiis*, "Preface", III, ANF, IV, 239. Justin Martyr, *Dialogue with Trypho* XXXIX, ANF, I, 214.

[154] Swete, *The Holy Spirit in the Ancient Church*, p. 384.

Summary and Conclusions

According to early Christian thought the Holy Spirit was a personal manifestation of the presence of God. Consistent with Jewish thought, the Spirit was understood to be the breath of a personal God. As the breath of God the Spirit was associated with the power of God and the speech of God, that is prophecy. The Spirit was the power of God to create and to destroy. Prophecy was the work of the Spirit whereby God made known Himself and his will. Christians also associated their experience of the Holy Spirit with the Jewish theme of a new age, a time when God's Spirit would again be active in the earth.

Christian understandings of the Spirit broke with Jewish thought with the development of a personal identity for the Spirit. The Christian experience of Jesus and the Spirit forced a reinterpretation of Jewish monotheism. A personal identity for the Spirit was intimated by the Pauline concept of the Spirit of Christ. In the Johannine Paraclete sayings the Spirit was explicitly described in personal terms. Post-apostolic writers expressed the personhood of the Spirit through the unorthodox identification of him as an angel and ultimately through the formation of the orthodox doctrine of the Trinity.

The Paraclete sayings of John served as the fountainhead of the church's imagery of the Spirit as a teacher. The Paraclete's status as a teacher was based upon his intimate, tandem and ongoing relationship with Jesus. He was of the same nature as Christ and was sent by the father and Son to help the disciples in their needs. The teaching activities of the paraclete included reminding, witnessing, exposing, guiding, speaking and proclaiming. In essence, his function was to speak the words of Jesus after him. However, this speaking after meant a fresh and living interpretation of the words of Christ and was inclusive of prophetic revelations. The Spirit communicated to the disciples "all things" which Jesus wished to tell them. As teacher the Spirit brought into the lives of the disciples the immediacy of Christ and his teachings.

Five themes on the Spirit as teacher emerged from the Paraclete sayings which were corroborated by other early Christian writings. First, the Holy Spirit teaches by bringing an experiential knowledge of God through direct personal encounter with him. Second, the Spirit teaches by serving as an internal witness to the standards of life in Christ. Third, the Spirit teaches by guiding disciples in their confrontation with the world. Fourth, the Spirit teaches by causing followers of Jesus to have a heightened understanding of the Word of God. Finally, the Spirit teaches through prophetic proclamation which requires the participation of the community of disciples with the Spirit.

Chapter 3

THE HOLY SPIRIT AND THE PEDAGOGY OF THE CHURCH

During the formative period of Christianity, pedagogy was an integral aspect of the community life of the church. Teaching and learning were constitutive elements of being the covenanted people of God. Formal and informal instruction permeated the gatherings of the believers.[1] The objective of this chapter is to descriptively analyze early Christianity's understanding of the role of the Holy Spirit in the pedagogical dimensions of the life of the church.

The method of inquiry is twofold. First, the historical-theological background of early Christianity's perception of the relationship between the Holy Spirit and the church is considered. Of special interest is the place of the Holy Spirit in the identity of the church. Second, three pedagogical issues relative to the existence of the church as the community of the Spirit are investigated: (1) What were the objectives of instruction associated with the Holy Spirit? (2) What was the environment for learning constituted by the church as a gathering with the Spirit? and (3) What was the role of the Spirit in relation to the human teachers of the church?

---

[1] The central place of instruction in the early church was established in the New Testament. Matthew recorded the Great Commission in essentially pedagogical terms, "Go therefore and *make disciples* of all the nations, baptizing them in the name of the Father, and the Son, and the Holy Spirit, *teaching them to observe all that I commanded you*; and lo, I am with you always, even to the end of the age" (Matt. 28-19-20 NAS, emphasis added). In the aftermath of Pentecost the Jerusalem believers attached themselves to the apostles for instruction (Acts 2:42). Peter's initial confrontations with the Jerusalem authorities centered on the fact that he was teaching the people and filling the city with his doctrine (Acts 4:2; 5:28). Likewise, Paul was depicted as preaching and teaching throughout his journeys (Acts 20:20). Acts closed with a picture of the Apostle to the Gentiles under custody at Rome "teaching concerning the Lord Jesus Christ, with all openness, unhindered" (Acts 28:31 NAS). Perhaps the most revealing was the prominence given to the office of teacher in the earliest communities (Acts 13:1; 1 Cor. 12:28; Eph. 4:11; Rom. 12:6).

THE HOLY SPIRIT AND THE IDENTITY OF THE CHURCH

Early Christianity understood the Holy Spirit to be the agent of the eschatological renewal of the people of God; he was the Spirit of the new age.[2] The Spirit's work within the church was evidence par excellence that God was at work in the world calling a people unto himself.[3] The renewed manifestation of God's Spirit was the fulfillment of prophecy (Acts 2:14-21), and the keeping of a promise (Acts 2:33). On the day of Pentecost Peter spoke of the powerful demonstration of the Spirit as a "gift" from God (Acts 2:38), adding "for the promise is for you and your children, and for all who are far off, as many as the Lord our God shall call to Himself," (Acts 2:39 NAS). In that setting the cornerstone of the church's identity was laid. The repentant followers of the crucified, resurrected, and exalted Jesus the Nazarene were a people called by God, called out of a perverse generation and into a life of the Holy Spirit (Acts 2:22-42). From that sense of calling they took their identity as the *ekklesia*, the called out ones.[4]

THE MEANING OF *EKKLESIA*

In the English language "church" is the common translation of the Greek word *ekklesia*.[5] While the term was only used twice in the Gospels

[2] The association of the Spirit with the eschatological renewal of the people of God was based upon the Hebrew Scriptures which had pointed to the restoration of Israel accompanied by the Spirit of God. The Spirit's association with the renewal of Israel was succinctly stated in Isaiah 44:1-5 as well as Joel 2:28-32. See the discussion of the Spirit of the new age above chapter 2, pp. 35-37.

[3] Justin argued that the presence of the prophetic gifts of the Spirit within the church was proof that Jesus was the Messiah according to Isaiah 11:1-2. *Dialogue with Trypho* LXXXVII, The Ante-Nicene Fathers, ed. Alexander Roberts and James Donaldson (Grand Rapids: Wm. B. Eerdmans, 1956), I, 243. Through Christ the gifts had been transferred to the church "for the prophetical gifts remain with us, even to the present time. And hence you ought to understand that the gifts formerly among your nation (Israel) have been transferred to us," *Dialogue* LXXXII, ANF, I, 240. "Now, it is possible to see amongst us women and men who possess gifts of the Spirit of God . . . ." *Dialogue* LXXXIII, ANF, I, 243; 88.

[4] W. Bauer, "Ekklesia," *A Greek-English Lexicon of the New Testament and Other Early Christian Literature*, trans. and ed. by W. F. Arndt and F. W. Gingrich (Chicago: University Press, 1957), 240-241.

[5] The English word "church" is derived from the Old English *kirk* and the German *kirche* which are generally considered to have been taken from the Greek word *kyrisken* which meant "belonging to the Lord." However, Karl Barth has indicated two other possibilities. The root may have been the same as that of the Latin word circa and would have indicated the circumscribed sphere in which the *ekklesia* gathered. Also, it may have come from the Greek term *kerugeia* for the office of a herald so that the church was those persons gathered around

(Matt. 16:18; 18:17), it was clearly the common designation for the primitive Christian community from its earliest days. The early Christian understanding of *ekklesia* reflected an awareness of its classical Greek usage but was more closely aligned with that of the LXX.

Classical Greek Usage. In classical Greece *ekklesia* was predominantly a political term referring to the assembly of full citizens of the polis. Functionally the *ekklesia* was rooted in the constitutions of the various city-state democracies which called for certain political and judicial decisions to be made by the full citizens when "called out" from the remainder of the populace.[6] Luke used *ekklesia* in this classical sense in reference to the assembly at Ephesus that gathered to hear accusations against Paul (Acts 19:32).

Hebrew Antecedents. The primary New Testament use of *ekklesia* closely paralleled the Old Testament use of the Hebrew words *qahal* and *'edah*. The Hebrew *qahal* was predominantly translated as *ekklesia* in the LXX although it was also translated as *synagoge* 21 times. The *qahal* probably derived its meaning from the verb *qol*, to voice, and thus depicted an assembly which had been summoned in the sense of mustering. Such an assembly varied in purpose from military service to political consultation or judicial hearing, to assembly for worship. It was frequently used of special ceremonial assemblies constituted by God's covenant with his people (Lev. 16:17-33; 1 Kgs. 8:14-65; 2 Chr. 6:3-13, etc.).[7]

A related but more technical Hebrew term was *'edah*. In the LXX *'edah* was almost exclusively translated *synagoge*.[8] The word appeared most frequently in the Pentateuch (123 of 147 occurrences) and was related to the root *ya ad*, to appoint. Thus, the meaning of *'edah* was a "company assembled together by appointment."[9] The *'edah*, sometimes qualified with the addition of "of Israel" (for example, Exod. 16:9; Num. 1:2; Lev. 4:13), was an expression coined for the people of the Exodus as they gathered before the tent of meeting (Exod. 33:7-16). The people would assemble at the tent outside of

---

the herald of God, the bishop. Karl Barth, *Church Dogmatics*, Vol. IV, *The Doctrine of Reconciliation* (Edinburgh: T & T Clark, 1974), p. 651.

[6] Luther Coenan, "Church, Synagogue," *New International Dictionary of New Testament Theology*, ed. Colin Brown (Grand Rapids: Zondervan Publishing House, 1979), I, 219-292.

[7] Ibid.

[8] In classical Greek usage synagoge referred to any collection of things and found broad application from objects such as books or letters to persons in a guild. Progressively the meaning shifted from activity of gathering to the place of assembly. Wolfgang Schrage, "Synagoge," *Theological Dictionary of the New Testament*, ed. Gerhard Kittel and trans. Geoffrey W. Bromiley (Grand Rapids: Wm. B. Eerdmans Publishing Company, 1964), VII, 806-807.

[9] Francis Brown, S. R. Driver, and Charles A. Briggs, ed., "edah," *A Hebrew and English Lexicon of the Old Testament* (Oxford: Clarendon Press, 1962), p. 417.

their encampment to seek God because it was there that God would come down in a pillar of cloud and meet "face to face" with Moses. It was the presence of God that made them a distinguished people (Exod. 33:16). Before him they stood as recipients of his covenant and of his Law.

According to Lothar Coenan 'edah expressed "a concept of corporateness" with the stress falling not on the total of individuals, but on "the unity of the fellowship."[10] The 'edah was the corporate community appointed to serve the Lord. Yet it represented the community as a people in all of its functions, of which even the most secular was not without connection with the law and the sanctuary. Of special significance was the fact that 'edah was never used of any people other than Israel.[11]

In summary, the 'edah, predominantly translated synagoge in the LXX, was the unambiguous and permanent term for Israel as the covenant community of God. It connoted their corporate nature as the people of God. The qahal, usually translated ekklesia in the LXX, stood for any assembly of persons but was frequently used as a ceremonial expression for the assembly which resulted from the covenant, that is, those mustered out for service.

New Testament Usage. In the New Testament synagoge described either the meeting place of the local Jewish community or the congregation itself which represented the total number of Jews living in the community. With only one exception (Jas. 2:2) the New Testament did not use synagoge to represent the Christian community or its meetings.[12] This was perhaps due to the fact that the synagogue had become a symbol of the Jewish religion with all its traditions.[13] However, it probably also reflected the church's sense of belonging to the nation of Israel and its early refusal to be cast into the role of a new religion.[14]

On the other hand, the verb synago appeared in the New Testament with a clearly eschatological meaning of the end time gathering of the people of God. It was applied to the people who came to Jesus as the salvation of God (Mark 2:2; 4:1; 5:21; 6:30; 7:1) and it also denoted the coming together of the Christian congregation (Acts 4:31; 15:6, 30; 20:7).[15] But the noun used to designate the assembly was most often ekklesia.

Paul gave the fullest meaning in the New Testament to the Christian ekklesia. For him it was foremost an event, the event in which God fulfilled

---

[10] Coenan, "Church, Synagogue," p. 294.

[11] Ibid.

[12] Ibid., pp. 296-297.

[13] Schrage, "synagoge," p. 829.

[14] See below, "The True Israel," pp. 60-62. In the post-apostolic writings synagoge became common designation for Christian worship gatherings and meeting places. It was used as such by Ignatius, Hermas, Justin, Clement of Alexandria and others. Schrage, "synagoge," p. 840.

[15] Coenan, "Church, Synagogue," p. 298.

his election through his personal call (Rom. 8:28-30). The church grew out of the proclamation of Christ through which the call was issued. Thus, the Christian community was the congregation of the *kletoi*, the called (Rom. 1:1-7; 1 Cor. 1:2) and the *ekklesia* was the embodiment of God's offer of reconciliation (2 Cor. 5:18-19). It represented God's new creation, the eschatological order of salvation which stood before God face to face as his people. As the *ekklesia tou theou*, the congregation of God (1 Cor. 1:2; 11:16; 2 Cor. 1:1; Gal. 1:13; 1 Thess. 2:14; 2 Thess. 1:4), the church was understood to exist only through an ongoing relation with him and thus stood in contrast to other forms of society.[16]

The *ekklesia* event found tangible expression in the localized gatherings of its members. It existed in concrete settings where the called lived in both the sphere of the new creation (2 Cor. 5:17) and in the midst of the old world. The *ekklesia* represented a new citizenship in a higher kingdom (Phil. 3:20) but without fully nullifying citizenship in the old.[17]

The *ekklesia* transcended a single event in time and space. It was spoken of in the plural form in 20 of the 50 Pauline uses. Thus, it was described and ordered in terms of particularized settings which were simultaneously ongoing. Yet, there was a sense in which there was one *ekklesia* (1 Cor. 15:9; Gal. 1:13; Phil 3:6). It was one because the Lord of the church was one (1 Cor. 12:12-13). This cosmic corporateness was expressed not only in singleness of faith but also in common rules and ordinances (1 Cor. 7:17; 11:16; 16:1).[18]

In Acts where the word *ekklesia* appeared 16 times, Luke echoed the Pauline understanding. He used it to depict Christian congregations living and meeting in particular places (Acts 5:11; 8:1; 11:22; 12:1, 5; 13:1; 14:23; 15:41; 16:5). But ultimately the *ekklesia* was one as the singular and plural forms of the word were qualitatively identical,

> The *ekklesia* is those who follow the call of God, come together (cf. the *synagein* of 14:27) and yet even when their meeting is over still retain their quality of *ekklesia*. It is one throughout the whole world and yet is at the same time fully present in every individual assembly.[19]

Revelation, James and Hebrews used *ekklesia* in the sense of localized congregations, the single exception being Hebrews 12:23. There the word

---

[16] Karl L. Schmidt, "ekklesia," TDNT, III, 505.

[17] For example, Paul made full use of his Roman citizenship in defending his right to preach the Gospel (Acts 22:25-29; 23:27).

[18] Coenan, "Church, Synagogue," p. 301.

[19] Ibid., p. 303.

occurred in a series of eschatological terms taken from Jewish tradition (Mount Zion, city of the living God, heavenly Jerusalem) and was qualified as the congregation of the first-born whose names are written in heaven. The imagery was clearly that of the eschatological community of the new covenant.[20]

In summary, the New Testament understanding of the Christian *ekklesia* was as the people called before God to be reconciled to him through Jesus Christ. The call was issued through the preaching of Jesus. It was given to individuals but resulted in the formation of a single community belonging to God through an ongoing relationship with him. The *ekklesia* found tangible expression in localized meetings but was ultimately considered a single ongoing event transcending time and locations. The church was one cosmic assembly with a single faith and covenant and yet was fully constituted by individual assemblies.

IMAGES OF THE CHURCH

The early Christian understanding of the church was further clarified by the various images associated with the people of God. Five dominant images are here reviewed: the true Israel, the kingdom of God, the saints, the habitation of God, and the body of Christ.[21] Except for the latter, these portraits of the church were rooted in Old Testament concepts associated with eschatological expectations for Israel. Each of the images was also dependent upon the Christian understanding of the Holy Spirit for proper interpretation.

The True Israel. The early church identified itself with the eschatological gathering of the true Israel.[22] As such it was the *qahal* of the *'edah*, the final mustering of a faithful remnant. The initial followers of Christ were Jews who focused their mission on the salvation of Israel. The concern of the Christian community for Israel was demonstrated by the content of their preaching (Acts 2:14-40; 3:12-26; 4:8-12; 5:29-32) and the extension of John's baptism of repentance (Acts 2:38-42). The gathering of the twelve

---

[20] Schmidt, "ekklesia," p. 513.

[21] Paul S. Minear identified 96 *Images of the Church* in the New Testament. He grouped them into four major categories: the People of God; the New Creation; the Fellowship of Faith; the Body of Christ. Paul S. Minear, *Images of the Church in the New Testament* (Philadelphia: The Westminster Press, 1960).

[22] The phrase "true Israel" was not used in the New Testament but does accurately reflect the early Christian understanding of the church as the fulfillment of the Abrahamic covenant. Jesus Christ was the promised seed. In the words of Justin, "As, therefore, Christ is the Israel and the Jacob, even so we, who have been quarried out from the bowels of Christ, are the true Israelitic race," *Dialogue* CXXXIV, ANF, XI, 267.

disciples by Jesus carried overtones of the restoration of the twelve tribes of Israel (Eze. 37; 39:23-29; 40-48).[23] The circle of the Twelve was reconstituted at Jerusalem with the selection of a replacement for Judas Iscariot. In the recording of these actions the early Christian community demonstrated its self-consciousness as the eschatological gathering of the true Israel.[24]

In the context of Jerusalem the church clearly identified itself with the Hebrew *qahal* which was mustered before Yahweh as the people of the covenant (Deut. 23:2-9). That identity continued as the church was dispersed and Paul extended the limits of the true Israel to cover Gentile Christians by applying the rubric of descent from Abraham (Rom. 4; Gal. 3). Salvation belonged to the "seed of Abraham," but true descent was the product of believing as Abraham believed. Thus, all who believed in Christ were the true descendents of Abraham, the chosen people of God.[25]

As the people of promise, early Christians saw themselves as those who stood under the new covenant of God (2 Cor. 3:6), the covenant promised by Jeremiah (Jer. 31:31-34; Heb. 8:8-12; 10:16-17). Four parallel New Testament passages (Matt. 26:28; Mk. 14:24; Lk. 22:20; 1 Cor. 11:25) pointed to Christ's own identification with the new covenant.[26] In each case it was connected with the cup of the Lord's Supper. The concept of shedding or pouring out of blood made the association with the covenant blood of the Old Testament clear (Ex. 24:5-8).[27]

Paul included in his account of the Lord's Supper aspects of the covenantal blessings and curses (1 Cor. 11:27-32). Later writings such as the

---

[23] Gerhard Lohfink, *Jesus and Community: The Social Dimension of Christian Faith* (Philadelphia: Fortress Press, 1985), pp. 10, 75-76.

[24] F. F. Bruce, *The Spreading Flame: The Rise and Progress of Christianity from Its First Beginnings to the Conversion of the English* (Grand Rapids: Wm. B. Eerdmans, 1979), p. 72.

[25] Paul described the inheritance of Israel as belonging to the seed (not seeds) of Abraham, that is Christ (Gal. 3:16). Christians share in the promise in that they have been baptized into Christ and have clothed themselves in him (Gal. 3:27). It is because they belong to Christ that they share in his inheritance. Thus, Paul could describe Christians as having Abraham for their father (Rom. 4:12); heirs of Abraham (Gal. 3:29); children of God's promise (Gal. 4:28); the beloved (Rom. 1:7); the elect (Rom. 8:33); the sons of God (Rom. 8:16; Gal. 3:26). Consider also the description of the faithful in Ephesians 1:3-14 which was followed by the admonitions, "therefore remember, that formerly you, the Gentiles in the flesh, who are called 'Uncircumcision' by the so-called 'Circumcision,' . . . that you were . . . excluded from the commonwealth of Israel, and strangers to the covenants of promise, having no hope and without God in the world. . . . So then you are no longer strangers and aliens, but you are fellow citizens with the saints, and are of God's household (Eph. 2:11-19 NAS)."

Peter echoed the theme of a chosen race via divine election; compare 1 Pet. 2:4-10 with Deut. 7:6-11 and 10:12-22.

[26] Paul and Luke included the adjective "new." Some later manuscripts have it added to the accounts of Matthew and Mark.

[27] Joachim Guhrt, "Covenant," NIDNTT, I, 369-370.

Didache provided the structure of the covenant ritual associated with the Lord's Supper.[28]

The new covenant was not a replacement of the old one; the new fulfilled the old bringing it to its intended end. Paul argued that the covenant of God with Israel was made with Abraham and consisted of the promise. The law came as an addendum at Sinai (Rom. 5:20) and could not annul that promise which was already being fulfilled in the church (Gal. 3:16). The law served only as a custodian (*paidagogos*) of Israel until Christ came to bring the promise (Gal. 3:24). The new covenant was the fulfillment of the Abrahamic covenant (Gal. 4:23) in that it brought life and liberty to those who belong to Christ (Gal. 4:26). In Christ they now, like Moses in ancient times, stood face to face with the maker and keeper of the covenant as heirs of his promise.[29]

The writer of Hebrews expanded on the relationship of the new covenant to the old. The new covenant was the better covenant because its guarantor and mediator was Christ (Heb. 7:22; 8:6; 12:24). The very promise of the new covenant (Jer. 31:31-34) declared the old obsolete (Heb. 8:8-13). It had been overtaken and fulfilled by the new. The old was but a pattern (Heb. 8:5) of the one covenant which had become a reality through the sacrifice of Christ (10:1-18; 9:13-15). In sum, the *ekklesia* was the true Israel because it existed in the true covenant of God.[30]

The Kingdom of God. The early church further identified itself with the kingdom of God. Inter-testamental Judaism was characterized by a belief in the coming Messiah who would establish the kingdom of God on earth. The apocalyptic writings gave preeminence to the expected arrival of the "son of Man" who would possess the kingdom. The kingdom would be characterized by liberation from the total misery of human society; it would be a kingdom of "peace," "joy," and "freedom."[31]

The roots of the kingdom idea lay in the Old Testament doctrine of the theistic monarchy; Yahweh alone is king and only those he appoints rule. Israel originally existed as a sacred confederation of tribes with a central cultic sanctuary. In the conquest of Canaan, Israel understood itself to be in a holy war, with Yahweh himself serving as commander-in-chief of the army (Exod. 14:14; Jos. 23:10; Judges 7:22). In time God approved and anointed the

---

[28] *The Didache* or *The Teaching of the Twelve Apostles*, is perhaps the earliest non-canonical description of Christian practices being dated by some as early as the seventh decade of the first century. Included is a directive on the giving of thanks during the Eucharist, *The Teaching of the Twelve Apostles* II & III, ANF, VII, 377-378.

[29] F. F. Bruce, *The New Testament Development of Old Testament Themes* (Grand Rapids: Wm. B. Eerdmans, 1977), pp. 51-55.

[30] Ibid., pp. 55-57.

[31] French L. Arrington, *Paul's Aeon Theology in 1 Corinthians* (Washington, D.C.: University Press of America, 1977), pp. 90-91.

concept of a surrogate human monarchy (1 Sam. 9:1-10:16; 11:1-11) and entered into an everlasting covenant with the house of David to fill that post.[32] With the failure of the kings of Judah to live up to the standards of the covenant, the expectation of an eschatological messianic king grew. The lordship of Yahweh was combined with the hoped-for lordship of the Messiah. The messianic son of David would be appointed by God and draw his authority as the representative of the kingly rule of Yahweh (Isa. 9:7; 11:1f). Thus, Yahweh would one day rule over the whole earth. His throne would be in Jerusalem where all nations would gather to worship him (Isa. 24:23; Zech. 14:9; Obad. 21).[33]

In the New Testament, God and Christ alone have full right to the title king. Jesus was described as the messianic king of the Jews, the promised son of David. At his trial he responded to the question of the high priest, "Are you the Christ?" with the unequivocal statement, "I am; and you will see the son of man sitting at the right hand of power, and coming with the clouds of heaven" (Mk. 14:62). For Jesus the kingdom of God was both a coming event and a present reality. He stressed the immanence of the future kingdom (Mk. 1:15; Matt. 3:2; 5:17; Lk. 21:31), as the rule of God was at hand (Matt. 24:32f; Mk. 13:28f; Lk. 21:29f). However, for him the kingdom of God was also already present (Mk. 2:19; Matt. 9:15; Lk. 5:34; 17:20f) because he, the son of David, was already present. The future rule of God had, in his personhood, become a reality in word and deed.[34]

The kingdom of God terminology was less prominent in early Christian literature outside of the Synoptic Gospels.[35] However it must be remembered that the title "Christ" was rooted in the Jewish expectation of the kingdom of God so that any association of the title "Christ" with the church was a direct association with the kingdom of God motif.[36] The Christological kerygma substituted the crucified and resurrected Jesus for the kingdom of God. The

---

[32] The northern kingdom refused to recognize the Davidic covenant and retained in principle the ideal of a charismatic leader.

[33] Bertold Klappert, "King, Kingdom," NIDNTT, II, 372-376.

[34] Ibid., pp. 378-383.

[35] The phrase "kingdom of God" did remain in common use, however. The Johannine Gospel and the Pauline epistles contain numerous references to the kingdom of God. Irenaeus made extensive use of the terminology especially in relationship to 1 Cor. 15:50, ". . . flesh and blood cannot inherit the kingdom of God." Christians are spiritual persons who have died to the flesh (without destroying it) and therefore participate in the kingdom of God. This is possible because flesh and blood "can be taken for an inheritance into the kingdom of God," *Against Heresies* V, 9-10, ANF, I, 334-336. The activities of the church on their day of worship, that is, distributing goods to the needy and celebrating the Eucharist marked it as living in the "times of the kingdom," *Against Heresies* V, 23, ANF, I, 562-563.

[36] Wolfhart Pannenberg, Avery Dulles, and Carl E. Braaten, *Spirit, Faith, and Church* (Philadelphia: The Westminster Press, 1970), p. 109.

church knew the exalted Christ as Lord (Phil 2:9-11; Acts 2:36) and thus began to speak of the kingdom of Christ (Eph. 5:5; 2 Tim. 4:1, 18; 2 Pet. 1:11; Rev. 1:9). In Christ, the community experienced the rule of God.[37]

The Saints. In association with the kingdom of God concept, the Christian community also identified itself with the Hebrew image of the saints. Daniel had prophetically applied the image of "holy ones" to the eschatological people of God. The decisive element of the Old Testament concept of the holy was relatively direct contact with divine power. Encounter with the divine demanded certain modes of response. Improper or profane response resulted in separation from the divine, that is, death. Thus, preparation for encounter with the holy meant a separation from the profane.[38]

The people called by God were to be a "holy people," separated from foreign practices and unto Yahweh (Deut. 7:6; 14:2, 21; 26:19). This holiness was to be through conformity to the law of Yahweh. On the basis of his law for them, Yahweh demanded, "You shall be holy for I am holy" (Lev. 19:2; 20:7). This holiness before the Lord covered all aspects of life but took on special significance in the realm of the cultus. Everything belonging to the worship of Yahweh was to be kept holy.[39] But the concept of the "saints" or "holy ones" received relatively little attention in the Old Testament.[40] Inter-testamental Judaism especially associated the concept of saints with those who knew the Scriptures and those of the coming kingdom.[41]

In the New Testament "saints" was used as a special reference for the members of the *ekklesia*. Churches were composed of those called to be saints (Rom. 1:7; 1 Cor. 1:2; 14:33). Thus, the designation virtually always

---

[37] So Justin said to Trypho, "And when Scripture says, 'I am the Lord God, the Holy One of Israel, who have made known Israel your king,' will you not understand that truly Christ is the everlasting king?" *Dialogue with Trypho* CXXXV, ANF, I, 267.

[38] Horst Seebass, "Holy," NIDNTT, II, 223-224.

[39] Otto Procksch, "'agios," TDNT, I, 91-97.

[40] Only rarely were the members of the holy nation called saints. Aaron was referred to as a saint (Ps. 106:16) as were the Nazarites (Num. 6:18). In the Psalms the saints were equated with those who fear Yahweh (Ps. 34:9; 16:3) and Psalm 89:7 mentioned the assembly of the saints. Zechariah 14:5 foretold the eschatological coming of the saints with God. In Daniel those who stood by Yahweh in his future war with the world powers were called saints and were promised the keys to the kingdom (Dan. 7:18). However, Daniel also used the term for the heavenly companions of God (Dan. 7:21).

[41] Inter-testamental Judaism made "holy" a common designation for the Scriptures. Similarly, the Spirit who spoke in the Scriptures became increasingly the Holy Spirit. Those who obeyed the Torah, especially the pupils of the scribes, were regarded as holy ones. And the Qumran community identified itself with the saints of Yahweh gathered together as the eschatological community "in which the ordinances of purification which were originally obligatory only for the priests were made binding on all members." Seebass, "Holy," p. 227.

appeared in the plural form as a synonym for the *ekklesia*.[42] The emphasis was upon belonging to God as his own. The saints were at every point circumscribed by the Holy Spirit so that their lives were determined and empowered by him. This association with the Spirit marked them as the eschatological community.[43] It was they who would one day return with Christ to rule the world (1 Cor. 6:2; 1 Thess. 3:12; 2 Thess. 1:10; Jude 14).[44]

The Habitation of God. Another set of images adopted by the church portrayed the covenant community as the dwelling place of God. The primary idea was that the *ekklesia* constituted a temple inhabited by God.

Paul spoke of the redeemed community as the temple of God in respect to both the local congregation (1 Cor. 3:16-17) and the church as a whole (Eph. 2:21). He used the Greek word *naos*[45] which was used in the LXX as a translation of the Hebrew *hekal*, palace or temple, but only when it referred to the temple of God. It developed as a purely cultic concept, referring exclusively to the true temple of God. It was in that sense that Paul developed his imagery. The church was God's temple because God's Spirit dwelt in her (1 Cor. 6:19).[46] Barnabas described the church as "the incorruptible temple."[47] A similar image was projected by Peter in his description of Christians as "living stones" being built into a "spiritual house" (1 Pet. 2:5). Ignatius described the church as "the divine edifice of the Father."[48] In the visions of Hermas the church was a tower being carefully constructed under the supervision of the Lord.[49]

---

[42] There was only one New Testament use of the singular "saint," Phil. 4:21.

[43] Minear, *Images of the Church*, pp. 136-139.

[44] The New Testament usage was most concentrated in the *Epistle to the Ephesians* where there were nine references to the saints with clear eschatological overtones. The epistle was addressed to the saints at Ephesus (1:1) who were currently being blessed with every spiritual blessing in the heavenly realm in Christ (1:3). They were the ones who had been chosen by God to be holy and blameless before him (1:4, see also 5:27; Col. 1:22; 2 Tim. 1:9). Among their blessings was the knowledge of the mystery of God concerning Christ and the "fullness of the times" (1:9-10; also see Col. 1:26). Special emphasis was placed on the heavenly realms where Jesus and the saints were currently sitting together (1:3, 20; 2:6; 3:10). The saints were specifically citizens of God's kingdom (2:19) and members of his household (2:19) who were heirs of the riches of glory (1:18; see also Col 1:12). They had once followed the "prince of the power of the air" (2:2) but now were alive together with Christ (2:5) and were in battle with those evil forces (6:10-20).

[45] The other Greek word for temple, to hieron, was never used in the sense of God's habitation or temple, Wichmann von Meding, "Temple," NIDNTT, III, 781-782.

[46] In another passage Paul referred to the church as "God's building," but without specific indication that he would inhabit the building' 1 Cor. 3:9.

[47] *The Epistle of Barnabas* XVI, ANF, I, 147.

[48] Ignatius, *Letter to the Ephesians* IX, ANF, I, 53.

[49] Believers were depicted as both the stones out of which the tower was built and the inhabitants of the tower; *The Pastor of Hermas*, Similitude VIII, ANF, II, 41, 42. Believers were

The central idea behind these images was that the church constituted a glorious building constructed for the pleasure of God and was the focal point of communion between God and his creation. In a similar fashion Mount Zion and Jerusalem were used as metaphors for the church (Gal. 4:21-31; Heb. 12:22-23).[50] Christians were citizens of the holy city, the new Jerusalem in which God dwelt. John the Revelator saw the fulfillment of that habitation and heard a voice declare, "Behold, the tabernacle of God is among men, and He shall dwell among them, and they shall be his people, and God himself shall be among them . . ." (Rev. 21:3). The church was the place where God was known.[51]

The Body of Christ. Paul expressed the divine unity of the church with the imagery of the *soma Christou*, the body of Christ. In 1 Corinthians 12:12-30 he adopted the Greek thought of the organism to demonstrate the necessity of different functions within the body. But essentially Paul kept the Hebrew understanding of wholeness, that is, the several members do not constitute the whole. Rather the various tasks of the members highlights their corporate nature. The *soma* constituted their unity, a unity based on Christ himself.[52]

The character of the church as the body of Christ was most clearly expressed by the word *koinonia*, meaning fellowship. The root idea was the commonness of their existence, the communion they shared.[53] It denoted a unanimity and unity brought about by the Spirit. In Acts this was expressed in the sharing of material goods according to need (Acts 2:42; 4:32). Similarly, Paul's collections for the saints at Jerusalem were tangible expressions of the fellowship (*koinonia*) of the churches (2 Cor. 9:13).[54]

Paul always used *koinonia* in a religious sense. When applied to the church it referred strictly to the relationships established by faith in Christ. Believers shared the fellowship of the Son (1 Cor. 1:9), and his sufferings (Phil. 3:10). They also shared the fellowship of the Holy Spirit (2 Cor. 13:13), the fellowship in the gospel (Phil. 1:5), and the fellowship of faith (Phlm. 6).

---

also depicted as the dwelling place of the Spirit; Commandment V, ANF, II, 23. Further, the Lord is said to dwell with the believer; Commandment IV, ANF, II, 22; Similitude IX, ANF, II, 43.

[50] Minear, *Images of the Church*, pp. 90-98.

[51] God was understood to dwell in the church by the Spirit so that the two were inseparable; Irenaeus, *Against Heresies* I.3.24.1, ANF, I, 458. Also, Tertullian, *On Baptism* VI, ANF, III, 672.

[52] Siegfried Wibbing, "Body," NIDNTT, I, 232-238.

[53] Lohfink has pointed out the significance to the church's self-understanding of the oft overlooked reciprocal pronoun "one another" (allelon). It appeared 47 times in the New Testament epistles in reference to the character of Christian relationships. The life of a Christian was that of a shared journey; Lohfink, *Jesus and Community*, pp. 99-102.

[54] Johannes Schattenmann, "*Koinonia*," TDNT, I, 639-644.

The Lord's Supper meant the *koinonia* of the body and blood of Christ and thus union together with the exalted Christ (1 Cor. 10:16).[55]

But the imagery of the body of Christ was more than an expression of unity; it was a proclamation of hope. As members of the body of Christ, believers understood themselves to be participants in his resurrection (Rom. 6:5-11).[56] Participation in Christ Jesus was participation in an order in which eternal life rules. Believers had followed Christ in death to sin (Rom. 6:10; 7:2) having been baptized into his death (Rom. 7:3). Paul instructed,

> "You also were made to die to the law *through the body of Christ*, that you might be joined to another, to him who was raised from the dead, that we might bear fruit for God" (Rom. 7:4, NAS emphasis added).

Participation in the body of Christ thus meant participation in both his death and his resurrection. The transition, however, could not be completed until the coming redemption of the believer's body (Rom. 8:23). In the meantime the Spirit infused the believer with the life of Christ (Rom. 8:5-11) and called forth the hope of his inheritance (Rom. 8:12-25).[57]

It was in the Eucharist that the church most clearly celebrated its participation in the body of Christ.

> Is not the cup of blessing which we bless a sharing in the blood of Christ? Is not the bread which we break a sharing in the body of Christ? Since there is one bread, we who are many are one body; for we all partake of the one bread (1 Cor. 10:16-17, NAS).

At the one table they affirmed their union with him and with one another.[58]

The responsibility of every believer was to build up the body of Christ (Rom. 12:3-8; 1 Cor. 10:23-24; 12:7, 12-31; Eph. 4:12). Unity in Christ did not destroy individuality (1 Cor. 12:27); it did call forth the exercise of various gifts and ministries for the good of the body. However, since life was in the Spirit, the Holy Spirit was the source of all of the gifts of life.[59]

---

[55] Ibid., p. 643.

[56] The entire being of the believer participated in the life of Christ so that the resurrection of the dead was essential to the Gospel. Irenaeus queried, "How then is it not the utmost blasphemy to allege, that the temple of God, in which the Spirit of the Father dwells, and the members of Christ, do not partake of salvation, but are reduced to perdition?" *Against Heresies* V.6.2, ANF, I, 532.

[57] Minear, *Images of the Church*, pp. 173-178.

[58] Irenaeus, *Against Heresies* V.2.2-3, ANF, I, 528.

[59] Minear, *Images of the Church*, pp. 190-195. Also, see Tertullian, *On Repentance* X, ANF, III, 664.

Summary. The early church expressed its self-understanding through a variety of images. The church identified itself with the eschatological gathering of the true Israel. As spiritual descendants of Abraham and recipients of God's promise to him they lived in the realities of the new covenant. The church further identified itself with the kingdom of God which was present in the Spirit of the resurrected Christ and was yet to come in fullness when he returned with the saints of the ages. The image of the saints accented the church's perception of itself as an eschatological community. The church further understood itself to be the habitation of God, especially as the living temple in which God dwelt. In them God was present in the world. The doctrine of the body of Christ gave expression to the church's unity and to the hope of the final resurrection.

THE COMMUNITY OF THE SPIRIT

The Holy Spirit as the Spirit of Christ was the thread which tied the various images and understanding of the church together in one common identity. Gerhard Lohfink correctly surmised, "It is impossible to discuss the self-understanding of the early church without considering its consciousness of the living presence of the Spirit in its midst."[60] It was that consciousness which most clearly delineated the ecclesiological context in which the Spirit was understood to function as teacher.

Called by the Spirit. The *ekklesia* was understood to be called and constituted by the Spirit. The call as issued through the apostolic proclamation of Christ was understood to be the cooperative effort of the apostles and the Spirit. Their preaching was in the power of the Spirit and was accompanied by signs and wonders worked by the Spirit (Acts 13:6-12; Rom. 15:18-19; 1 Cor. 2:4; 1 Thess. 1:5; Heb. 2:3-4).[61]

The Spiritual Israel. A constitutional relationship of the Holy Spirit to the church was evident in the various images applied to the church. The Old Testament prophets had presented the Spirit both as God's gift to the eschatological gathering of nations and as God's power to create the eschatological Israel (Isa. 32:15; Ezek. 11:19; 36:26- 27; 37:14; Joel 3:1-2). Thus, the church was known to be the true Israel precisely because the Spirit was at work within it (Gal. 3:1-5).[62]

Further, Christians were the true Israel because they, in keeping with God's promise to Abraham, were born according to the Spirit (Gal. 3:14; 4:29) which set them free from the law of sin and death (Gal. 5:18; Rom. 7:6;

---

[60] Lohfink, *Jesus and Community*, p. 82.

[61] Ibid. See also, Chap. 2, "Spirit of the New Age," pp. 35-37.

[62] Justin, *Dialogue with Trypho* XXXIX, ANF, I, 214; LXXXVII-LXXXVII, 242-243.

8:2). The Spirit was writing the new covenant within them (2 Cor. 2:3) and the sign of their covenant with God was a circumcision of the heart by the Holy Spirit (Rom. 2:29; Phil. 3:3; compare Col. 2:11).[63] Being led by the Spirit, believers were the children of God (Rom. 8:14; Gal. 4:6-7), heirs with Christ (Rom. 8:16-17). Irenaeus depicted the Spirit as leading the disciples to open the new covenant to the Gentiles. At Pentecost the Spirit joined into unity distant tribes making them the first fruits of all nations, the spiritual Israel.[64]

The Kingdom of the Spirit. It was the Holy Spirit who made the lordship of Jesus a reality in the church (2 Cor. 3:17-18) and the realities of the Spirit which thus identified the kingdom. "The kingdom of God is righteousness and peace and joy in the Holy Spirit" (Rom. 14:17).[65] Only the righteous would inherit the kingdom and it was the Spirit of God who was making the church fit for the kingdom (1 Cor. 6:9-11; Gal. 5:16-25). Specifically, the believers' status as saints was the result of the Holy Spirit's sanctifying work within them (1 Cor. 6:11; 2 Thess. 2:13; 1 Pet. 1:2).[66]

Hoisted by the Spirit. The Holy Spirit was the agent of the church's construction and the means of God's inhabitation (Eph. 2:17-22; 1 Cor. 3:16). Ignatius described the church as "the divine edifice of the Father" whose members are "chosen stones . . . who are raised up on high by Christ, who was crucified for you, making use of the Holy Spirit as a rope, and being borne up by faith . . ."[67] Novatian echoed the words of Paul in describing the church as being prepared by the Spirit to be God's temple, his house, and inhabiting the individual members to affect their holiness.[68]

The Life Giving and Unifying Spirit. The Holy Spirit was further perceived as the life giving and unifying agent in the body of Christ. It was the Spirit who baptized believers into the body (1 Cor. 12:13) and equipped them to function together as complementary dimensions of the whole (1 Cor.

---

[63] The early church developed a didactic imagery for the believers' circumcision by the Spirit. The *Epistle of Barnabas* interpreted this circumcision as referring to the ears. By it the believers were able to hear (understand) the Word of God, ANF, I, 142-143.

Justin understood this circumcision to be a cutting off of evil from the lives of believers. The utensil used by the Spirit was the "sharp stones" of the words of the apostles; stones taken out of the good rock, Jesus. *Dialogue with Trypho* CXIV, ANF, I, 256.

[64] Irenaeus, *Against Heresies* III.17.2, ANF, I, 444.

[65] Irenaeus understood the kingdom to be present in the church and future in the coming of Christ. He described the kingdom of the church's experience as "tranquil and peaceful" which he attributed to the work of the Spirit who was of "the most gentle manner" while vivifying humanity. Ibid., IV.20.10, ANF, I, 490.

[66] Irenaeus also taught that the Spirit had worked through the Old Testament prophets to assure that all who belonged to God, including the prophets, would be sanctified and instructed in the things of God. Ibid., IV.20.8, ANF, I, 490.

[67] Ignatius, *Epistle to the Ephesians* IX, ANF, I, 53.

[68] Novatian, *Treatise Concerning the Trinity* XXIX, ANF, V, 641.

12:4-11, 20-27).[69] The unity of the body was effectuated by the unity of the Spirit (Eph. 4:1-6).[70] Tertullian expanded upon the imagery by describing the church as the body of the Father, Son, and Holy Spirit.[71]

The unity between the Spirit and the church was further expressed by Irenaeus in his polemical work against gnosticism at the close of the second century. The Spirit could not be experienced outside of the church for, "Where the church is, there is the Spirit of God; where the Spirit of God is, there is the church and every grace."[72]

Irenaeus' polemic foreshadowed a recurring debate on the relationship of the church to the Spirit. Does the church by virtue of apostolic succession constitute the presence of the Spirit in the world, or does the Spirit constitute the presence of the church? The issue was catapulted to the front by the Montanist movement. The Montanists held that the Spirit was by means of prophecy directing the church into a more rigorous discipline in preparation for the second coming of Christ. A part of that discipline was a refusal to forgive major sins after baptism. The Catholic position held the power to forgive sins rested in the bishops.

The Montanist argument was articulated by Tertullian. Only by the power of the Spirit can the church remit sins. The Apostles forgave sin by the power of the Holy Spirit working within them, not as an act of discipline. Therefore, the church was constituted by the powerful presence of the Spirit.[73] "For the very church itself is, properly and principally, the Spirit himself . . . ."[74] That is, the effects of the presence of true church are the effects of the presence of the Spirit. The church functions only at the discretion of the Spirit.

Hippolytus, like Tertullian a rigorist opposed to laxity in the readmission of adulterers, held, contrary to Tertullian, that the Spirit was transmitted within the church through a succession of office as constituted by right belief. However, the officer works under the direction of the Spirit and therefore is careful "to impart to all without grudging whatever the Holy Ghost supplies . . . ."[75] By the mid-third century Cyprian[76] argued only the successors to the Apostles by the laying on of hands had the Spirit and their

---

[69] Paul expressed the same thought in Rom. 8:3-8 and Eph. 4:11-16 but without direct reference to the Spirit.

[70] Irenaeus wrote of the union of the souls of the believers by means of the Holy Spirit. *Against Heresies* III.17.2, ANF, I, 445.

[71] Tertullian, *On Baptism* VI, ANF, III, 672.

[72] Irenaeus, *Against Heresies* III.24.1, ANF, I, 470-474.

[73] Tertullian, *On Modesty* , ANF, IV, 98-100.

[74] Ibid., p. 99.

[75] Hippolytus, *The Refutation of all Heresies* , "Preface," ANF, V, 10.

[76] Ironically, Cyprian was an avid student of the writings of Tertullian.

presence was required for forgiveness. Christ, the Holy Spirit, the church and baptism could not be separated.[77] The point of departure for all was the same. The church existed because the Holy Spirit was at work within it. The Spirit and the church were ontologically distinct but phenomenologically inseparable. The church was the community of the Spirit.

CONCLUSIONS

The theological context in which the Holy Spirit was understood to operate as teacher was that of the church as the eschatological community of God. It was the Spirit who called out and constituted the *ekklesia* as the gathering of God's people. Thus, the church was the true, spiritual Israel marked by the Spirit and bound together under the Lordship of Jesus. The church was the dominion of God where his presence and sovereignty were presently realized through the Spirit.

THE ROLE OF THE SPIRIT IN THE PEDAGOGY OF THE CHURCH

The early church's understanding of itself as the community of the Spirit was reflected in the pedagogical aspects of its existence. Three educational issues of the church as community were especially influenced by Christianity's Spirit-consciousness: pedagogical objectives, the environment for learning, and the role of the (human) teacher. These issues reflected the pedagogical context in which the Spirit was perceived to function as teacher.

PEDAGOGICAL OBJECTIVES

The pedagogical objectives associated with the Holy Spirit by Christians of the first three centuries were rooted in the church's concept of divine mission. Educational aims were inseparable from the community's sense of identity and purpose.

Mission of the Church. The missionary vision of the church was rooted in Jewish apocalyptic thought.[78] A common theme of the Old Testament prophecy was the gathering of nations before the Lord on Mount Zion (Isa. 2:2-3; 60:2-3). In the last days God would bring about the salvation

---

[77] Cyprian, *Epistle 74: To Bishop Pompey* IV-V ANF, V, 387-388.

[78] E. Glenn Hinson, *The Evangelization of the Roman Empire: Identity and Adaptability* (Macon, Georgia: Mercer University Press, 1981), p. 16.

of the nations through Israel.[79] Jesus identified with those prophecies and focused his ministry on the calling of Israel to repentance. He portrayed a seemingly ambivalent attitude toward the Gentiles.[80]

However, Jesus also projected a consciousness of the universal impact of his mission. Joachim Jeremias analyzed the apparent contradictions in Jesus' attitude toward Gentiles and concluded that the incorporation of the Gentiles "was expected and announced by Jesus as God's eschatological act of power, as the great final manifestation of God's free grace."[81] Elsewhere, Jeremias wrote "the *sole* meaning of the entire activity of Jesus is the gathering of God's eschatological people."[82] Jesus came to Israel *because* his mission was for the entire world.

Lohfink concluded that foundational to the mission of Jesus was:

> . . . the idea that God has selected a single people out of all the nations of the world in order to make this people a sign of salvation. His interest in the other nations is no way impeded by this. When the people of God shines as a sign among the nations (cf. Isa. 2:1-4), the other nations will learn from God's people; they will come together in Israel in order to participate, in Israel and mediated through Israel, in God's glory. But all this can happen only when Israel really becomes recognizable as a *sign of salvation*, when God's salvation transforms his people recognizably, tangibly, even visibly.[83]

As the true Israel the church understood itself to be the object of the mission of Jesus, and, consequently, the extension of that mission to the Gentiles. The foundational objective of the church was to be the spiritual Israel which served as a sign for the nations. Even after the church moved out from Jerusalem it maintained a strong sense of being the symbolic presence of the people of God among the nations.[84]

---

[79] Lohfink, *Jesus and Community*, p. 19.

[80] Jesus restricted his own ministry to Israel and forbade his disciples to preach to non-Jews during his lifetime (Matt. 10:5). On the other hand Jesus did minister to Gentiles and marveled at their faith (Lk. 7:2-10). He further promised them a share in the salvation of Israel (Matt. 12:15-21).

[81] Joachim Jeremias, *Jesus' Promise to the Nations* , trans. S. H. Hooke, "Studies in Biblical Theology," No. 24 (London: SCM Press, 1958), p. 70.

[82] Joachim Jeremias, *New Testament Theology* (New York: Charles Scribner's Sons, 1971), p. 167.

[83] Lohfink, *Jesus and Community*, p. 28.

[84] Ibid., pp. 139-147.

The ante-Nicene writers spoke frequently of God's gathering the church from among all peoples and sanctifying it unto himself. A Eucharistic prayer in the *Didache* read:

> Remember, Lord, Thy Church, to deliver it from all evil and to make it perfect in Thy love, and gather it from the four winds, sanctified for Thy kingdom which Thou hast prepared for it; for Thine is the power and the glory forever.[85]

Clement of Rome exhorted the Corinthians to draw near to God:

> . . . lifting up pure and undefiled hands unto Him, loving our gracious and merciful Father, who has made us partakers in the blessings of His elect. For thus it is written. . . "Behold, the Lord taketh unto Himself a nation out of the midst of the nations, as a man takes the first-fruits of his threshing-floor; and from that nation shall come forth the most Holy." Seeing, therefore, that we are the portion of the Holy One, let us do all these things which pertain to holiness . . . .[86]

In a similar fashion the *Epistle of Barnabas* depicted the church as "a light to the nations."[87] The primary mission of the church was to be the people of God in the midst of the world, the means whereby the nations might discover the glorious reign of Christ.

The continuity of the mission of Jesus with the mission of the church was maintained through the Holy Spirit. The Spirit was the power and presence of Christ whereby his will was known and fulfilled.[88] The church was thus able to continue the mission of Jesus, extending it to the Gentiles as they perceived he intended. The pattern of the church's mission, "to the Jew first and also to the Gentile" (Rom. 2:10), was received from Christ and was mandated by the Scriptures.[89]

The continuity of the two missions was further expressed by the essentially spiritual manner in which they were interpreted. Just as Jesus stated his kingdom was not of this world (John 18:36), so the church understood its struggle as "not against flesh and blood, but against the powers, against the world forces of this darkness, against the spiritual forces

---

[85] *Didache* X.5, ANF, VII, 380.

[86] Clement, *Epistle to the Corinthians* XXIX-XXX, ANF, XI, 12-13.

[87] *Barnabas* XXIV, ANF, I, 146.

[88] See above, Chapter 2, pp. 30-32, 34-37.

[89] The first record of the use of the Old Testament by the church to defend its mission to the Gentiles was at the Jerusalem Council of Acts 15. James appealed to Amos 9:11-12 to justify the ministry of Paul and *Barnabas* to the Gentiles (Acts 15:13-18).

of wickedness in the heavenly places" (Eph. 6:12 *NAS*). Hence, the church ministered as Jesus ministered, proclaiming the good news of God's impending kingdom and confronting the powers of darkness especially as they fostered human misery. The church, like Jesus, was characterized by love and the power to overcome evil.[90]

Pedagogical Objectives Associated with the Spirit. The mission of the church mandated pedagogical objectives suitable for life in the kingdom of God. The objectives associated with the Holy Spirit were invariably directed toward the ultimate goal of union with God, an eternal state of unencumbered fellowship between the saints and their Creator. Such was to be life in the kingdom. The Spirit was portrayed as working in and through the church to prepare believers for this destiny through the transformation of their character, the development of their faith, and their salubrious incorporation into the body of Christ.

The ultimate goal of union with God was two faceted. First, in a very real sense union with God was attainable in the present life through the communion of the Holy Spirit.[91] Believers had God's Spirit dwelling in them mingling with their souls[92] and their flesh,[93] making them the temple of the Holy Spirit (1 Cor. 6:19). For the Lord "has also poured out the Spirit of the

---

[90] The ante-Nicene Church made frequent references to the continuation of two of the signs of the kingdom associated with the Spirit of Power, healing and the casting out of demons. See above, chap. 2, pp. 30-32. Also Justin Martyr, *Second Apology* VI, ANF, I, 190. Tatian, *Admonition to the Greeks* XV, XVIII, ANF, II, 71, 73. Origen, *Against Celsus* I.6, I.46, ANF, III, 398, 415. Novatian, *Treatise Concerning the Trinity* XIX, ANF, V, 641. Cyprian, *The Epistles of Cyprian* LXXIV.10, ANF, 393.

[91] Irenaeus clearly saw union with God as a present reality preparatory for immortality: Jesus "has poured out the Spirit of the Father for the union and communion of God and man, imparting indeed God to men by means of the Spirit, and, on the other hand, attaching man to God by His own incarnation, and bestowing upon us at His coming immortality durably and truly, by means of communion with God . . . ." *Against Heresies* V.1.1, ANF I, 527. In general the concept of communion with the Spirit was applied to all Christians. However, Tatian argued that the communion of the Spirit, while attainable by all believers, was the product of special grace realized by only a few; *Admonition to the Greeks* XIII, ANF, II, 71.

[92] Clement of Alexandria described the Spirit mingling with the believer's soul during the Eucharist. However, it was the Word through the bread which mingled with the flesh. *Instructor* II.2, ANF, II, 242-243.

[93] Irenaeus, *Against Heresies* V.8-5.10, ANF, I, 533-537. Irenaeus dealt at length with the role of the Holy Spirit indwelling in the believer. The Holy Spirit transformed the entire person (body, soul, and spirit) into a spiritual person nulifying the lusts of the flesh which bring death. "Rightly therefore does the apostle declare, "Flesh and blood cannot inherit the kingdom of God;" and "Those who are in the flesh cannot please God: not repudiating (by these words) the substance flesh, but showing that into it the Spirit must be infused. And for this reason, he says, "this mortal must put on immortality and this corruptible must put on incorruption." *Against Heresies* V.10.2, ANF, I, 536.

Father for the union and communion of God and man, imparting indeed God to men by means of the Spirit . . .".[94] Furthermore, the Spirit worked to draw persons into the church where communion with God was tangibly actualized especially in the Eucharist.[95] Pedagogical objectives associated with this union with God stressed moral and mental preparation for participation in the life of the church. Union with the church became functionally synonymous with union with God.[96]

In a second sense, union with God was yet to be fully realized. The believer's experience of the Spirit was considered preparatory for a future and final union with God. If the Spirit caused believers to even now cry "Abba, Father,"

> what shall the complete grace of the Spirit effect, which shall be given to men by God? It will render us like unto Him, and accomplish the will of the Father; for it shall make man after the image and likeness of God.[97]

Thus, early Christianity primarily understood the Holy Spirit's pedagogical objective to be the preparation of Christians for their ultimate glorious destiny in God.

However, distinctions between present and future realities were not always clearly maintained by the early church. The encounter of God within the church by the Holy Spirit was essentially the same as future union with him. The Spirit was the "first installment" or pledge from God of what the final state of the believer would be (2 Cor. 1:22; 5:1-5; Eph. 1:13-14).[98] Hence, preparation for union with the church was preparation for union with God and union with the church brought a foretaste of union with God.[99]

---

[94] Ibid., V.1.1, ANF, I, 527.

[95] Justin, *First Apology* LXVI, ANF, I, 185. Clement of Alexandria, *Instructor* II.2, ANF, II, 242- 243.

[96] "For this gift of God has been entrusted to the Church, as breath was to the first created man, for this purpose, that all the members receiving it may be vivified; and the [means of] communion with Christ has been distributed throughout it, that is, the Holy Spirit, the earnest of incorruption, the means of confirming our faith, and the ladder of ascent to God. . . ." For where the Church is, there is the Spirit of God; and where the Spirit of God is, there is the Church." Irenaeus, *Against Heresies* III.24.1, ANF, I, 458.

[97] Irenaeus, *Against Heresies* V.8.1, ANF, I, 533.

[98] A pledge which "Pays a part of the purchase price in advance and so secures a legal claim to the article in question . . .," Bauer, "arrabon," *A Greek-English Lexicon*, p. 109.

[99] Origen articulated the present-future realities of Christian union with God, "But both Jesus Himself and His disciples desired that His followers should believe not merely in His Godhead and miracles, as if He had not also been a partaker of human nature, and had assumed the human flesh which "lusteth against the Spirit;" but they saw also that the power

One primary pedagogical objective of the Spirit was the preparation of persons for union with God through the training of their characters in moral discipline, especially the control of the flesh. Irenaeus expressed it as follows,

> But we do now receive a certain portion of His Spirit, tending towards perfections, and preparing us for incorruption, being little by little accustomed to receive and bear God; Those persons, then, who possess the earnest of the Spirit, and who are not enslaved by the lusts of the flesh, but are subject to the Spirit, and who in all things walk according to the light of reason, does the apostle properly term "spiritual," because the Spirit of God dwells in them.[100]

Likewise, Tertullian described the Spirit as working against human tendencies:

> Whereas the reason why the Lord sent the Paraclete was, that, since human mediocrity was unable to take in all things at once, discipline should, little by little, be directed, and ordained, and carried on to perfection, by that Vicar of the Lord, the Holy Spirit . . . . What, then, is the Paraclete's administrative office but this: the direction of disciplines, the revelation of the Scriptures, the reformation of the intellect, the advancement toward the "better things?"[101]

For him the Holy Spirit was "the Determiner of discipline itself," that is the one who shapes moral character.[102]

Origen postulated that the Holy Spirit was not even in the morally deficient;

> In those persons alone do I think that the operation of the Holy Spirit takes place, who are already turning to a better life . . . who

---

which had descended into human nature, and into the midst of human miseries, and which had assumed a human soul and body, contributed through faith, along with its divine elements, to the salvation of believers, when they see that from Him there began the union of the divine with the human nature, in order that the human, by communion with the divine, might rise to be divine, not in Jesus alone, but in all those who not only believe, but enter upon the life which Jesus taught, and which elevates to friendship with God and communion with Him every one who lives according to the precepts of Jesus." *Against Celsus* III.28, ANF, IV, 475.

[100] Irenaeus, *Against Heresies* V.8.1-2, ANF, I, 533-534.

[101] Tertullian, *On the Veiling of Virgins* I, ANF, IV, 27.

[102] Tertullian, *On Modesty* XI, ANF, IV, 85.

are engaged in the performance of good actions, and who abide in God.[103]

The Spirit accomplished this transformation by turning the mind and imagination toward the things of God.[104]

Tatian described the Spirit as a trainer preparing the body for immortality.

> For our bodies are both trained in Him and by Him to advance to immortality, by learning to govern themselves with moderation according to His decrees . . . . This is He who restrains insatiable desires, controls immoderate lusts, quenches unlawful fires, conquers reckless impulses, repels drunkenness, checks avarice, drives away luxurious revelings . . . .[105]

Stated in positive form, the aim of the Spirit was to transform believers into "spiritual" persons suitable for being "planted in the paradise of God."[106] For Irenaeus this was a recapitulation of the original state of humanity, a rediscovery of "the pristine nature of man--that which was created after the image and likeness of God."[107] So the Holy Spirit was "a sanctifying power,"[108] rendering unto the faithful the holiness of God.[109]

A second primary pedagogical object of the Spirit was the preparation of believers for union with God through the perfecting of their faith. Faith was strengthened by hearing what the Spirit had said through the inspired teachers in the church[110] and through the prophecies of the Scriptures.[111] Faith was also strengthened by seeing signs and wonders performed by the Spirit in the church.[112] The Spirit worked within the heart and mind of individuals to help them "conform" to the faith of the church.[113] He wrote salvation upon their hearts through the proclamation of the ancient tradition of the church.[114]

---

[103] Origen, *De Principiis* I.3.5, ANF, IV, 253.

[104] Origen, *Against Celsus* IV.95, ANF, IV, 539.

[105] Tatian, *Treatise Concerning the Trinity* XXIX, ANF, V, 641.

[106] Irenaeus, *Against Heresies* V.10.1, ANF, I, 536.

[107] Ibid.

[108] Origen, *De Principiis* I.1.3, ANF, IV, 242.

[109] Ibid., I.3.8, ANF, IV, 255.

[110] Hippolytus, *Apostolic Tradition* XXV.3, trans. Burton Scott Easton, The *Apostolic Tradition* of Hippolytus (Cambridge: Cambridge University Press, 1935), p. 54. Also, Irenaeus, *Against Heresies* III.24.1, ANF, I, 458.

[111] Origen, *Against Celsus* I.2, ANF, IV, 397-398.

[112] Ibid.

[113] Irenaeus, *Against Heresies* III.24.1, ANF, I, 458.

[114] Ibid., III.4.2, ANF, I, 417.

The Spirit was further depicted as strengthening faith through providing understanding of the Scriptures.[115]

A third primary pedagogical objective of the Spirit was the preparation of believers for their final union with God through their salubrious union with the body of Christ. The Spirit was perceived as working in the life of every Christian to place them within the church in a manner that contributed to its well-being and that of its members. Specifically, the *charismata*, or gifts of the Spirit, were administered through various individuals for the good of others (1 Cor. 12:12-31).[116] Visions and other gifts from the Spirit existed in the church "for a testimony to unbelievers, to believers for a benefit."[117] The Holy Spirit was always operating for the edification of the church through its members.[118] In this manner God was perfecting the church; perfect gifts profited the church unto perfection.[119] The Spirit's objective was that each member of the body find perfection as a contributing member of the body as it and they moved toward perfection and their final destiny in God.

From these observations it may be concluded that the Holy Spirit was indeed a primary factor in the early church's self-identity as expressed in terms of mission and pedagogical objectives. The tandem relationship of the Spirit with Jesus revealed in the Paraclete sayings of John was evident in the expressed mission of the church to be the sign among nations, in this the church continued and extended the mission of Jesus. The pedagogical objectives of the church precisely fulfilled the promised function of the Paraclete to bring a knowledge-by-encounter of God. The proposed "internal witness" of the Paraclete was amplified in the church's commitment to the training of character in moral discipline. Finally, the Spirit's prescribed role in bringing understanding of the Word found expression in the church's aim to perfect the faith of the believers.

THE ENVIRONMENT FOR LEARNING

Little can be said with certainty about the formal educational programs of the early church. Schools for specialized training and evangelism apparently existed from the time of the apostles but there is little recorded

---

[115] Novatian, *Treatise Concerning the Trinity* XXIX, ANF, V, 640-641. Also, Origen, *De Principiis* II.7.2, ANF, IV, 285.

[116] In general these were considered gifts for the good of the church. However, they also served as a tool for evangelism. The nation marked by such good gifts was indeed a light to others. Irenaeus, *Against Heresies* II.32.4, ANF, III, 409.

[117] *The Passion of the Holy Martyrs Perpetua and Felicitas*, "Preface," ANF, III, 699.

[118] Ibid., VI.4, ANF, III, 705-706.

[119] Clement of Alexandria, *The Instructor* IV.21, ANF, II, 434. Also, Novatian, *Treatise Concerning the Trinity* XXIX, ANF, V, 541.

about the character of those institutions and there is no indication that they were integral parts of the common life of the church.[120] Rather, the education that would have been normative took place in the environment of the relationships and gatherings of the local assembly.

Social Environment. The social environment of early Christianity was that of an eschatological community living out the present realities of an age and kingdom which was yet to come. The kingdom of God called forth radically different standards for human relationships. Standards that were rooted in the character of Christ and actualized through the conviction of his presence as Lord through the person of the Holy Spirit. Thus, the church presented itself as a "contrast-society,"[121] the only reasonable alternative to the existing pagan social order. The church provided the world a model of what society ought to be, indeed, was destined to be.[122] Three dominant themes characterized the social environment of the church.

---

[120] Hinson, *Evangelization of the Roman Empire*, p. 40. The earliest certain school was that of Pantaenus in Alexandria in the mid-second century. However, information on the school is sketchy and it might be better to say that he was in charge of teaching catechumens. At any rate, "school" should not connote a formal organization or special building as instruction would have taken place in the teacher's residence. Pantaenus' student and successor, Clement, made effective use of the school as a tool of evangelism. Under Clement and his successor, Origen, students were educated in the classical literature as a means of pointing them to the giver of truth, Jesus Christ. John Ferguson, *Clement of Alexandria* (New York: Twayne Publishers, Inc., 1974), p. 15. Later tradition and modern scholarship has suggested that some of the Gospels and other New Testament literature were the products of schools founded by the Apostles and their followers. K. Stendahl argued that Matthew was written as a manual of instruction for teachers and church leaders. K. Stendahl, *The School of St. Matthew and Its Use of the Old Testament.* John's Gospel has been especially seen to lend itself to this view on the basis of internal evidence and patristic writings. Alan Culpepper has added a strong external argument that the Johannine literature was probably the product of a school. His conclusion was based upon an analysis of ancient schools from which he demonstrated that the Johannine community shared the primary characteristics of a school. R. Alan Culpepper, *The Johannine School: An Evaluation of the Johannine School Hypothesis Based on the Investigation of the Nature of Ancient Schools* (Missoula, Montana: Scholars Press, 1975).

[121] Lohfink, *Jesus and Community.*

[122] Origen expressed the contrast, "For if, in the words of Celsus, "they do as I do," then it is evident that even the barbarians, when they yield obedience to the word of God, will become most obedient to the law, and most humane; and every form of worship will be destroyed except the religion of Christ, which will alone prevail. And indeed it will one day triumph, as its principles take possession of the minds of men more and more every day." *Against Celsus* VIII.68, ANF, IV, 666. And again, "But we recognize in each state the existence of another national organization, founded by the Word of God, and we exhort those who are mighty in word and of blameless life to rule over Churches. Those who are ambitious of ruling we reject; but we constrain those who, through excess of modesty, are not easily induced to take a public charge in the Church of God. And those who rule over us well are under the constraining influence of the great King, whom we believe to be the Son of God, God the Word. And if

First, the nature of the church as a covenant community established a sense of exclusive and "mysterious" participation, a sense of belonging. Christians described themselves as belonging to an intimate family.[123] This imagery was strengthened by the fact that Christians principally met in homes.[124] Members entered the family through a universal rite of initiation, baptism, and associated with that rite the reception of a special knowledge withheld from all others.[125] The familial identity was realized through the common experience of the Spirit which bound believers together as heirs and joint heirs with Christ, the anointed one from whom their own anointing came.

The Eucharist early became a checkpoint for adherence to the covenant (1 Cor. 11:28).[126] Nonbelievers were withheld, and even the baptized who were living in a manner morally unworthy of communion with the saints were barred from participation. The result of these practices was a sense of separation from the world through moral purity[127] and, perhaps more significantly, a sense of exclusive belonging to the family of God.

---

those who govern in the Church, and are called rulers of the divine nation--that is, the Church--rule well, they rule in accordance with the divine commands, and never suffer themselves to be led astray by worldly policy. And it is not for the purpose of escaping public duties that Christian decline public offices, but that they may re- serve themselves for a diviner and more necessary service in the Church of God--for the salvation of men." Ibid. VIII.75, ANF, IV, 668. Also, *Barnabas* VI, ANF, I, 141.

[123] The image of the Christian community as a family was vividly portrayed by Aristides: "They love one another. They do not neglect widows. Orphans they rescue from those who are cruel to them. Every one of them who has anything gives ungrudgingly to the one who has nothing. If they see a traveling stranger they bring him under their roof. They rejoice over him as over a real brother, for they do not call one another brothers after the flesh, but they know they are brothers in the Spirit and in God. If one of them sees that one of their poor must leave this world, he provides for his burial as well as he can. And if they hear that one of them is imprisoned or oppressed by their opponents for the sake of their Christ's name, all of them take care of all his needs. If possible they set him free. If anyone among them is poor or comes into want while they themselves have nothing to spare, they fast two or three days for him. In this way they can supply any poor man with the food he needs." Aristides, *Apology* 15, 16, quotation from Eberhard Arnold, *The Early Christians: A Sourcebook on the Witness of the Early Church* (Grand Rapids, Michigan: Baker Book House, 1979), pp. 104-105.

[124] On the physical environment for the gatherings see Gregory Dix, The *Shape of the Liturgy* (London: Dacie Press: 1975), pp. 19-27.

[125] Hinson, *Evangelization of the Roman Empire*, pp. 73-95.

[126] Paul warned that each individual must conduct a self-examination before participating in the Eucharist. The context of the warning was the presence of factions in the church (1 Cor. 11:17-19), factions which denied the of the body of Christ by ignoring the suffering of its members (1 Cor. 11:20-21).

[127] Consider again the Eucharistic prayer from the *Didache* X.5, ANF, I, 380. Also, Justin stated, "And thus do we also, since persuasion by the Word, stand aloof from them (i.e., the demons), and follow the only unbegotten God through His Son--we who formerly delighted in

Second, the character of the church as fellowship fostered an attitude of support for weak and needy members. Converts were sponsored by established believers through what became a lengthy period of preparation for baptism.[128] In terms of physical care even the pagans took note of the manner in which Christians provided for their widows, orphans, and sick.[129] Belonging to the kingdom of Christ included tangible assurances of sharing in the blessings of his kingdom; it meant belonging to a family that provided for the needs of its members.[130]

Third, the church provided an environment of radical social order. Christianity insisted on the nobility and worth of the individual with no consideration of economic or political status (James 2:1-9). The Spirit elevated all to equal rank in the kingdom of God. There was neither bond nor free, Jew nor Gentile, male nor female (Gal. 3:28). Slaves and women, who were nonentities in the Hellenistic world, were able to rise to positions of leadership in the Christian *ekklesia*. Even marriage barriers between social classes were broken down.

Fundamental for the new social order was a denouncement of the use of power to control others. Christians served God and each other out of a sense of freedom and love.[131]

---

fornication, but now embrace chastity alone; we who formerly used magical arts, dedicate ourselves to the good and unbegotten God; we who valued above all things the acquisition of wealth and possessions, now bring what we have into a common stock, and communicate to everyone in need; we who hated and destroyed one another, and on account of their different manners would not live with men of a different tribe, now, since the coming of Christ, live familiarly with them, and pray for our enemies, and endeavor to persuade those who hate us unjustly to live comfortably to the good precepts of Christ, to the end that they may become partakers with us of the same joyful hope of a reward from God the ruler of all." *First Apology* XIV, ANF, I, 167.

[128] Hippolytus made a requirement of as much as three years of instruction before baptism and the Pseudo-Clementine writings demanded a six-year catechumenate! Hinson, *Evangelization of the Roman Empire*, p. 76.

[129] Bruce, *The Spreading Flame*, pp. 188-191.

[130] Tertullian described the "brotherhood" as follows: "But we are your brethren as well, by the law of our common mother nature, though you are hardly men, because brothers so unkind. At the same time, how much more fittingly they are called and counted brothers who have been led to the knowledge of God as their common Father, who have drunk in one Spirit of holiness, who from the same womb of a common ignorance have agonized into the same light of truth! But on this very account, perhaps, we are regarded as having less claim to be held true brothers, that no tragedy makes a noise about our brotherhood, or that the family possessions, which generally destroy brotherhood among you, create fraternal bonds among us. One in mind and soul, we do not hesitate to share our earthly goods with one another. All things are common among us but our wives." *Apology* XXXIX, ANF, III, 46.

[131] Bruce, *The Spreading Flame*, pp. 191-192.

82

The Christian Gatherings. The immediate environment for learning in the early Church was that of the Christian gatherings. Life in the kingdom of God was cultivated and reinforced through the regular patterns of corporate existence. There were four dominant types of Christian meetings which continued throughout the ante-Nicene period: daily gatherings for prayer, household feasts of celebration, Sunday services, and special gatherings.[132]

Christians gathered on a daily basis for prayer services (Acts 2:46; 3:1)[133] These were morning and evening assemblies which provided opportunity for personal exhortation and mutual support in response to the moral and spiritual challenges of the day.[134] Emphasis was placed upon the need of the body of Christ to continually assemble under the headship of its Lord.[135] Instruction in the Word of God, the acknowledgement of transgressions, the singing of psalms, and prayers of praise and petition were included.[136] The presence of spiritual teachers was an important aspect of these gatherings[137] and where possible the bishop was included.[138]

Feasts were also a common type of Christian gathering which gave tangible expression to the familial precepts of the church.[139] Life in the church was depicted as an eternal feast, members partaking of a table prepared by God. The pattern of Jesus in frequenting feasts was adopted and his instructions concerning the giving of feasts were taken literally, that is, emphasis was placed on feeding the lame, blind, and poor (Luke. 14:12-13).[140] Thus, these feasts were given the name love, or *agape*.

Love feasts apparently began as a part of the Sunday observance of the Lord's Supper, the Eucharist being incorporated into the meal as Jesus had done (Matt. 26:20- 29; Mark 14:17-25; Luke 22:14-38; 1 Cor. 11:17-34). But

---

[132] This classification of the gatherings was based upon a reading of the primary texts and represents a consensus. Practices varied slightly from region to region and generation to generation. These four categories were universal.

[133] Dugmore recognized the Jewish precedence for meetings of this type but pointed out that the Christian practice took on a radically different form. Clifford W. Dugmore, *The Influence of the Synagogue Upon the Divine Office* (Westminster: The Faith Press, 1964), pp. 42-45.

[134] Dix, *Apostolic Tradition*, p. 61.

[135] *The Teaching of the Twelve Apostles* III, ANF, VII, 378.

[136] *Constitutions of the Holy Apostles* II.7.59, ANF, VII, 422-423; *Canons of the Church of Alexandria* XXVII, ANF, V, 258; *Epistle of Barnabas* XIX, ANF, I, 148.

[137] *Constitutions of the Holy Apostles* VII.1.9, ANF, VII, 467.

[138] *Constitutions of the Holy Apostles* VIII.4.35, ANF, VII, 496.

[139] Jungmann has suggested that early Christians adapted the Jewish chaburah meal, a routine gathering of friends to celebrate the Sabbath meal, as the basis for weekly feasts; Josef A. Jungmann, *The Early Liturgy* (Notre Dame, Indiana: University of Notre Dame Press, 1977), p. 31.

[140] Irenaeus, *Against Heresies* V.33.2, ANF, I, 562.

the Eucharist was early separated from the meal and the feasts were moved to more private settings throughout the week.[141]

Emphasis was placed on the character of the festivals. Clement of Alexandria described the feasts as a divine orchestra in which the human instruments were played by the Spirit. They were occasions for righteous singing in contrast to the frivolous feasts of the pagans.[142] Tertullian gave a vivid description of the character of these gatherings.

> Yet about the modest supper room of the Christians alone a great ado is made. Our feast explains itself by its name. The Greeks call it *agape*, i.e., affection. Whatever it costs, our outlay in the name of piety is gain, since with the good things of the feast we benefit the needy; not as it is with you, do parasites aspire to the glory of satisfying their licentious propensities, selling themselves for a belly-feast to all disgraceful treatment,--but as it is with God himself, a peculiar respect is shown to the lowly. If the object of our feast be good, in the light of that consider its further regulations. As it is an act of religious service, it permits no vileness or immodesty. The participants, before reclining, taste first of prayer to God. As much is eaten as satisfies the cravings of hunger; as much is drunk as befits the chaste. They say it is enough, as those who remember that even during the night they have to worship God; they talk as those who know that the Lord is one of their auditors. After manual ablution, and the bringing in of lights, each is asked to stand forth and sing, as he can, a hymn to God, either one from the holy Scriptures or one of his own composing,-- a proof of the measure of our drinking. As the feast commenced with prayer, so with prayer it is closed. We go from it, not like troops of mischief-doers, nor bands of vagabonds, nor to break out into licentious acts, but to have as much care of our modesty and chastity as if we had been at a school of virtue rather than a banquet.[143]

---

[141] Dix, *Shape of the Liturgy*, pp. 96-102. However, the continuation of a combined Agape and Eucharist was evident in the *Didache* IX-X, ANF, VII, 379- 380; and as late as Tertullian's *Apology* XXXIX, ANF, III, 46-47.

[142] Clement of Alexandria, *The Instructor* II.4, ANF, II, 248; also, *The Instructor* II.1, ANF, II, 238.

[143] Tertullian, *Apology* XXXIX, ANF, III, 43. The pedagogical significance of these events is stressed by Tertullian's assertion that their affect was that of a "school of virtue." See also *The Octavius of Minucius Felix* XXXI, ANF, IV, 192.

Where possible the bishops attended these festivities to bless the meal and give instruction from the Scriptures.[144] Traveling prophet-teachers also frequented these gatherings and gave instruction.[145]

Sunday was the great festival day of the early church which called forth regular gatherings of distinctive significance.[146] The importance of Sunday was established by its association with the resurrection and post-resurrection appearances of Jesus (Matt. 28:1; Mark 16:2, 9; Luke 24:1; John 20:1, 19, 26). Sunday was the Lord's day, the eighth day of the week. As such it both fulfilled the Jewish Sabbath and age, and inaugurated the new creation brought forth in the resurrection. Sunday became the symbolic embodiment of the new age of the kingdom.[147] It signified the realities of the new which were proclaiming the death of the old. Therefore, the Sunday gatherings conveyed a sense of realized eschatology to all participants.[148]

The essential character and elements of the Sunday gatherings were presented by Justin:

> And on the day called Sunday, all who live in cities or in the country gather together to one place, and the memoirs of the apostles or the writings of the prophets are read, as long as time permits; then when the reader has ceased, the president verbally instructs, and exhorts to the imitation of these good things. Then we all rise together and pray, and, as we before said, when our prayer is ended, bread and wine and water are brought, and the president in like manner offers prayers and thanksgivings, according to his ability, and the people assent, saying Amen; and there is a distribution to each, and a participation of that over which thanks have been given, and to those who are absent a portion is sent by the deacons. And they who are well to do, and

---

[144] Bishops were not to fast except when the entire church was called to a fast so that they could attend these gatherings daily. Thus, they also became a means of supplying the needs of the bishop as well as deacons and other clergymen. Consider the instructions in the *Constitutions of the Holy Apostles* II.4.28, ANF, VII, 411.

[145] These teachers sometimes exhorted the believers to conduct a feast but were not to eat of it if they had instigated the event. *Didache* XIX, ANF, VII, 380.

[146] Ignatius gave instruction, "let every friend of Christ keep the Lord's Day as a festival, the resurrection-day, the queen and chief of all the days (of the week). Looking forward to this, the prophet declared, "to the end, for the eighth day," on which our life both sprang up again, and the victory over death was obtained in Christ . . ." *Epistle to the Magnesians* XI, ANF, I, 163. Like- wise, fasting and kneeling in worship were forbidden on the Lord's day. Tertullian, *The Chaplet* III, ANF, III, 94.

[147] So Justin argued that the celebration of the Eucharist on Sunday (the eighth day) was the true circumcision, cutting away deceit and iniquity. *Dialogue with Trypho* 41, ANF, I, 215.

[148] Ignatius, *Epistle to the Magnesians* IX, ANF, I, 63. See Jungmann, *Early Liturgy*, pp. 20-24; Dix, *Shape of the Liturgy*, p. 337.

willing, give what each thinks fit; and what is collected is deposited with the president, who succours the orphans and widows, and those who, through sickness or any other cause, are in want, and those who are in bonds, and the strangers sojourning among us, and in a word takes care of all who are in need. But Sunday is the day on which we all hold our common assembly, because it is the first day on which God, having wrought a change in the darkness and matter, made the world; and Jesus Christ our Saviour on the same day rose from the dead.[149]

From this passage it is clear that preeminence was given to the reading of the Scriptures, instruction and exhortation from the Scriptures read, prayer, the Eucharist, and offerings for the needy.

Amplification was added by Tertullian. Prayer was offered up in united force as if with violence in order to please God by wrestling with him in supplications. Intercession was given "for the emperors, for their ministers and for all in authority, for the welfare of the world, for the prevalence of peace, for the delay of the final consummation."[150] Scripture readings were selected as needful for the "peculiarity of the times"[151] in order to nourish faith, animate hope, make confidence steadfast, and confirm good habits. Exhortations from the Scriptures included rebukes, sacred censures and judgments against individuals.[152]

The climax of the Sunday gatherings was the celebration of the Eucharist. Prior to that ceremonial meal the unbaptized and those deemed unworthy of the sacred communion of Christ and his church were dismissed. Only those walking in harmony with Christ and the church were allowed to eat of the celestial food which infused the believer with the very life of Christ.[153] Thus, a cloak of secrecy enveloped this aspect of the gathering.

Christians also gathered for special ecclesiastical events. Chief among those were baptisms, ordination services, and common feast days such as Easter and Pentecost. In general, special events culminated in the celebration of the Eucharist. Thus, the environment was essentially the same as Sunday

---

[149] Justin, *First Apology* LXVII, ANF, I, 186.

[150] Tertullian, *Apology* XXXIX, ANF, III, 46.

[151] Ibid.

[152] In Tertullian's setting the offerings were received monthly to care for the poor, orphans, the aged, those who have suffered shipwreck, and imprisoned believers. Ibid.

[153] The determining factor of worthiness was unity with the body of Christ. Transgressions were to be confessed and thanksgiving offered for forgiveness. "But let no one that is at variance with his fellow come together with you (at the Eucharist), until they be reconciled, that your sacrifice may not be profaned." *Didache* XIV, ANF, VII, 381.

gatherings but with intensified meaning.[154] Each contributed to the aura and conceptualization of belonging to the covenant of the Lord Jesus.[155]

The Presence of the Spirit. A distinctive factor in the environment of the early church was the sense of the presence of the Holy Spirit. The church understood the impetus of its existence as a contrast society to be its infusion with the Spirit of God.[156] The leaders and activities of the Christian gatherings were perceived to be under the immediate direction of the Spirit.[157] But perhaps the greatest impact of the Spirit upon the church as a learning environment was through the ongoing presence of the *charismata*. The gifts of the Spirit, especially prophetic utterances and healings, were common to the church until the end of the second century and clearly continued to a lesser degree throughout the ante-Nicene period.[158] It would be difficult to overstate the impact of that kind of manifestations. Their presence made the church a place of expectation. To meet together was to meet with God who attested his presence through signs, wonders, and gifts by the Holy Spirit.

The assembly of the saints was not a school to learn about God; it was a living temple in which God dwelt by his Spirit and therefore was known by encounter. In the church truth was an experience of the ultimate (God) rather than a mere pursuit of reason. Thus, the church constituted an environment for learning which, because of the dynamic presence of the Spirit, placed the believer in a tension between the realities of the two worlds. Life in the kingdom of God was both a future expectation implanted by the Spirit and a present reality fulfilled by the Spirit.

---

[154] Justin, *First Apology* 44-47, ANF, I, 184-186. Tertullian, *Apology* 39, ANF, III, 46-67; *The Chaplet* 3, ANF, III, 94-95; *On Baptism* 6-8, ANF, III, 672-673; Cyprian, *Epistle* 69, ANF, V, 376; *Didache* 7, 9, 10, 14, ANF, VI, 379-381.

[155] Hinson, *Evangelization of the Roman Empire*, pp. 73-95; 131-146.

[156] So Irenaeus said of the Holy Spirit that he was the gift of God to the Church vivifying its members for incorruption in contrast to those without the Church and Spirit who "defraud themselves of life through their perverse opinions and infamous behavior." Irenaeus, *Against Heresies* III.24.1, ANF, I, 458.

[157] Hippolytus described the ordination of bishops, presbyters and deacons with a special emphasis upon their reception of the Spirit to aid them in their ministries. Hippolytus, The *Apostolic Tradition*, 3-10, Easton, 34-39. See, John E. Stam, *Episcopacy in the Apostolic Tradition* of Hippolytus (Basil, 1969), pp. 17-29.

[158] For a study of the evidence for the continuation of the gifts see A.N. Kydd, *Charismatic Gifts in the Early Church: An Exploration into the Gifts of the Spirit During the First Three Centuries of the Christian Church* (Peabody, MA: Hendrickson Publishers, Inc., 1984), pp. 5-87.

THE ROLE OF THE TEACHER

The third pedagogical issue impacted by the early church's identity as the community of the Spirit was that of the role of the human teacher within the community. Two types of teachers emerged in early Christianity. Both types were closely associated with the work of the Holy Spirit as teacher but represented different modes of divine operation.

Pastor-teachers. One type of teacher recognized by the early church was that of the pastor-teacher. Pastor-teachers were characterized by their pastoral relationship with the people, and their functions of preserving and transmitting the traditions of the apostles. By the end of the first century or early second century the pastor-teacher was incorporated into the office of the bishop and remained thus throughout the early church. Deacons, presbyters and others functioned as pastor-teachers, but only as extensions of the bishop.[159]

The pastor-teacher, in the office of the bishop, served as guardian of the faith. This pattern was set in the Pauline schemata of ministry in which the overseer, or bishop, was to be able to teach (1 Tim. 3:2), "holding fast the faithful word which is in accordance with the teaching, that he may be able both to exhort in sound doctrine and to refute those who contradict" (Titus 1:9 NAS).[160] Bishops were understood to be shepherds of the true flock[161] who by the Holy Spirit served in the place of the apostles.[162] In the generations following the apostles, the preeminence of the bishop was portrayed by Ignatius, who exhorted, "For as many as are of God and of Jesus Christ are also with the bishop."[163] Another writer described the function of the bishop, "he is the minister of the word, the keeper of knowledge, the mediator between God and you in the several parts of your divine worship."[164] The overseer served as Moses for the church.[165]

---

[159] Three quotes from the *Constitutions of the Holy Apostles* illustrate the relationships of the various teachers to the bishop: "The bishop, he is the minister of the word, the keeper of knowledge . . . the teacher of piety . . . ." "Let the presbyters be esteemed by you to represent us the apostles, and let them be the teachers of divine knowledge . . . ." Constitutions 2.26, ANF, VII, 410. "For now the deacon is to you Aaron, and the bishop Moses." Constitutions 2.30, ANF, VII, 411. ". . . let the presbyters one by one, not all together, exhort the people, and the bishop in the last place, as being the commander." *Constitutions* 2.56, ANF, VII, 421. Compare, *Shepherd of Hermas*, 1.5, ANF, II, 14.

[160] Origen, *Against Celsus* III.48, ANF, IV, 483.

[161] Commodianus, *Instructions* II., ANF, IV, 216.

[162] Cyprian understood the Apostles to be the first bishops, *Epistles* XXXXIV.3, ANF, V, 366.

[163] Ignatius, *Epistle to the Philadelphians* III, ANF,I, 80.

[164] *Constitutions of the Holy Apostles* 2.4.26, ANF, VII, 410.

[165] Ibid., p. 411.

Pastor-teachers were considered gifts from Christ (Eph. 4:11-12) who functioned under the leadership of the Holy Spirit. At their ordination bishops received a special anointing of the Spirit whereby they bestowed the Spirit on others at baptism and invoked the Spirit's presence at the Eucharist.[166] As guardians[167] of the sacred truths of the church they were to be esteemed as prophets[168] as it was believed that the Spirit protected them from error.[169]

Gregory Dix has summarized the teaching role of the bishop:

> The power of prophecy no less than the power of priesthood was conveyed in the bishop's ordination. Passages are numerous which refer to this special grace of 'teaching' as a unique sacramental endowment of his office, and not an exercise of such intellectual powers as he might possess. 'We ought', advises Irenaeus, 'to hearken to those elders who are in the *ecclesia*, to those who have the succession from the apostles, who with the succession in the episcopate have received the *unfailing spiritual gift of the truth* (*charisma veritatis certum*) according to the Father's good pleasure. But others who are outside the original succession, and who hold meetings where they can, we ought to hold suspect as being either heretics and men of evil doctrine, or else as creating a schism and self-important and self- pleasing, or again as hypocrites, doing what they do for the sake of gain and vain-glory.' It was as an inspired teacher 'according to the Father's good pleasure' that the bishop taught from the 'throne' or *cathedra*--the official 'chair' of his church which he shared with no one else but inherited from all his dead predecessors back to the first apostolic missionaries to that church. The bishop's 'throne' is not so much a seat of government (he is not the 'ruler' but the 'watchman' of his church according to Hippolytus' definition above) as a 'teacher's chair'; 'for the *cathedra*', says Irenaeus, 'is the symbol of teaching.'[170]

Thus, pastor-teachers served the primary function of preserving and transmitting the sacred traditions of the church. Centralized in the office of

---

[166] Gregory Dix, ed. and trans., *The Treatise on the Apostolic Tradition of St. Hippolytus of Rome* (London: S.P.C.K., 1937), pp. 2-6.

[167] Hippolytus wrote of the bishop, "Being found successors of the Apostles, and partakers with them of the same grace (charis) of high priesthood and the teaching office, and watchmen of the church," *Philosophumenor* 1.1. Quoted in Dix, Liturgy, p. 31.

[168] *Didache* XV, ANF, VII, 381. *Constitutions* 2.4.20, ANF, VII, 411. By the early second century the office of prophet was apprently absorbed into that of the bishop; see James L. Ash, Jr., "The Decline of Ecstatic Prohecy in the Early Church," *Theological Studies*, 37 (1976), 236.

[169] Ignatius, *Epistle to the Philadelphians* VII, ANF, I, 83.

[170] Dix, *Liturgy*, p. 31.

the bishop, these teachers served as watchmen over the Body of Christ protecting it from error in practice or faith. Yet, it should not be forgotten that these guardians of the truth were understood to function as agents of the Holy Spirit. It was the Spirit working through them that preserved and communicated the faith. It was the Spirit's anointing upon them which gave them authority.

Prophet-teachers. A second type of teacher recognized by the early church was that of the prophet-teacher.[171] These gifted persons taught through a form of ecstatic prophecy. They apparently served no other official function in church than to speak "in the Spirit." They characteristically traveled from one community to the next but were known to also exist as resident teachers. Because of their mobility and lack of accountability strict guidelines were imposed on them and their activities.[172]

The prophet-teacher was considered to bring instruction directly from the Holy Spirit. The shepherd described for Hermas the manner in which the Spirit operated through these instructors.

> When, then, a man having the Divine Spirit comes into an assembly of righteous men who have faith in the Divine Spirit, and this assembly of men offers up prayer to God, then the angel of the prophetic Spirit, who is destined for him, fills the man; and the man being filled with the Holy Spirit, speaks to the multitude as the Lord wishes. Thus, then, will the Spirit of Divinity become manifest. Whatever power therefore comes from the Spirit of Divinity belongs to the Lord.[173]

A true teacher of this type did not answer questions or respond to requests for instruction for the Holy Spirit "speaks only when God wishes it to speak."[174] Rather, the Spirit responded to the prayers of the righteous who

---

[171] The phrase "prophet-teacher" was selected in order to convey their character as inspired speakers. Prophets and teachers were distinguishable in the earliest period of Christianity but the basis of distinction has been lost. Prophets were understood to teach through their prophecies and some teachers functioned in the same manner as prophets. Their close association makes it reasonable to class them together as one type of divine instruction within the church, instruction rendered under the direct influence of the Spirit. *Hermas* 2.10-11, ANF, II, 26-28, *Didache* XI-XV, ANF, VII, 380-381. Justin, *Dialogue with Trypho* XXXIX, ANF, I, 214. Novatian, *Concerning the Trinity* XXIX, ANF, V, 640-641.

[172] Kydd, *Charismatic Gifts*, pp. 66-68.

[173] *Hermas* II.11, ANF, II, 27-28. The reference to angel of the prophetic Spirit is difficult to apprehend. It is analogous to the state of being "filled with the Holy Spirit" so that the reference to "angel" seems to serve to emphasize the nature of this experience as being that of delivering a message.

[174] Ibid.

had faith in the Spirit.[175] These teachers served as direct channels of communication from God to the righteous without dependence upon personally acquired knowledge. The requirements for such a teacher were a life in the Spirit attested to by moral uprightness and selection by a sovereign God.[176]

The mode of delivery for these messages from God varied. The direct prophetic speech described above by the Shepherd seems to have been the most common but a variety of others were also recorded. Visions and dreams were especially present[177] as were glossolalia with interpretations, and xenolalia.[178]

The extent of these phenomenon is difficult to ascertain. Irenaeus wrote in the late second century that there were many in the church

> who possess prophetic gifts, and who through the Spirit speak all kinds of languages, and bring to light for the general benefit the hidden things of men, and declare the mysteries of God."[179]

Hippolytus wrote of them in the early third century encouraging believers to attend the gatherings where they ministered:

> for grace will be given to the speaker to utter things profitable to all, and thou wilt here new things, and thou wilt be profited by what the Holy Spirit will give thee through the instructor; so thy faith will be strengthened by what thou hearest, and in that place thou wilt learn thy duties at home; therefore, let everyone be zealous to go to church, the place where the Spirit abounds.[180]

---

[175] The same paragraph implied that faith in the Divine Spirit was the product of having the Divine Spirit. Tertullian later wrote that prophecy continued among the Montanist because they acknowledged the gifts of the Spirit, that is, they believed they were important. Kydd, *Charismatic Gifts*, p. 68.

[176] This does not imply that they were ignorant of the Scriptures or doctrine as these were closely associated with life in the Spirit.

[177] Kydd, *Charismatic Gifts*, pp. 44, 67, 68.

[178] Harold Hunter, "Tongues-Speech: A Patristic Analysis," *Journal of the Evangelical Theological Society*, 23 (1980), 125-127. Xenolalia refers to speaking in a known language that has not been learned by normal means. By comparison, glossolalia involves speech which does not correspond to any known language.

[179] Irenaeus, *Against Heresies* V.6.1, ANF, I, 531.

[180] Dix, *Apostolic Tradition*, p. 54.

In the mid-third century Novatian[181] and even Cyprian referred to the continuation of these activities.[182] However, in time the prophet-teacher was also absorbed into the office of the bishop who became the single channel through which the Spirit was understood to bestow the charismata and teach.[183]

In summary, there were two types of teachers recognized by the early church, both originating during the period of the apostles and both attributing their authority to the Holy Spirit. One type, the pastor-teacher, was typified by the office of the bishop and served to preserve and communicate the sacred traditions of the church as a means of facilitating and effectuating communion between God and the church. The pastor-teacher was understood to function with an anointing of the Holy Spirit received at ordination. The second type, the prophet-teacher, was typified by the wandering prophet and served as the immediate voice of God concerning practical matters of Christian living. The prophet-teacher was understood to operate under the immediate influence of the Spirit as indicated by their behavior. At least until the mid-third century this type of teacher was fully endorsed by the church and apparently provided regular instruction for all believers. Together they provided the church a pedagogical link to both the historical Jesus of Nazareth and the resurrected Lord.

CONCLUSIONS

The early church's understanding of itself as the eschatological community of God by the Holy Spirit established the pedagogical patterns it followed. The corporate experiences of the church created a sense of the realized kingdom and fostered a powerful drive for final union with God. The Holy Spirit was perceived to be directing the church toward that end. Specifically, the church aimed at three prerequisites for union with God: moral discipline, faith, and union with the church.

---

[181] Novatian's language and list were comparable to those of Paul in 1 Cor. 12:8-10 making clear his emphasis on the function of prophet-teachers rather than an elected office; Novatian, *Treatise Concerning the Trinity* XXIX, ANF, V, 640-641.

[182] Cyprian, *The Epistles of Cyprian* IV.4, ANF, V, 290. Cyprian here referred to children who were filled with the Spirit and through visions and ecstatic utterances gave instruction concerning the treatment of the lapsed. However, for Cyprian all instruction and the charismata centered in the bishop so that these actions by children were directed toward him to confirm his position on the issue. On Cyprian and the Charismatic Gifts see Kydd, *Charismatic Gifts*, pp. 71-74; also Burgess, *The Spirit and the Church*, pp. 84-86.

[183] Ash, "Decline of Ecstatic Prophecy," p. 252.

The church's perceived, favored position before God fostered a radical social and spiritual environment for learning. In essence the church offered a foretaste of the future consummation. To experience life in the church was to know the rule of God. His presence brought forth a new social order in which relationships were governed by love. Furthermore, the presence of the charismata brought tangible demonstrations of the blessings of life with God. Thus, the environment for learning was a representation of the ultimate goal of union with God, for in the church the koinonia and gifts of the Spirit were the basis of divine-human encounter.

The two classes of teachers in the church served to reinforce the concept of being the eschatological people of God. Pastor-teachers by serving as communicators and guardians of the traditions of the church provided a link to the historic but timeless revelations of God. Like the Johannine Paraclete they functioned to remind (in the sense of bringing to life) the church of the words and commandments of Jesus.

Prophet-teachers served as the immediate voice of God. Through prophetic speech and activity they contributed to the Paraclete's function of leading into all truth. By bringing forth words direct from God they provided tangible expression for the Lordship of the resurrected Jesus over his church.

Chapter 4

THE HOLY SPIRIT AND THE PROCESSES OF CHRISTIAN
FORMATION

Early Christian writers were unanimous in their opinion that it was impossible to belong to Jesus without experiencing something of the Holy Spirit.[1] The purpose of this chapter is to describe the early church's perception of the role of the Holy Spirit in the process of Christian formation. The method of inquiry is twofold. First, the historical-theological issue of the Spirit's relationship to the individual in Christian formation is considered. Second, the pedagogical questions of the role of learner, the content of education, and the methods of instruction are addressed with emphasis being placed upon the church's perception of the Spirit's involvement with the learner.

THE HOLY SPIRIT AND THE INDIVIDUAL

The early Christian understanding of human existence focused upon the questions of sin and redemption. In contrast to Greek thought, the church adopted a basically Old Testament view of human beings which stressed the relationship of their whole being with God.[2] The work of the Holy Spirit with the individual thus circumscribed the process of redemption. Christian formation was the affective dimension of personal redemption and reflected a total transformation of the nature of human existence.

---

[1] Eduard Schweizer, *The Holy Spirit*, trans. Reginald H. and Ilse Fuller (Philadelphia: Fortress Press, 1980), p. 75.

[2] Geoffrey W. Bromiley, "Anthropology," *The International Standard Bible Encyclopedia* (Grand Rapids: William B. Eerdmans Publishing Company, 1979), I, 131-136.

CONTRASTING VIEWS OF HUMAN EXISTENCE

The early church was confronted by two basic understandings of the nature of human existence. Greek thought focused on the material and nonmaterial aspects of life. Hebrew thought began with the presupposition of a personal God from whom the identity of human existence was taken.

Greek Views of Human Existence. The anthropology of the Greek world was a complex mixture of varying strands of ancient concepts. However, one theme pervaded virtually all systems of thought; humanity was distinguished from the rest of nature by the individual's capacity for reason. At the heart of the varying systems was a deeply-rooted dualism which contrasted matter and reason and distinguished between the person as body and the person as mind.[3] In general the result was to understand the individual as a composite of two or more parts which worked against each other.[4]

The Old Testament View of Human Existence. In the Old Testament the different aspects of human existence were always seen as dimensions of a whole. People were not composites of diverse elements. They were an order of creation which had specific diverse features, the chief of which were flesh, soul, heart, and spirit.[5]

The concept of "flesh" conveyed the transitoriness of being human. The aspect of humanness referred to as "soul" designated life and vitality as being bound up with the body. The dimension of human existence referred to as the "heart" described the essential inner nature of the human being. And the concept of "spirit" portrayed people as living, breathing beings.[6]

Human nature found its focal expressions in the creation and fall of Adam and Eve. At creation they were said to be made in the image of God and it was his breath which made them living souls. As originally formed, they existed in dignity with sovereignty over nature in a fashion analogous to God's own dignity and sovereignty. In the absence of sin, they enjoyed an unimpaired relationship with their maker and each other.[7] In sum, the

---

[3] Harold B. Kuhn, "The Nature of Man," *The Zondervan Pictoral Encyclopedia of the Bible*, ed. Merrill C. Tenney (Grand Rapids: Zondervan Publishing House, 1976), IV, 53-55.

[4] The Greek language provided three primary parts: the body (soma), the soul (psyche), and the mind (nous); Herwart Vorlander, "Anthropos," NIDNTT, II, 564.

[5] Edmond Jacob, "Psyche," *Theological Dictionary of the New Testament*, ed. Gerhard Kittel, and trans. Geoffrey W. Bromiley (Grand Rapids: Wm. B. Eerdmans Publishing Company, 1964), I, 617-631.

[6] Vorlander, "Anthropos," *The New International Dictionary of New Testament Theology* , ed. Colin Brown (Grand Rapids: Zondervan Publishing House, 1975), I, 564-565.

[7] Karl Barth, *Church Dogmatics*, Vol. 3, trans. G. W. Bromiley (Edinburgh: T&T Clark, 1956), pp. 207-220.

Hebrew view of the first humans was conveyed with the words, "And God saw all that He had made, and behold, it was very good" (Gen. 1:31 NAS).

The impact of the fall on human nature was illustrated rather than spelled out in the Old Testament. The choice to disobey God resulted in alienation and tension in relationships. Adam reproached Eve in an attempt to escape responsibility. Eve was destined to cleave to her husband and in time brother slew brother. Driven from the face of God, succeeding generations knew him not and turned their hearts toward evil continually (Gen. 6:5; 8:21). In gist, the Old Testament view of human nature stressed its original design for fellowship with God and its distortion due to sin which made it inclined toward evil. To be human was to need redemption unto God.[8]

The Early Christian View of Human Existence. The early Christian view of human existence was primarily an extension of Hebrew thought but was clearly influenced by interaction with the Hellenistic world. The Greek word for the human species was *anthropos*, a masculine noun generally translated "man" but inclusive of the more generic "human being."[9] According to Joachim Jeremias, in the New Testament *anthropos* almost always expressed "the limited nature of human thinking and conduct in contrast to God and His revelation."[10] Herwart Vorlander further deduced from the New Testament that the human being, always appears as man vis-a-vis God: in his creatureliness (as distinct from other creatures and from God), in being addressed and chosen by God, in his transitoriness and disobedience, and as subject to the wrath and grace of God.[11] Thus, the essential questions of human existence were those concerning sin and redemption.[12]

Largely in response to Hellenistic dualism as seen in gnosticism, the patristic writers stressed the application of the redemptive work of Christ for the total human being. However, in the process of apologetics they accommodated themselves to a partite view of the species; humans were a composite of body, soul, and spirit. Precedence for this shift in thought was taken from New Testament passages such as 1 Thessalonians 5:23 ("and may your spirit and soul and body be preserved . . ." NAS) and Hebrews 4:12

---

[8] G. C. Berkouwer, *Man: The Image of God*, trans. James E. Davidson (Grand Rapids: William B. Eerdmans, 1976), pp. 20-32.

[9] W. Bauer, "Anthropos," *A Greek-English Lexicon of New Testament and Other Early Christian Literature* trans. and ed. by W. F. Arndt and F. W. Gingrich (Chicago: University Press, 1957), pp. 35-37.

[10] Joachim Jeremias, "Anthropos," TDNT, I, 364.

[11] Vorlander, "Anthropos," p. 565.

[12] Ibid.

("as far as the division of soul and spirit . . ." *NAS*).[13] The body was composed of mortal flesh and was the receptacle of the immortal soul and spirit.[14] Irenaeus expressed the relationship of the three as follows:

> There are three things out of which, as I have shown, the complete man is composed--flesh, soul and spirit. One of these does indeed preserve and fashion (the man)--this is the spirit; while to another it is united and formed--that is the flesh; then (comes) that which is between these two--that is the soul, which sometimes indeed, when it follows the spirit, is raised up by it, but sometimes it sympathizes with the flesh, and falls into carnal lusts.[15]

However, it should be noted that in this passage Irenaeus adopted the basic New Testament understanding of the soul as the seat of life, or, as Gunther Harder stated, "the soul is simply that area in which decisions are made concerning life and death, salvation and destruction."[16] Furthermore, consistent with the Scriptures, the Spirit was understood to be the life force which had its origin in God.[17] The thrust of this and other ante-Nicene references to the body, soul and spirit centered on the totality of God's redemptive work in Christ Jesus. The entire substance of the believer was destined to salvation.[18]

Early Christian thought also accommodated to the Greeks in its perception of humans as having the ability to improve themselves through reason as a faculty of the mind. Paul used the words *nous* and *noema*, both translated as "mind," to portray the conscious and rational dimension of human existence.[19] However, he understood the mind (*nous*) of sinners to be depraved (Rom. 1:28), vain (Eph. 4:17; Col. 2:18), corrupt (1 Tim. 6:5; 2 Tim 3:8), defiled (Titus 1:15), and therefore in need of renewal (Rom. 12:2; Eph. 4:23). The god of this age has blinded the minds (*noena*) of unbelievers (2 Cor. 4:4) and believers must have theirs guarded by God (Philippians 4:7). Indeed, at the heart of the New Testament understanding of becoming a believer was the concept of repentance which was taken from the word *metanoia*, literally

---

[13] Tertullian, *On the Resurrection of the Flesh*, XLVII, ANF, III, 581.

[14] Irenaeus, *Against Heresies* XIII, ANF, I, 540. Mathetes even described the soul as imprisoned in the body; Mathetes, *Epistle to Diognetue* VII, ANF, I, 27. Origen accepted the Platonic view of the pre-existence of the soul. However, Tatian held that the soul was mortal and could obtain immortality by union with the Holy Spirit, Tatian, *Admonition to the Greeks* XIII, ANF, II, 70-71.

[15] Irenaeus, *Against Heresies* V.9, ANF, I, 534.

[16] Gunther Harder, "Soul," NIDNTT, V, 686.

[17] See above, Chapter 2, pp. 26-30.

[18] Irenaeus, *Against Heresies* V.9, ANF, I, 534.

[19] Vorlander, "Man," NIDNTT, II, 567.

meaning "change of mind."[20] For the earliest Christians the mind was but one aspect of human existence which, like all others, needed transformation. Humanity had forfeited the right and ability to know God and thereby attain unto eternal life (Rom. 1:18-32).[21]

The patristic writers maintained the orthodox position that the knowledge of God comes only by grace,[22] but they also developed an elevated view of the human capacity for reason as complementary to the work of the Spirit. So Irenaeus termed "spiritual" those who "walk according to the light of reason."[23] Athenagoras hinted at this when he wrote that God was, "apprehended by the understanding only and the reason . . . ."[24] Tertullian appealed to reason as God's gift whereby believers understood the "why" of church tradition.[25] Clement of Alexandria represented ante-Nicene thought when he repeatedly proclaimed believers the true gnostics of the world because they superseded other systems of learning:

> I call him truly learned who brings everything to bear on the truth;
> so that, from geometry, and music, and grammar, and philosophy
> itself, culling what is useful, he guards the faith against assault . . . .
> And how necessary is it for him who desires to be partaker of the
> power of God, to treat of intellectual subjects by philosophizing![26]

Later in the same work he reiterated,

> . . . philosophy, being the search for truth, contributes to the
> comprehension of truth; not as being the cause of comprehension,
> but a cause along with other things, and co-operator, perhaps also
> a joint cause.[27]

In gist, for Clement individuals should exercise the soul through reason so that it might become susceptible to the reception of knowledge.[28]

Origen displayed a similar view of the benefits of academic pursuits. For him humans drew their existence from God the Father, their rational natures

---

[20] Bauer, "Metanoia," *Lexicon*, p. 513.

[21] D. M. Lake, "Mind," ZPEB, IV, 229.

[22] So Justin asked, "Will the mind of man see God at any time it is uninstructed by the Holy Spirit?" Justin, *Dialogue* IV, ANF, I, 196.

[23] Irenaeus, *Against Heresies* V.8, ANF, I, 534.

[24] Anthenagoras, *A Plea for the Christians* X, ANF, II, 133.

[25] Tertullian, *The Chaplet* IV, ANF, III, 95.

[26] Clement, *The Stromata* I.9, ANF, II, 309-310.

[27] Clement, *The Stromata* I.20, ANF, II, 323.

[28] Clement, *The Stromata* VII.12, ANF, III, 543.

from having been created by Christ, and their holiness from the Spirit.[29] As reason comes to all from Christ, "Truly it is no evil to have been educated, for education is the way to virtue. . . ."[30]

While there was no unanimity in the value attributed to pursuits in the realm of reason and the knowledge of God retained its subjective character,[31] obviously the church was rapidly influenced by the Greek understanding of personal knowledge as an intellectual looking at in which the object of knowledge was externalized and contemplated from a distance.[32]

In summary, the early church defined human existence in terms of relationship to God. To be human was to belong to a race of creatures living in rebellion against God their creator. It was to be a personal entity answerable to a personal God, a multi-dimensional entity retaining something of the image of God but marred by sin so as to be totally incapable of self-deliverance. Yet, to be human was to be the object of God's love and redemptive act in Jesus Christ. It was to have the potential of knowing God in the highest sense of being united to him; the potential of being transformed from sinner to saint, from an enemy of God to a member of his family.

THE WORK OF THE SPIRIT IN THE REDEMPTION OF PERSONS

The results of redemption through Jesus Christ were for the early church a total transformation of human existence. To be joined to Jesus was to become a whole new creation (2 Cor. 5:17). The Holy Spirit was understood to be the powerful presence of God in the world whereby he was effecting the new creation and ushering in the new age. In this the Spirit was perceived to principally work with people.

Early Christian writings used a variety of concepts and images to describe the work of the Holy Spirit in the redemption of persons. In general they fell into three categories; (1) those which portrayed the new life obtained in redemption, (2) those which portrayed cleansing or sanctification as an aspect of redemption, and (3) those which connoted personal encounter with God by the Holy Spirit.

New Life. Perhaps the most comprehensive image associated with the Holy Spirit and redemption was that of regeneration, or new life. Hendrikus

---

[29] Origen, *De Principiis* I.3, ANF, IV, 255.
[30] Origen, *Against Celsus* III.49, ANF, IV, 484.
[31] See above, Chapter 2, pp. 48-50.
[32] Rudolph Bultmann, "Ginosko," TDNT, I, 697.

Berkhof has identified this as the dominating concept of the Spirit and the individual in the Scriptures:

> The Spirit is the life-giver; he is God breathing the breath of life into man. That is the essence of his work in redemption as well as in creation. Redemption as the work of the Spirit means "rebirth." The heart of stone is replaced by a heart of flesh (Ezek. 36:26), breath comes into the dry bones (37:10). So we become children of God, not born of the will of man but of God (John 1:13). For "unless one is born anew, he cannot see the kingdom of God" (3:3). "Therefore, if anyone is in Christ, he is a new creation" (2 Cor. 5:17), similar to the first creation: "For it is the God who said, 'Let light shine out of darkness,' who has shone in our hearts to give the light of the knowledge of the glory of God in the face of Christ" (2 Cor. 4:6). This light is life, for the Spirit gives life (2 Cor. 3:6). When you were dead, he made you alive (Eph. 2:1). God brought us forth of his own will by the word of truth (James 1:18), by which he has caused us to be born anew to a living hope through the resurrection of Christ (1 Peter 1:3).[33]

However, in the mind of the early church the term "regeneration" did not stand for a sharply defined concept.[34] It was generally associated with water baptism and the forgiveness of sins. Hippolytus referred to baptism as the "laver of regeneration by the Holy Spirit" by which sins were remitted.[35] It was the Spirit according to Novatian "who effects with water the second birth, as a certain seed of divine generation. . ."[36] Likewise Cyprian rejected the baptism of schismatics because they should "consider and understand that spiritual birth cannot be without the Spirit . . . ."[37] So with Ireneaus, the individual who "receives the quickening Spirit, shall find life."[38]

The new life associated with the Spirit permeated the inner and outer realms of the individual affecting both soul and body. Hence, Tatian argued,

> The soul is not in itself immortal, O Greeks, but mortal . . . if it continues solitary (lives alone), it tends downward towards matter, and dies with the flesh; but, if it enters into union with Divine

---

[33] Hendrikus Berkhof, *The Doctrine of the Holy Spirit* (Atlanta: John Knox Press, 1977), p. 9.

[34] L. Berkhof, *Systematic Theology* (Grand Rapids: Wm. B. Eerdmans Publishing Co., 1969), p. 465.

[35] Gregory Dix, ed. and trans., *The Treatise on the Apostolic Tradition of St. Hippolytus of Rome* (London: S.P.C.K., 1937), p. 38.

[36] Novatian, *Treatise Concerning the Trinity* XXIX, ANF, V, 641.

[37] Cyprian, *Epistles* LXXIV.8, ANF, V, 392.

[38] Irenaeus, *Against Heresies* V.12.2, ANF, I, 538.

Spirit, it is no longer helpless, but ascends to the regions whither the Spirit guides it.[39]

And *Pseudo-Clement* spoke of the life given to the flesh, "So excellent is the life and immortality which this flesh can receive as its portion, if the Holy Spirit be joined to it."[40]

Cleansing. A second image of redemption closely associated with the Holy Spirit by the early church was sanctification or cleansing. The New Testament understanding of sanctification was largely derived from the Old Testament concept which had its basis in the Hebrew word *qadosh*. The root meaning of *qadosh* was to "cut off" or to "separate" which conveyed the spiritual message of holiness or apartness.[41] The Greek term for sanctification was *hagiasmos* which connoted a state of sanctity in the sense of consecration or holiness.[42] The verb *hagiazo* expressed the act of sanctifying and in several cases meant moral purification.[43]

In early Christian thought the Holy Spirit was the agent whereby the individual was sanctified (2 Thes. 2:13; Rom. 15:16).[44] It was the Spirit who gave believers "an insatiable desire for doing good,"[45] having remitted their sins[46] and returned them to the pristine nature for which they were created, refashioning them into the very likeness of God.[47] In the words of Irenaeus, those who establish the Spirit of God in their hearts,

> shall be properly called both "pure," and "spiritual," and "those living to God," because they possess the Spirit of the Father, who purifies man, and raises him up to the life of God.[48]

By the Holy Spirit the individual was understood to participate in the very holiness of God.[49] Origen wrote

---

[39] Tatian, *Admonition to the Greeks* XIII, ANF, II, 70-71.

[40] *Second Epistle of Clement*, XIV, in J. B. Lightfoot, *The Apostolic Fathers* (Grand Rapids: Baker Book House, 1980), pp. 49-50.

[41] Francis Brown, S.R. Driver and Charles A. Briggs, eds., "Qadosh," *A Hebrew and English Lexicon of the Old Testament* (Oxford: Clarendon Press, 1975), pp. 871-873.

[42] Bauer, "Hagiasmos," *Lexicon*, p. 9.

[43] Ibid., "Hagiazo," pp. 8-9.

[44] Irenaeus, *Against Heresies* V.11, ANF, I, 537. Origen, *De Principiis* I.3.5, ANF, IV, 255; also I.1.3, ANF, IV, 242. Tertullian, *On Baptism* IV, ANF, III, 671.

[45] Clement, *Epistle to the Corinthians* II, ANF, I, 5.

[46] Tertullian, *On Baptism* VI, ANF, III, 672.

[47] Irenaeus, *Against Heresies* V.10, ANF, I, 536. Irenaeus, *The Demonstration of Apostolic Preaching*, ACW, 16, 73-74. Tertullian, *On Baptism* V, ANF, III, 672.

[48] Irenaeus, *Against Heresies* V.9, ANF, I, 535.

[49] Clement of Alexandria, *Stromata* VII.14, ANF, II, 548.

On this account, therefore, is the grace of the Holy Ghost present, that those beings which are not holy in their essence may be rendered holy by participating in it.[50]

For Clement of Alexandria this was actualized in the Eucharist for "they who by faith partake of it are sanctified both in body and soul."[51] But most often sanctification was associated with baptism, "the mark of complete purification."[52]

Personal Encounter with the Spirit. The dominant images associated by the early church with the individual and the Holy Spirit were those which portrayed personal encounter or, at the very least, contact and interaction between the two. New life and cleansing were results of the Spirit's work on the believer. But they were in one respect only means toward an end. The objective the Spirit worked toward was redemption unto union and communion with God. Early Christian literature abounds with references which connote personal interaction with God through the Holy Spirit.

Intimacy between the believer and the Spirit was foreshadowed in John's prophecy, "I baptize you with water but he (Jesus) will baptize you with the Holy Spirit" (Mark 1:8; Matt. 3:11; Luke 3:17; John 1:33). Other images of interaction included the Spirit coming upon the believer, the Spirit being poured out on the believer, the Spirit filling the believer, the believer receiving the Spirit and the believer having the Spirit dwell within. Modern scholarship has generally interpreted these images from the perspective of Pauline theology without consideration of their Old Testament antecedents or recognition of the fact that they were predominantly Lukan terms.[53]

Roger Stronstad in his study of the charismatic theology of Luke reviewed the descriptions in LXX of human encounters of the charismatic Spirit and the charismatic element of prophecies concerning the messianic age. On the latter he concluded,

> . . . as the prophets describe it, the gift of the Spirit of God in the age to come will be characterized by two dimensions. In the first place, God will pour out His Spirit on a universal scale. Certainly the community of the new age will have a uniquely chosen, equipped, and sent charismatic leader, but for the first time the community itself will be charismatic.

---

[50] Origen, *De Principiis* I.33.5, ANF, IV, 255.

[51] Clement of Alexandria, *The Instructor* II.2, ANF, II, 242.

[52] Origen, *Against Celsus* III.51, ANF, IV, 484.

[53] Clark H. Pinnock, "Forward," in Roger Stronstad, *The Charismatic Theology of St. Luke* (Peabody, MA: Hendrickson Publishers, 1984), p. 7-12.

In the second place, in the age to come God's people will experience a totally new dimension of the Spirit--the indwelling of the Spirit. By his Spirit God will cleanse and purify his people from their sins, create new life in them, and impart to them the ability to keep his covenantal demands. The inward renewal of the Spirit, which results from the indwelling of the Spirit, complements the charismatic gift of the Spirit.[54]

His review of the LXX treatment of personal encounters with the Spirit of God revealed several recurring themes. First, the Spirit principally acted upon persons to endow them with the ability to fulfill an assignment from God. Secondly, prophetic speech activity was a common sign of the Spirit's presence in a person. Third, the anointing of the Spirit was frequently transferred from one person to another. Fourth, the Old Testament prophets applied the same images of the Spirit and people to the coming Messiah and the members of the messianic community. The experience of the members of the messianic community would differ from their Old Testament counterparts in only two ways. Theirs would be an ongoing, shared encounter of the entire community. And they would experience a new dimension of the Spirit--the indwelling of the Spirit as the means of keeping the covenant of God.[55]

The early church interpreted its experience of the Spirit in light of this background of Old Testament experiences and prophecies. Two dominant themes emerged. First, the Spirit of God was at work in the church empowering its members for messianic activity accompanied by signs. Second, the Spirit of God was indwelling the members of the church that they might achieve the fullness of life in the kingdom. The first theme gained prominence in the writings of Luke, the latter in the writings of Paul. Both themes were rooted in the Old Testament as filtered through the common experiences of the church.

For Luke the primal image for Spirit-believer encounters was a "baptism in the Spirit" (Luke 3:16; Acts 1:5; 11:16). Each of the Gospels recorded John's identification of Jesus as the administrator of such a baptism (Matt. 3:11; Mark 1:8; Luke 3:16; John 1:33).[56] All of these references juxtaposed the

---

[54] Roger Stronstad, *The Charismatic Theology of St. Luke*, p. 26.

[55] Ibid., pp. 22-27. Stronstad concluded this Spirit would provide two types of power: charismatic and moral.

[56] Paul also used a construct of the phrase in 1 Corinthians 12:13 ("for by one Spirit we were all baptized into one body . . ."NAS). Dunn treated this as a "crucial" passage for understanding the early Christian concept of a baptism in the Spirit; Dunn, *Baptism in the Holy Spirit*, p. 127.

However, Ervin argued the instrumental use of en with pneuma in verses 3 and 9 set a contextual precedence favoring an instrumental en in v. 13, that is, "by one Spirit." Therefore, the Spirit is the one who does the baptizing. Ervin, *Baptism in the Holy Spirit*, pp. 98-99.

baptism by Jesus in the Spirit with John's baptism in water. The two baptisms converged with the descent of the Spirit upon Jesus at his baptism in water by John (Matt. 3:13-17; Mark 1:9-11; Luke 3:21-22; John 1:29-34). The Gospel of John made the connection explicit, "He upon whom you see the Spirit descending and remaining upon Him, this is the one who baptizes in the Holy Spirit" (John 1:33, NAS).

The significance of the Spirit's descent upon Jesus was twofold. First, it made manifest the presence of the messiah in the world and thereby proclaimed the inauguration of the messianic age.[57] In this event the Father proclaimed Jesus to be his son (Matt. 3:17; Mark 1:11; Luke 3:22) and John confessed that the reason he came baptizing with water was that Jesus as Messiah "might be manifested to Israel . . ." (John 1:31). A common patristic interpretation emphasized the resting of the Spirit upon Jesus in order that he might distribute the Spirit and the gifts of the Spirit to the church as the eschatological gathering of God's people.[58]

However, the significance of the Spirit's descent upon Jesus also included his personal reception of the Father's anointing with the Spirit as the means with which he would fulfill his ministry of healing and teaching. In essence he was baptized in the Spirit himself whereby he received the power which gave direction and authenticity to his ministry.[59] So, it was the Spirit who drove Jesus into the wilderness and it was by the power of the Spirit that he healed the sick and cast out demons.[60] Further, it was because he had received the Spirit in this manner that he could baptize others in the Spirit.[61]

---

[57] Lampe contended the baptism was a "foreshadowing and symbolical summing up of his mission as Son and Servant of God, of his death, resurrection, and ascension and of the New Covenant to be inaugurated in these events, and, secondly, as an event which prefigured and made possible the Pentecostal fulfillment of the ancient hope of a universal outpouring of the Spirit upon the people of God." Geoffrey W. H. Lampe, *The Seal of the Spirit: A Study in the Doctrine of Baptism and Confirmation in the New Testament and the Fathers* (London: S.P.C.K., 1967), p. 33.

Dunn placed greater significance on the event itself, "the experience of Jesus at Jordan is far more than something merely personal--it is a unique moment in history: the beginning of a new epoch in salvation history--the beginning, albeit in a restricted sense, of the End-time, the messianic age, the new covenant." Dunn, *Baptism in the Holy Spirit*, p. 24.

[58] Justin, *Dialogue with Trypho* LXXXVIII, ANF, I, 243-244. Novatian, *Treatise Concerning the Trinity* XXIX, ANF, V, 641. Tertullian, *On Baptism* VII-X, ANF, III, 672- 675. Irenaeus, *Against Heresies* V.8, ANF, I, 533-534. Dix, *Apostolic Tradition*, p. 4.

[59] See above, "The Holy Spirit in Early Christian Thought," chapter 2, pp. 29-41.

[60] G. R. Beasley-Murray, "Jesus and the Spirit", in *Melanges Biliques*, ed. Albert Descamps and Andre de Halleux (Gembloux: Duculot, 1970), pp. 471-473.

[61] Dunn, *Baptism in the Holy Spirit*, p. 32. Dunn concluded, "For us the most important ministry for which the descent of the Spirit equipped Jesus was his messianic task of baptizing in the Spirit."

In the Lukan tradition the believer's baptism in the Spirit was clearly associated with the reception of power, the fulfillment of mission, and the glorification of God.[62] These themes were also portrayed by other images of the Holy Spirit interacting with believers. What Jesus had promised in Acts 1:5, Luke recorded in terms of being "filled" with the Holy Spirit in Acts 2:4. This latter phrase was for Luke a dominant description of believer-Spirit encounters.[63] It was especially related to prophetic-speech activity[64] which glorified God (Luke 1:41-45; 61-68; Acts 2:4-11) and pronounced the arrival of the eschatological age (Luke 1:15-17, 41-45, 61-79; Acts 4:8-12, 31; 7:55-56; 13:9-12). It was further used in conjunction with individuals being directed by the Spirit in confrontations with forces opposing the kingdom of God (Luke 4:1; Acts 4:8-12; 13:9-12).[65]

Closely associated with the image of being full of the Spirit were those of having the Spirit "come upon" the individual or having the Spirit "poured out" upon the believer. These images were also connected with prophetic speech activity especially in relation to the proclamation and activities of the kingdom of Christ (Luke 4:18; Acts 1:8; 2:17-18; 10:44, 45; 11:15; 19:6).

An inverse description of the Spirit-believer encounter used by Luke was that of the individual "receiving" the Spirit (Acts 2:38; 8:15, 17; 10:47; 19:2). This act by the believer was concomitant with the Spirit's coming upon or filling the believer.[66] The encounter was mutually participatory. The image was one of God embracing the individual in a manner that allowed the human to accept the embrace as God's eschatological gift (Luke 11:13; Acts 2:38; 10:45; 11:17; 15:8) and thereby participate in God's eschatological activity, that is, the ushering in of the kingdom. The experience was an act of

---

[62] James D. G. Dunn, *Jesus and the Spirit: A Study of the Religious and Charismatic Experience of Jesus and the First Christians as Reflected in the New Testament* (Philadelphia: The Westminster Press, 1975), pp. 152-156, 163-170; James D. G. Dunn, "Spirit, Holy Spirit," NIDNTT, III, 698-670; Eduard Schweizer, "Pneuma," TDNT, VI, 404- 415.

[63] In the New Testament the image of being filled with or full of the Spirit is almost exclusively Lukan. The single Pauline reference was Ephesians 5:18.

[64] For Luke the phrase "filled with the Spirit" always described an experience of inspiration. Even in Acts 13:52 the recorded outcome of "joy" connoted inspiration, see Luke 10:21. Stronstad, Charismatic Theology in St. Luke, p. 54.

[65] Compare themes associated with the Paraclete, above, chapter 2, pp. 48-53.

[66] The 120 were "filled with the Spirit" (Acts 2:4) which Peter described to the multitude as "the gift of the Holy Spirit" (Acts 2:38) which they too could receive. Because the Holy Spirit had not yet "come upon" any of the Samaritans, Peter and John prayed that they might "receive" the Holy Spirit. As they laid their hands upon the people they did "receive" (Acts 8:15-17). The encounter between the Spirit and the people at the house of Cornelius was described as the Spirit being "poured out" and "coming upon" the people (Acts 10:44,45) and their having "received" the Spirit (Acts 10:47). The images of "receiving" and "coming upon" were also used of the Spirit and the disciples at Ephesus (Acts 19:1-7).

grace which in no wise detracted from the believer's humanness but rather served to fulfill and perfect the creature through the restoration of communion with the Creator.[67]

In the development of the theme of the indwelling Spirit, Paul also made reference to believers "receiving" the Spirit (Gal. 3:2, 14; 1 Cor. 2:12).[68] His meaning has been widely debated without clear resolution.[69] However, it is noteworthy that both Galatians passages tied the reception of the Spirit to faith, a condition of the believer. Also, in the same context, the gift of the Spirit was associated with miracles (Gal. 3:5).[70] Furthermore, the Corinthian passage emphasized the effects of receiving the Spirit; believers gained a knowledge of "the things freely given to us by God" (1 Cor. 2:12 NAS) and they spoke of those things taught by the Spirit (1 Cor 2:13). Thus, for Paul, like Luke, the reception of the Spirit was associated with both knowing and speaking things learned from God.

However, the prevailing Pauline image was that of the Spirit dwelling in the believer (Rom. 8:9, 11; 1 Cor. 3:15; 2 Tim. 1:14) which closely resembled the image of the believer being the temple of God (1 Cor. 3:16; 6:19; 2 Cor. 6:16). On this point Paul was emphatic, one could not belong to Christ without the indwelling of the Spirit (Rom. 8:9). To be an heir of the new covenant was to have the Spirit within the heart crying out, "Abba! Father!" (Gal. 4:6). In this

> The Spirit Himself bears witness with our spirit that we are children of God, and if children, heirs also, heirs of God and fellow-heirs with Christ, . . . (Rom, 8:16-17 NAS).

Furthermore, it was the indwelling of the Spirit which brought new life to the believer (Rom. 8:2, 5-6, 9-10) and gave hope for the resurrection (Rom. 8:18-25). On these points the indwelling of the Spirit was virtually synonymous with regeneration.[71]

In other passages Paul depicted the indwelling Spirit as facilitator of sanctification helping believers separate themselves from evil and participate in the righteous will of God. The Spirit served as a helper and intercessor between the believer and God

---

[67] The imagery of "receiving" was built upon the Greek word *lambano* meaning literally "to take," "to take hold of," "to grasp," and is used of persons and things. Bauer, Arndt and Gingrich, "Lambano," pp. 465-466.

[68] Possibly also Rom. 8:15, "you have received a spirit/the Spirit of adoption."

[69] For a polemical review of the major arguments see Dunn, *Baptism in the Holy Spirit*, pp. 107-109.

[70] Erwin, *Baptism in the Holy Spirit*, p. 85.

[71] Lampe, *Seal of the Spirit*, pp. 3-18.

> And in the same way the Spirit also helps our weakness; for we do not know how to pray as we should, but the Spirit Himself intercedes for us with groanings too deep for words; and He who searches the hearts knows what the mind of the Spirit is, because He intercedes for the saints according to the will of God (Rom. 8:26-27 *NAS*).

It was the Spirit within which helped the individual overcome the weakness of "the flesh" (Rom. 8:1- 14). And the Spirit preserved sound doctrine (2 Tim. 1:13-14) by working within the believer to provide understanding of the grace of God (1 Cor. 2:12-14).[72]

In summary, Paul and Luke used a variety of images to portray a personal encounter between the Spirit and the individual. Each of the images was associated with the arrival of the messianic age and the believer's response to the Spirit by participating in the arrival of that age. For Luke, the encounter of the Spirit primarily connoted empowerment for mission and was accompanied by signs of the Spirit's presence. Paul was more concerned with the inward work of the Spirit. He referred to believers "receiving" the Spirit in a manner that reflected the arrival of the new age but he focused on the Spirit's role in the transformation of believers. Thus, the dominant image for Paul was the indwelling of the Spirit which he understood to be essential to the believer's redemptive relationship with the Father, both present and future. The indwelling of the Spirit made the individual spiritually alive.

The writings of Paul and Luke show that the early church was impacted by two sets of images of the personal relationship between the Holy Spirit and individuals. The Holy Spirit was at work *in* believers effectuating the new covenant of Jesus Christ, the image prevailing in the writings of Paul. The Holy Spirit was at work *in and through* believers to make manifest the new covenant offered by God through Jesus Christ, the image prevailing in the writings of Luke. Both images were evident in the didactic portrayal of the Spirit as Paraclete in the Gospel of John. The Paraclete would be *in* the disciples communicating the words of Jesus (which were words of life) in a fresh and living manner. He would also work *through and with* the disciples in their confrontations with the world.[73] In the mission of the church the two themes were complementary and inseparable. God was by the Spirit calling forth a people to be his own, a light set upon a hill to make manifest the glories of his kingdom (1 Peter 2:9).

The patristic writers of the ante-Nicene period reflected both Pauline and Lukan priorities in describing encounters between the Holy Spirit and individuals. The Spirit who regenerated and sanctified was also the Spirit of

---

[72] See above, the discussion of the "Spirit of the New Age," Chapter 2, pp. 35-37.

[73] See above, chapter 2, pp. 42-53.

prophecy and power. Hermas vividly portrayed both themes. The indwelling Spirit was sensitive to the condition of the believer's spirit which affected his function as intercessor and confessor:

> Wherefore remove grief from you, and crush not the Holy Spirit which dwells in you, lest he entreat God against you, and he withdraw from you. For the Spirit of God . . . does not endure grief nor straitness.[74]

Cheerful people do what is good. Sorrowful people do evil in grieving the Holy Spirit,

> ... not entreating the Lord nor confessing to Him. For the entreaty of the sorrowful man has no power to ascend to the altar of God . . . so grief mixed with the Holy Spirit does not produce the same entreaty (as would be produced by the Holy Spirit alone).[75]

A similar warning occurred in *Commandment Five*:

> If you be patient, the Holy Spirit that dwells in you will be pure . . . . But if any outburst of anger takes place, forthwith the Holy Spirit, who is tender, is straitened, not having a pure place, and He seeks to depart. . . . For the Lord dwells in longsuffering, but the Devil in anger. The two spirits, then when dwelling in the same habitation, are at discord with each other, and are troublesome to that man in whom they dwell.[76]

However, Hermas also knew of a different encounter with the Spirit as illustrated by the traveling prophet-teachers. These spokespersons for God were said to have the divine Spirit "attached" to them at their arrival at a meeting and were "filled" with the Spirit during the gathering which resulted in their speaking "as the Lord willeth."[77]

Tatian made use of both themes. Concerning the Spirit's work in believers he taught persons to seek "to unite the soul with the Holy Spirit,

---

[74] *Shepherd of Hermas* II.10.2, ANF, II. 27, Swete has pointed out that there is no biblical basis for the Spirit accusing the believer before God. Henry Barclay Swete, *The Holy Spirit in the Ancient Church* (London: Macmillan, 1912), pp. 26-27.

[75] Ibid.

[76] *Hermas* II.5.1, ANF, II, 23; Burgess has pointed out that this is the only known reference prior to the hagiographic literature in ancient Christian writings to the possibility of simultaneous possession by the Holy Spirit and an evil spirit. Stanley M. Burgess, *The Spirit and the Church: Antiquity* (Peabody, MA: Hendrickson Publishers, 1984), pp. 23-24.

[77] *Hermas* II.11, ANF, II, 25.

and to strive after union with God" as a basis for true knowledge.[78] The Spirit served three functions within the believer: he represented God within the soul of the individual,[79] and he served as the wings of the soul in communion with God,[80] and he provided protection against evil spirits and the material inclinations of the body.[81] But the Spirit was not within all believers,

> the Spirit of God is not with all, but, taking up its abode with those who live justly, and intimately combining with the soul, by prophecies it announces hidden things to other souls."[82]

Thus, the Spirit was understood by Tatian to operate in two different modes within believers; one mode was that of a teacher, source of divine communion, and protector, while the other mode was that of a provider of prophetic instructions for others.

By the early third century the two themes on Spirit-believer encounters were associated with distinct institutions of the church. The work of the Spirit within the individual to give new life, sanctify, transform into a child of God, and illumine with divine truth was tied to the act of baptism. The reception of the Spirit as a source of divine impetus was linked to a separate ceremony immediately following baptism. A distinction between the two rites was maintained and clarified by Cyprian, Tertullian, and Hippolytus.

Cyprian wrote about the two ceremonies in the context of a polemic in which he insisted that persons baptized by schismatics must receive both true baptism and true unction. His argument presented simple deductions: (1) the Holy Spirit can only come upon someone who is sanctified, (2) sanctification can only take place if the Holy Spirit is present at baptism, (3) the Holy Spirit is present only in the true church and responds only to the prayers of those who have the Spirit, and therefore, (4) one must be baptized in the true church before one can receive the unction of the Spirit.[83]

Cyprian was no doubt influenced by the writings of his "master," Tertullian. The great Roman theologian had treated baptism and the receiving of the unction as parts of a single ceremony but with separate and clearly defined functions of the Holy Spirit in each activity.[84] The waters,

---

[78] Tatian, *Admonition to the Greeks* XV, ANF, II, 71.

[79] Ibid.

[80] Ibid., XX, ANF, II, 73-74.

[81] Ibid., XVI, ANF, II, 72; ibid., XV, ANF, II, 71.

[82] Ibid., VIII, ANF, II, 71.

[83] Cyprian, *Epistles* LXIX-LXXII, ANF, V, 375-382.

[84] However, in one ample description of baptism, Tertullian made no reference to the unction. He referred instead to the eating of milk and honey. Tertullian, *The Chaplet* III, ANF, III, 94.

> . . . in virtue of the pristine privilege of their origin, do, after invocation of God, attain the sacramental power of sanctification; for the Spirit immediately supervenes from the heavens, and rests over the waters, sanctifying them from Himself; and being thus sanctified, they imbibe at the same time the power of sanctifying.[85]

Thus, the waters cleanse and prepare the individual to "obtain the Holy Spirit."[86]

> After this, when we have issued from the font, we are thoroughly anointed with a blessed unction . . . (which) runs carnally, (i.e., on the body), but profits spiritually; in the same way as the act of baptism itself too is carnal, in that we are plunged in water, but the effect spiritual, in that we are freed from sins.
>   In the next place the hand is laid on us, invoking and inviting the Holy Spirit through benediction . . . then, over our cleansed and blessed bodies willingly descends from the Father the Holiest Spirit.[87]

Tertullian applied two significant analogies to this unction. First, he considered the practice to have been derived from "the old discipline, wherein on entering the priesthood, men were want to be anointed with oil from a horn, ever since Aaron was anointed by Moses."[88] Second, he considered the experience to have been based upon Christ's own anointing with the Spirit. The implication was that Tertullian considered the unction of the Spirit to be a form of ordination for lay ministry.[89]

During the interval of only decades between the writings of Tertullian and Cyprian, Hippolytus made clear the connection between the unction and the believer's call to serve God. He actually recorded three anointings with oil. The first, the "Oil of Exorcism," was administered immediately prior to baptism as an act of final and total deliverance from evil spirits. The second, the "Oil of thanksgiving," was administered immediately after baptism apparently as a seal upon the work accomplished in the waters. The third anointing came after the baptized had gathered with the entire church.[90] In this final anointing the bishop restated the Lukan theme of the connection between being filled with the Spirit and serving God:

---

[85] Tertullian, *On Baptism* IV, ANF, III, 671.

[86] Ibid., VI, ANF, III, 672.

[87] Ibid., VII-VIII, ANF, III, 672-673.

[88] Ibid.

[89] Ibid. Tertullian was specific that the Spirit brought the peace of God and "animated" the believers union into the body of the church.

[90] Dix, *Apostolic Tradition*, pp. 33-38.

> And the Bishop shall lay his hand upon them invoking and saying:
> O Lord God, who didst count these thy servants worthy of
> deserving the forgiveness of sins by the power of regeneration,
> *make them worthy to be filled with thy Holy Spirit* and send upon them
> thy grace, *that they may serve thee* according to thy will. . . .[91]

The anointing with oil was followed by sealing (the sign of the cross) on
the forehead and receiving the kiss of peace from the bishop. Of significance,
was the directive for the newly anointed to first pray with the faithful, which
they had previously been prohibited from doing,[92] and to then *give* them the
kiss of peace. In these actions they were accepted as contributing members of
the body of Christ worthy to participate in the communion of the church
which followed.[93] Hippolytus concluded his description of the day's activities
with an admonition to the newly initiated:

> . . . let each one be zealous to perform good works and to please
> God, living righteously, devoting himself to the church, performing
> the things which he has learnt, advancing in the service of God.[94]

The incorporation of the themes on Spirit-believer encounters into the
institutional rites of the church was not the product of their existential
demise in earlier times. Testimonies of powerful, transforming conversion
experiences remained normative throughout the first three centuries of the
church[95] as did the charismatic gifts, especially of healing and prophecy.[96]
Throughout the period under consideration believers were understood to
experience the Spirit as a reality in their lives.

In summary, the patristic writers maintained the two prevailing images
of Spirit-believer encounters with varying degrees of synthesis. On the one
hand, individuals were understood to encounter the Spirit as a source of
internal regeneration, sanctification and fortification. Closely associated with
that image were the Spirit's functions of interceding for the believer before
God and communicating the knowledge and righteousness of God to the
believer. On the other hand, individuals were understood to encounter the
Spirit as an indwelling power for service making the believer a channel for
gifts from God to others, especially gifts of prophetic utterance. By the early
third century the two images were incorporated into the rites of baptism and

---

[91] Ibid., p. 38, emphasis added.

[92] Justin, *First Apology* LXV, ANF, I, 185.

[93] Dix, *Apostolic Tradition*, pp. 39-42.

[94] Ibid.

[95] MacMullen, *Christianizing the Roman Empire*, pp. 25-42.

[96] See above, "The Spirit of Power" and "The Spirit of Prophecy," Chapter 2, pp.30-35.

holy unction. However, the continuing testimonies of conversion and the charismatic gifts indicated the experiential basis for the two themes on Spirit-believer encounters remained an existential reality in the church throughout the ante-Nicene period.

SUMMARY

The early church principally understood human beings as objects of God's love and redemptive sacrifice of his only begotten Son, Jesus Christ. Through the atoning work of Jesus people had access to an eternal union and communion with God. The Holy Spirit was understood to be the divine agent who brought the provisions of Christ to people and thus served as an active participant in their redemption.

Three sets of images of the Spirit's involvement in personal redemption were prominent; the Spirit as the source of new life, the Spirit as the agent of cleansing, and the Spirit as the means of personal encounter with God. It was the latter set which most dominated Christian perceptions of the Spirit. The Spirit was variously described as filling, coming upon, and being poured out on believers. People were further described as being baptized in the Spirit and receiving the Spirit.

The images of Spirit-believer encounters portrayed the Christian experience of the Spirit as fulfillment of Old Testament prophecies concerning the eschatological end-time. Two complementary themes from the Old Testament were applied to the church's experience. Paul especially identified with the concept that the Spirit of the new age would dwell within the members of the kingdom bringing direct communion with God, intercession, and an internalized knowledge of the new covenant. Luke emphasized the promised role of the Spirit in the ministry of the Messiah and the messianic people. The Spirit's presence working on, in, and through persons was evidence par excellence that the messianic age had arrived in the advent of Jesus.

The recognition of the theological significance of biblical narrative precludes the validity of interpreting Luke by Paul and makes evident that the earliest Christians perceived their relationship to the Spirit as being multi-dimensional and multi-episodic. Luke, and probably John,[97] understood the reception of the Spirit as the eschatological gift to be an experience distinguishable from conversion and baptism but essential to the identity of the people of God. Luke especially tied his concept of receiving the Spirit to

---

[97] Even Dunn conceded of John 20:22 that it may not be possible to equate Spirit-baptism with regeneration; Dunn, *Baptism in the Holy Spirit*, p. 182.

prophetic-speech activity as a sign the individual was empowered by God for participation in the messianic mission.

The post-canonical ante-Nicene writers reflected both themes on the relationship of the Holy Spirit to individuals. Hermas and Tatian juxtaposed the two themes. By the late second century the two modes of the Spirit's operation in persons were identified with separate institutions of the church, baptism and holy unction. However, it was noted that the institutionalization of the themes was not the result of their existential demise in the church. Individual, personal encounter of the Holy Spirit continued as a reality throughout the ante-Nicene period.

THE SPIRIT AND THE LEARNER:
PATTERNS OF PEDAGOGY

In the early church the New Testament themes on Spirit-believer encounters found vivid fulfillment in the church's perception of the Spirit's involvement with believers as learners. The various teaching functions attributed to the Paraclete were also actualized in the lives of Christians as they were perceived to develop through recognized stages of Christian formation. Specific methods of instruction were attributed to the Spirit within each stage of the individual's growth in the faith and the content of spiritual learning was understood to vary according to each person's abilities and level of attainment.

LEVELS OF LEARNING

Truth, knowledge, wisdom and understanding, for the early Christian these were all gifts from God which ultimately could only be attained by union with him.[98] Anything less was dark and distorted. Thus, the answer to all human pursuits lay in the redemption offered by Christ and administered by the Holy Spirit. The beckoning cry of the revelator spanned across the ages, "He who has an ear, let him hear what the Spirit says . . ."(Rev. 2:17; 3:6, 13, 22; 13:9) for no one knows God unless the Spirit reveals him (1 Cor. 2:10-12).[99]

---

[98] This was a major theme of the second century apologists. Christianity was the true philosophy and all truth was grounded in God.

[99] See above, "The Knowledge of God," Chapter 2, pp. 48-50.

In the church, especially at baptism, believers were understood to see God and receive eternal illumination.[100] The act was instant and in some mysterious way all encompassing.[101] Yet, there was for the early church a sense in which the Spirit taught in gradations, individuals gradually progressing to levels of greater understanding.[102] From the perspective of the church individuals could be divided into five distinct stages of spiritual knowledge. Each stage was defined largely in terms of relationship to the Spirit and the church. Individuals were either (1) outside the church, (2) catechumens of the church, (3) newly illuminated, (4) newly incorporated, or (5) spiritual persons.

Outside the Church. Persons living outside the active influence of the church were, although dead to God, not without instruction from him. All persons who exercised reason had received their knowledge from Jesus, the eternal Logos. The apologists were emphatic, all truth had its origins in God. The philosophers had either stolen it or received it from him. But ultimate truth and understanding, true gnosis, came only by the Holy Spirit as a gift from God through Jesus.[103]

While not learners of the church in the sense of disciples, this group of persons comprising the "world" was subject to instruction by the Spirit. It was the Spirit working through the church who proclaimed to the world the "good news" of Jesus Christ, proclamation authenticated by signs and wonders.[104]

These learners outside the church were assigned one fundamental task, to repent. The objective of this first phase according to Hinson was to "sift out those whose motives, occupations, behavior, or beliefs indicated they were shackled so firmly by the powers of evil that they could not escape."[105] The church expected those who presented themselves for discipleship to, in the words of John the Baptist, "bear the fruit of repentance" (Matt. 3:8; Luke 3:8). From the inception of the Gospel, a penitent heart was a prerequisite for membership in the kingdom of God (Matt. 3:2, 8; Mark 1:4, 15; Luke 3:8; Acts 2:38). As the church infiltrated pagan societies and sought to serve the destitute it became necessary to distinguish the sincere from the charlatans.

---

[100] Hinson wrote, "The concept of illumination, with its mystical connotation of spiritual awakening or enlightenment, held special charm for the philosophical mind and was frequently applied to baptism . . . ." Hinson, *Evangelization*, p. 177.

[101] A common reference was to the concept of "perfection" through baptism.

[102] The church maintained a view of gradual progress toward God even in the midst of its battles against gnosticism. See especially Origen, *De Principiis* I.3.8, ANF, IV, 255; *Against Celsus* III, 59, ANF, IV, 487.

[103] See above, Chapter 2, pp. 48-50.

[104] See above, Chapter 2, pp. 32-37.

[105] Hinson, *Evangelization*, p. 74.

Detractors accused Christians of inviting everyone "who is a sinner, who is devoid of understanding, who is a child, and, to speak generally, whoever is unfortunate" to enter the kingdom of God.[106] To this Origen responded the church indeed sought to cure the sick in soul and teach those in health the knowledge of divine things, but the church was careful to "first invite all men to be healed, and exhort those who are sinners to come to the consideration of the doctrines which teach men not to sin . . . ."[107] Before entering the tutelage of the church individuals were to show themselves sincere about achieving a virtuous life.[108]

Catechumens. A second level of spiritual learning was institutionalized during the early second century with the development of the catechumenate. The objective of this period of direct instruction by the church was two-fold. Persons preparing for baptism were to undergo a period of close ethical inspection accompanied by the spiritual support of a Christian sponsor. Also, disciples at this level were expected to learn the fundamental doctrines of the church, knowledge needed to enter into the covenant of the Lord. The catechumenate prepared persons to enter the kingdom of God.[109]

Catechumens were allowed to participate in limited fashion at certain functions of the church but were carefully segregated from the most sacred activities.[110] Clement of Alexandria described them as babes who were taught by the Spirit in that they drank the sincere milk of the word from the breast of the church. As such God had begun the process of healing their souls and forming their characters.[111] If sincere in their faith they were protected by the grace applied to the church but were in need of the perfection attained in baptism.[112] There they would be illumined and become one with Christ.

As apprentice members of the community, catechumens had almost daily interaction with members of the contrast society. They received a steady diet of private and group instruction, all of which bore the markings of control by the divine Spirit. They heard the Scriptures read and listened to

---

[106] Origen, *Against Celsus* III.59, ANF, IV, 487.

[107] Ibid., pp. 487-488.

[108] Ibid., III.51, ANF, IV, 484. Also, Hippolytus confirmed the church's willingness to take all persons provided they demonstrated proper motives. Certain occupations (magicians, soldiers, charioteers, and certain atheletes) as well as those bound by idolatry and immorality were not eligible to hear the Gospel taught, Dix, *Apostolic Traditions*, pp. 24-27.

[109] Hinson, *Evangelization*, pp. 38-40, 76-77.

[110] Hippolytus pointed out the catechumens were prohibited from the Eucharist, prayer with the faithful, and the kiss of peace; Dix, *Apostolic Tradition*, p. 39.

[111] Clement of Alexandria, *Instructor* I.6, ANF, II, 216-222.

[112] Cyprian admonished, "For those shall not be forsaken by the aid and assistance of the Lord, who meekly, humbly, and with true penitence have perservered in good works; but the divine remedy will be granted to them also . . . . let not the mercy of the Lord be denied to those that are imploring the divine favour." *Epistles* XII, ANF, V, 293.

homilies delivered in the tone of prophecy.[113] They participated in private agape feasts where they observed the *koinonia* of the Spirit and had things revealed to them by prophet-teachers who spoke in a form of ecstasy.[114] While not yet considered Christians, these sincere followers of Christ were already experiencing the internal working of the Spirit as the determiner of discipline, helping them to control their flesh. They may have already known the Spirit as healer or deliverer from demons.[115]

Catechumens underwent a period of intense preparation in the days immediately preceding their baptism. The *Didache*[116] and Justin[117] attested to the practice of fasting one or two days prior to baptism. Members of the church, especially their sponsors, fasted with them. By the early fourth century the fast had been expanded to forty days, that is, six weeks omitting Sundays. The fasts thus became associated with those of Moses (Exod. 34:38), Elijah (1 Kings 19:8), and Jesus (Matt. 4) and served the pedagogical function of making more distinct the boundaries of the kingdoms of Christ and Satan. While entrance to the catechumenate required sound motive, graduation was based upon a sound commitment to Christ. The baptism and unction which followed would begin, not end, their warfare with demonic powers.[118]

Persons entering the final phase of preparation were expected to have ceased sinning.[119] They presented themselves as morally clean and above reproach in conduct.[120] Sponsors and others were called upon to testify in their behalf to indicate whether they "lived piously while catechumens, whether they honored the widows, whether they visited the sick, whether they have fulfilled every good work."[121] If their testimony proved true, the

---

[113] See above, Chapter 3, pp. 78-86.

[114] Dix, *Apostolic Tradition*, p. 46.

[115] Justin argued these works of the Spirit were known throughout the empire: "For numberless demoniacs throughout the whole world, and in your city, many of our Christian men exorcising them in the name of Jesus Christ, who was crucified under Pontius Pilate, have healed and do heal, rendering helpless and driving the possessing devils out of the men, though they could not be cured by all the other exorcists, and those who used incantations and drugs," *Second Apology* V, ANF, I, 190.

[116] *Didache* VII, ANF, VII, 379.

[117] Justin, *First Apology* LXI, ANF, I, 183.

[118] Hinson, *Evangelization*, p. 78. In the East the fast lasted seven weeks omitting Saturdays and Sundays.

[119] Tertullian complained that some were using the catechumenate as a trial period to taper off from sin.

[120] *Constitutions* III.2; VII.40, ANF, VII, 431, 476.

[121] Dix, *Apostolic Tradition*, pp. 30-31.

candidates received further instruction in the gospel and were exorcised daily, that is, evil spirits that lingered around them were driven away.[122]

Justin summarized the catechumenate:

> As many as are persuaded and believe that what we teach and say is true, and undertake to be able to live accordingly, are instructed to pray and to entreat God with fasting, for the remission of their sins that are past, we praying and fasting with them.[123]

Illuminated. Water baptism became the critical experience in the process of becoming Christian. E. Glenn Hinson aptly summarized:

> In the baptismal rite itself new converts reached the summit of the process in which they dramatically renounced their fealty to Satan and sealed their new covenant with Christ. Although the exact nature of the primitive rite is difficult to reconstruct, it normally involved immersion by another, a confession of faith, possibly in response to interrogation, and some sort of pledge to live acceptably. By the beginning of the third century, Tertullian and Hippolytus confirmed, the rite had become a dramatic enactment of the passage of the baptizand from Satan's kingdom into Christ's. This event normally occurred on Easter Sunday at dawn, but Tertullian also allowed baptism at Pentecost, though "every day is the Lord's."[124]

Unwavering faith was placed in God's power to totally transform persons through this rite of washing. If properly administered the ceremonial cleansing would result in a spiritual cleansing and a new birth. In this event the believer received the knowledge of God, that is, saw God face to face so as to know him in redemption. Most often this gnosis was described by the word "illumination," or "enlightenment."[125] Clement of Alexandria portrayed Jesus, the supreme teacher, as calling humanity to the baptismal waters saying, "He invites to the laver, to salvation, to illumination."[126]

Cyprian described his own encounter with God in baptism as the climax of a long search for truth:

> While I was still lying in darkness and gloomy night, wavering hither and thither, tossed about on the foam of this boastful age,

---

[122] Ibid., p. 24. The fact that these exorcisms differed from possession was evident from the fact that Hippolytus did not allow "one who has a devil" to enter the catechumenate.

[123] Justin, *First Apology* LXI, ANF, I, 183.

[124] Hinson, *Evangelization*, p. 81.

[125] Justin, *First Apology* XLI, ANF, I, 183. Clement, *Instructor* I.6, ANF, II, 215-216.

[126] Clement of Alexandria, *Exhortation to the Heathen* X, ANF, II, 198.

and uncertain of my wandering steps, knowing nothing of my real life, and remote from truth and light, I used to regard it as a difficult matter, and especially as difficult in respect of my character at that time, that a man should be capable of being born again--a truth which the divine mercy had announced for my salvation,--and that a man quickened to a new life in the laver of saving water should be able to put off what he had previously been; and, although retaining all his bodily structure should be himself changed in heart and soul. "How," said I, "is such a conversion possible, that there should be a sudden and rapid divestment of all which, either innate in us has hardened in the corruption of our material nature, or acquired by us has become inveterate by long accustomed use? These things have become deeply and radically engrained within us. But after that, by the help of the water of new birth, the stain of former years had been washing away, and a light from above, serene and pure, had been infused into my reconciled heart,--after that, by the agency of the Spirit breathed from heaven, a second birth had restored me to a new man;--then, in a wondrous manner, doubtful things at once began to assure themselves to me, hidden things to be revealed, dark things to be enlightened, what before had seemed difficult began to suggest a means of accomplishment, which had been thought impossible, to be capable of being achieved; so that I was enabled to acknowledge that what previously, being born of the flesh, had been living in the practice of sins, was of the earth earthly, but had now begun to be of God, and was animated by the Spirit of holiness.[127]

A. D. Nock has shown that the term *photismos* from which illumination is translated while prominent among the mystery cults actually took its Christian meaning out of the light-darkness motif of Zoroastrian and Hebrew thought.[128] The church existed in the era and realm in which light was overcoming darkness, that is, good was proving victorious over evil (Rom. 13:12; 1 Cor. 4:5; 2 Cor. 4:6; 11:14; Eph. 5:8; Col. 1:12; 1 Thess. 5:5; 1 Pet. 2:9; Heb. 6:4). In that context, to be born again was to be born into the kingdom of light.[129] The light was from above and connoted the glory of the face of God. Thus, Clement of Alexandria described the results of baptism:

---

[127] Cyprian, *Epistles* I.3-4, ANF, V, 275-276.

[128] Arthur Darby Nock, *Early Gentile Christianity and Its Hellenistic Background* (New York: Harper & Row, 1964), p. 136.

[129] Justin, *Dialogue* VII, ANF, I, 198.

> We who are baptized have the eye of the Spirit, by which alone we can see God, free from obstruction and bright, the Holy Spirit flowing in upon us from heaven.[130]

Water baptism was thus considered the fountainhead of Christian knowledge. It precipitated the reception of the Spirit which brought union and communion with God, the ultimate goal of Christian pedagogy. Through this doorway the believer was placed in the realm of perfection which called forth growth unto perfection.

Incorporated. Baptism signified entrance into full participation in the kingdom of God. Not only was new life granted, a new way of life was attained. The immediate impact of the rite was to provide for the incorporation of the individual into the church as a contributing member and thereby introduce the believer to the mysteries of the kingdom.

Incorporation into the church was based upon the reception of the Spirit. Following the unction of the Spirit new converts were permitted to pray with the faithful for the first time. Prior to receiving the Spirit their prayers had no power to ascend to God and were polluted by other spirits. The Spirit, having brought to the believer the peace of God, enabled the convert to give the pure "kiss of peace" to the other members of the church, a practice also prohibited prior to the anointing of the *charismation* which qualified believers to participate in the full life of the church.[131]

The rites of incorporation culminated in the celebration of the Eucharist. On this occasion believers ate a mixture of milk and honey to signify entrance into the promised land and an oblation of water preceded the regular elements of bread and wine.[132] These rites of initiation were eventually cloaked in secrecy leading to their association with "mysteries." Hinson observed:

> . . . *mysteries* and cognate words took on a special significance with reference to the sacraments. *Mustogogein* and *mustagogia* designated initiation, instruction, or unfolding the meaning of the "mysteries." The priest became a *mustagogos*, initiator, instructor, or expounder of them. Catechumens were *amuatoi*, the Christian a *mustas*, an initiate, an expert or a confidant of "mysteries."[133]

---

[130] Clement of Alexandria, *Instructor* I.6, ANF, II, 215-216.

[131] Dix, *Apostolic Tradition*, p. 39.

[132] The bread and wine were eucharistized before the new converts ate the mixture of bread and honey but were not distributed until after the oblation of water. Ibid., pp. 40-42.

[133] Hinson, *Evangelization*, p. 180.

As time progressed there was a tendency to transpose pre-baptismal preparation into post-baptismal explanation. At first this occurred during the rites themselves.[134] After Nicea it was formalized into a period of intensive study.[135] The shift was not unprecedented. From the earliest days of the Christian faith believers were understood to have devoted themselves to a life marked by the study of the Scriptures and the continued pursuit of sacred truths (2 Tim. 3:16; Rom. 15:4; 2 Pet. 1:19-21).

Perfected Spiritual Persons. Christians of the early centuries understood themselves to be perfected and yet striving after perfection. They were spiritual persons, the true gnostics of the world. Clement of Alexandria said of them: "The Gnostic is consequently divine, and already holy, God-bearing, and God-borne."[136] On the other hand, Origen wrote:

> In this way, then, by the renewal of the ceaseless working of Father, Son, and Holy Spirit in us, in its various stages of progress, shall we be able at some future time perhaps, although with difficulty, to behold the holy and the blessed life, in which (as it is only after many struggles that we are able to reach it) we ought so to continue, that no satiety of that blessedness should ever seize us; but the more we perceive its blessedness, the more should be increased and intensified within us the longing for the same, while we ever more eagerly and freely receive and hold fast the Father, and the Son and the Holy Spirit.[137]

He continued by suggesting that should anyone attain the "highest and perfect summit" and there be satiated that person would gradually fall away.[138] The Christian life was one of continual growth and development or "backsliding." There was no standing still.

Cyprian tied believers' spiritual health to their conduct:

> Assuredly the same spiritual grace which is equally received in baptism by believers, is subsequently either increased or diminished in our conversation and conduct . . .[139]

---

[134] Hippolytus portrayed it as a simple response to questions during the rites; Dix, *Apostolic Tradition*, p. 41.

[135] Gregory of Nazianzus, *Orat.* 1.2, 2.95, *Orat. Cat.* 28.

[136] Clement of Alexandria, *Stromata* VII.13, ANF, II, 547.

[137] Origen, *De Principiis* I.3, ANF, IV, 255.

[138] Ibid.

[139] Cyprian, *Epistles* LXXV.14, ANF, V, 401.

Life after baptism was thus marked by a tension between the experience of the Spirit and the promise of the future. Final union with God required believers to learn the fullness of what it meant to be spiritual persons.

THE SPIRIT SPEAKS: THE CONTENT
OF CHRISTIAN INSTRUCTION

The most pervasive activity attributed to the Holy Spirit by the early church was that of speaking. The Spirit spoke through the Old Testament prophets, the apostles, pastor-teachers, prophet-teachers, the doctrines of the church and even the traditions of the church, including rituals. The Spirit brought the message of God and spoke it in a fresh manner to every generation of the church. Thus, the authoritative content of Christian pedagogy was the message of God as spoken by the Spirit.

Old Testament Scriptures. Until the middle of the second century the Old Testament Law and Prophets were the only canonical Scriptures. Swete summarized:

> The canonical Scriptures were the most conspicuous monument of the Spirit's handiwork. The Old Testament, more especially the Prophets of the Old Testament, formed the textbook of the primitive preacher, and the mainstay of the earlier apologists, who appealed to the "Spirit of prophecy" as their chief witness to the truth of the Gospel. The Spirit "preached through the prophets the dispensations and the Advents," exhibiting on the stage of history the Divine purpose to successive generations, till the Christ came.[140]

Three characteristics of the church's understanding of the inspiration of Scripture stood out; it was Christocentric, it was a verbal inspiration, and it was an active, ongoing reality.

The early church interpreted the Old Testament Scriptures through the lens of the advent of Jesus Christ, or as Lampe said:

> From the earliest stage to which the tradition of the Church can be traced, the Scriptures of the Old Testament had been interpreted as a book about Christ.[141]

---

[140] Swete, *Holy Spirit*, pp. 381-382.

[141] G.W.H. Lampe, "The Exposition and Exegesis of Scripture," in *The Cambridge History of the Bible*, Vol. 2, G.W.H. Lampe, ed. (Cambridge: Cambridge University Press, 1969), p. 155.

According to the Lucan Resurrection narratives, the procedure began with Jesus himself (Luke 24:26-27, 44-47). Irenaeus represented well the patristic understanding:

> If anyone, therefore, reads the Scriptures with attention, he will find in them an account of Christ, and a foreshadowing of the new calling (*vocationis*). For Christ is the treasure which was hid in the field, that is, in this world (for "the field is the world"); but the treasure hid in the Scriptures is Christ, since He was pointed out by means of types and parables. Hence, His human nature could not be understood prior to the consummation of those things which had been predicted, that is, the advent of Christ . . . it is a treasure, hid indeed in a field, but brought to light by the cross of Christ, and explained, both enriching the understanding of men, and showing forth the wisdom of God, and declaring His dispensations with regard to man, and forming the kingdom of Christ beforehand, and preaching by anticipation the inheritance of the holy Jerusalem . . .[142]

The early church adhered to a manic and plenary verbal view of the inspiration of the Old Testament Scriptures. The Spirit was the controlling force in the process, acting upon the prophets as if they were but musical instruments. Justin saw the harmony of the Scriptures as proof of this view. He added:

> For neither by nature nor by human conception is it possible for men to know things so great and divine, but by the gift which then descended from above upon the holy men, who had no need of rhetorical art, nor of uttering anything in a contentious or quarrelsome manner, but to present themselves pure to the energy of the Divine Spirit, in order that the divine plectrum itself, descending from heaven, and using righteous men as an instrument like a harp or lyre, might reveal to us the knowledge of things divine and heavenly.[143]

The words of the Scriptures *were* the words of the Holy Spirit.

The early church also approached the Old Testament Scriptures as if they were written for the age of the church. According to R. P. C. Hanson they held a view of the text that was essentially oracular. They were "obsessed" with the conviction that inspired writers knew a great deal about

---

[142] Irenaeus, *Against Heresies* IV.26.1, ANF, I, 496-497.
[143] Justin, *Address to the Greeks* VIII, ANF, I, 276.

Christ and the Christian doctrine.[144] Thus, the Spirit spoke through them truths hidden to their own time but evident to all who believe in Christ. The overall thrust was to approach the Scriptures as a medium through which the Spirit was currently speaking to the church.

The Teachings of Jesus. There was no stronger tradition about Jesus than that he was a teacher. He wandered about Galilee teaching openly in the synagogues and other public places. He claimed divine inspiration for his teachings. He accepted the Law and the Prophets as inspired, interpreted their meaning in an authoritative manner, and he claimed his own words superseded theirs. Thus, it was only natural for the teachings of Jesus to form the distinctive core of Christian teaching.

The earliest purely Christian content for instruction was no doubt a compilation of the teachings of Jesus.[145] The Pauline epistles antedated the written Gospels and contained numerous references to the words of Jesus often in a manner which assumed the readers were aware of the quotes given (1 Cor. 2:10; 9:14; 11:2, 23). For Paul the words of Jesus were authoritative and binding. He expected his widely dispersed readers would recognize the sayings of the Lord and obey them.[146]

The *Didache*, a first century handbook of Christian instruction,[147] opened with a homily on the "two ways," the way of life and the way of death. While the form was probably borrowed from a Jewish source, the content was apparently a compendium of the ethical teachings of Jesus, some canonical, others not. These "Commandments of the Lord" were apparently based upon an established oral tradition.[148] A variation of the "two ways" appeared in the second-century epistle attributed to Barnabas[149] and later in the *Apostolic Constitutions*.[150] Thus, the teachings of Jesus formed a distinguishable body of material for Christians to study. But authenticity of the sayings of Jesus early was tied to the traditions of the apostles.

The Apostles. The New Testament recorded a high level of veneration for the apostles of Jesus and their teachings. They served as a direct link to

---

[144] R. P. C. Hanson, "The Bible in the Early Church," The *Cambridge History of the Bible,* Vol. 1, From the Beginnings to Jerome (Cambridge: Cambridge University Press, 1970), pp. 419-422.

[145] Donald Guthrie, *New Testament Introduction* (Downers Grove, Illinois: Inter-Varsity Press, 1970), pp. 143-157.

[146] Dunn, *Jesus and the Spirit*, pp. 236-238; 277; 282-284. Bruce, *The Spreading Flame*, pp. 77-78.

[147] The dating of the *Didache* varies widely from first century to late second century. R. M. Grant suggested it was written as early as 70 A.D., *Cambridge History*, Vol. 1, p. 289.

[148] Ibid.

[149] *Epistle of Barnabas*, XVIII-XX, ANF, I, 148-149.

[150] *Apostolic Constitutions*, I, ANF, VII, 377.

Christ. With their passage from the scene even greater significance was given to their words. By the close of the first century a lineal connection through the apostles to Jesus was firmly established as a basis for authority.[151] Authentic Christian teaching came only through the legacy of the apostles, a legacy marked by the presence of the Spirit and a commitment to the life and words of the crucified and resurrected Lord.

In time the apostles were equated with the Old Testament prophets and were viewed as having taught through an equal or superior level of inspiration.[152] Novatian expressed the difference between the two groups:

> He is therefore one and the same Spirit who was in the prophets and apostles, except that in the former He was occasional, in the latter always. But in the former not as being always in them, in the latter as abiding always in them; and in the former distributed with reserve in the latter all poured out; in the former given sparingly in the latter liberally bestowed; not yet manifested before the Lord's resurrection, but conferred after the resurrection. [153]

Stress was placed upon the completeness of the apostles' instructions and the preservation of those precepts in oral form within the church. Clement asserted the apostles received the Gospel "from the Lord Jesus Christ."[154] Justin attributed the tradition he taught to the apostles who were instructed by Christ himself with special significance placed upon the period between the resurrection and the ascension.[155] Tertullian used the Johannine Paraclete sayings to argue the apostles indeed gained a complete understanding of all Jesus had taught.

> No doubt He had once said, "I have yet many things to say unto you, but ye cannot hear them now," but even then He added, "When He, the Spirit of truth, shall come, He will lead you into all truth." He (thus) shows that there was nothing of which they were ignorant to whom He had promised the future attainment of all truth by help of the Spirit of truth. And assuredly He fulfilled His promise, since it is proved in the Acts of the Apostles that the Holy Ghost did come down.[156]

---

151 H. von Campenhausen, *Ecclesiastical Authority and Spiritual Power in the Church of the First Three Centuries*, trans. J. A. Baker (London: Adam & Charles Black, 1969), pp. 9-20.

152 Origen, *De Principiis* I.3.1, ANF, IV, 252.

153 Novatian, *Concerning the Trinity* XXIV, ANF, V, 640.

154 *First Clement* XLII, ANF, I, 16.

155 Justin, *First Apology* LXII, ANF, I, 186.

156 Tertullian, *Against Heresies* XXII, ANF, III, 253.

Like Tertullian, Irenaeus attributed perfect knowledge to the apostles who then placed the whole truth in the church's hands.[157] In combating Gnosticism he attested not only the inspiration of these oral instructions but also the veracity of their preservation by the presbyters of the church so that if anyone did not accept the authority of the unwritten record, "he despises the companions of the Lord; nay more, he despises Christ Himself the Lord; yea, he despises the Father also . . . ."[158] The same tradition existed everywhere the same in the true church and effectuated the kingdom even in the absence of the written Scriptures:

> To which course many nations of those barbarians who believe in Christ do assent, having salvation written in their hearts by the Spirit, without paper or ink, and, carefully preserving the ancient tradition, . . . Those who, in the absence of written documents, have believed this faith, are barbarians, so far as regards our language; but as regards doctrine, manner, and tenor of life, they are, because of faith, very wise indeed; and they do please God, ordering their conversation in all righteousness, chastity, and wisdom.[159]

The exact nature and content of these oral traditions have been lost. In their wake two authoritative sources of inspired content arose, the New Testament canon and the "rule of faith."

The New Testament Scriptures. In spite of the esteem placed on the apostles, the gospels and epistles did not gain acceptance as Scripture until the middle of the second century. The Apostolic Fathers (Clement of Rome, the *Didache*, Papias, Ignatius, Polycarp and Barnabas) treated the sayings of Jesus and the Pauline epistles as authoritative for Christians, but refrained from using them in a manner equal to the Scriptures. R. M. Grant concluded:

> . . . as the early Church entered more fully into the Graeco-Roman world it placed an increasingly high value upon traditions about the Lord Jesus and upon the writings of the apostles, but the books of the apostles and their immediate successors were not yet viewed as scripture.[160]

Gnosticism prodded the church into the canonization of New Testament Scriptures. Marcion's self-proclaimed attempts in the middle of the second century to remove interpolations by Judaizers from the authentic

---

[157] Irenaeus, *Against Heresies* IV, "Preface," ANF, I, 462.

[158] Ibid., III.1, ANF, I, 415.

[159] Ibid., III.4, ANF, I, 417.

[160] Grant, "The New Testament Canon," p. 293.

teachings of Jesus resulted in a highly edited canon composed of a version of Luke's gospel and a compilation of ten abridged Pauline letters. In response, Irenaeus identified a canon of New Testament scriptures so that by the end of the second century, Christians generally made use of a collection of New Testament writings as Scripture.[161]

The Rule of Faith. Beginning late in the second century, and with great frequency during the third, the "rule of faith" was mentioned by Christian writers. Irenaeus was the first on record to use the phrase but its immediate appearance in the writings of Clement of Alexandria in another region of the empire indicated the idea had been widely circulating throughout the church for some time.[162]

The rule of faith was considered universal but was apparently not based upon a fixed formula. Variations in the rule were found not only between authors and regions but also within the works of a single author.[163] Gonzalez concluded:

> Therefore, it seems possible to say that the rule of faith was not a fixed text, which it was necessary to repeat word by word, but that it was rather a summary of the fundamental contents of the Christian message probably underlining those aspects of that message which the heretics denied.[164]

Thus, the "rule of faith" became a summary of the benchmark doctrines of the Church Catholic.[165]

Creeds and Hymns. Two of the earliest and most consistent forms of Christian content were creeds and hymns. From the time of the apostles reception of the rite of baptism was based upon a formal public confession of the faith, probably made in response to a definite question. The New Testament indicated the earliest creed was a simple profession of belief, "Jesus is Lord." In the title "Lord" converts among the Jews and God-fearers confessed the divine lordship of Jesus and surrendered to his sovereignty.[166] Matthew recorded an alternative form with the use of the threefold name: "In the name of the Father and of the Son and of the Holy Spirit" (Matthew

---

[161] Ibid., p. 295.

[162] R. P. C. Hanson, *Tradition in the Early Church*, p. 77.

[163] Tertullian presented three different forms of the rule; *Against Praxeas* II, ANF, III, 600; *The Shows* XIII, ANF, III, 82. *On Veiling Virgins* I, ANF, IV, 27.

[164] Gonzalez, *Christian Thought*, Vol. 1, pp. 157-158.

[165] The rule of faith as presented in essentially the same form by Irenaeus, Clement of Alexandria, Origen, and Tertullian.

[166] Bruce, *Spreading Flame*, pp. 238-240.

28:19). Before the end of the first century the threefold creed had become the standard confession for catechumens desiring baptism.[167]

In the early third century Hippolytus quoted an established baptismal formula which approximated what came to be called the Apostles' Creed:

> Dost thou believe in God the Father almighty? Dost thou believe in Christ Jesus, the Son of God, Who was born by the Holy Spirit from the Virgin Mary, Who was crucified under Pontius Pulsate, and died, and rose again on the third day living from the dead, and ascended into the heavens, and sat down on the right hand of the Father, and will come to judge the living and the dead? Dost thou believe in the Holy Spirit, in the holy Church, and in the resurrection of the flesh?[168]

In this form the early threefold confession was expanded to assure orthodoxy in the face of growing heresies. The confession of the true faith came to be known as the Roman Symbol, indicating its use as a sign or test of membership in the Church.[169]

Hymns were a popular means of expressing Christian truth. Some were embedded in the text of the New Testament. Psalms from the Jewish Scriptures were incorporated into Christian worship. Spirit inspired songs were apparently equated with prophecy (1 Cor. 14:13-17). In response to the Gnostic appetite for creative poetry, the Church Catholic largely restricted its worship services to Scriptural hymns or canticles. Other hymns were for family, or private use.[170]

Prophecy. A final form of authoritative content for Christian instruction was ongoing prophetic speech and activity. The nature of these prophecies varied according to the situation in which they were given. Some were extremely personal and directed toward individual situations. Others were more general and addressed the needs of the church during times of crises. Apocalyptic themes were common as were visions of angels and heaven. Most were considered special messages just for the given moment, but some were written down and circulated. In authenticated cases prophecy was considered an authoritative word from God, a message to be learned.[171]

---

[167] The threefold creed was included in the *Didache* VII, ANF, VII, 379.

[168] Dix, *Apostolic Tradition*, pp. 36-37.

[169] Latourette concluded, "the term 'symbol' comes from a word which in one of its usages meant a watchword, or a password in a military camp." It thus served as the "password" for entrance into the church. Kenneth Scott Latourette, *A History of Christianity, Vol. 1, Beginnings to 1500* (New York: Harper & Row, 1975), p. 135.

[170] Ibid, p. 206-208.

[171] See Above, "Prophet-Teachers," Chapter 3, pp. 89-91.

Conclusions. Early Christianity had a large body of content to incorporate into its educational processes. All content considered valid for instruction was believed to have the Holy Spirit as its author. The Scriptures, both those of the Old Testament and by the end of the second century those of the New Testament, were considered the primary channel through which the Spirit spoke. Through them the Spirit spoke directly and immediately to the church.

The Spirit was viewed to be speaking authoritatively through other sources as well. Oral traditions attributed to the apostles were considered equal to Scripture having originated in the first outpourings of the Holy Spirit. The doctrines of the "rule of faith" also drew their authority from association with the Spirit's work with the apostles. Through the ongoing practice of prophecy, the Spirit was perceived to continue to speak to the church. However, while the Spirit was credited with the origin of all of the primary sources of church tradition, only the Scriptures were projected as being taught through the Spirit's operation.

There were three overriding characteristics of the content of Christian instruction. First, it always centered on Christ. Second, it had the Holy Spirit as its author. And, third, all content, regardless of the date of its origin, was considered to be an immediate revelation of the Holy Spirit. That is, the Spirit remained active in the preservation and transmission of the Scriptures and traditions of the church.

METHODS OF INSTRUCTION

The critical question which remained was how the learner and content of instruction were brought together, or what were the methods of instruction associated with the Holy Spirit? In general the church portrayed the Spirit as gradually but powerfully engaging the individual in dialogue with divine truth in a manner that carefully transformed the individual into a truly spiritual person, one who enjoyed union and communion with God in the church. The methods attributed to the Spirit were essentially those of the Johannine Paraclete and were based upon the individual's ability to relate to the Spirit as a personal divine being.

A Call to Repentance. The first stage of Christian pedagogy was one of confrontation through proclamation, dialogue and demonstration. The church went everywhere "preaching the word" (Acts 8:4, 12; 15:35). Christians invaded the major cities of the empire "reasoning in the synagogue with the Jews and the God- fearing Gentiles, and in the marketplace every day with those who happened to be present" (Acts 17:17).[172] Those without the church were to hear clearly the reason of the hope that was within the believers presented in gentleness and reverence (1 Peter 3:15). But for the most part this took place among the masses as Christians went about their daily living.[173] Origen boasted that wool and leather workers, fullers, and uneducated persons were spreading the gospel everywhere.[174] Slaves and soldiers were especially noted for the spread of the gospel[175] which Celsus charged to be foolish doctrines believed only by children, slaves, and women.[176] Believers from every strata of society told of their experiences and understanding of Jesus.

However, the proclamation was not in words alone. It incorporated all that the church was, said, and did by the power of the Holy Spirit in the presence of the world. Ramsay MacMullen concluded it was the witness of ongoing miracles, especially the driving out of spirits and healings, which most appealed to the multitudes. In these, they were confronted with the Great God of the Christians, enticed to know more about him. He projected a not unlikely scenario:

> Testing to see if I can imagine in some detail a scene that conflicts with no point of the little that is known about conversion in the second and third centuries, I would choose the room of some sick person: there, a servant talking to a mistress, or one spouse to another, saying, perhaps, "Unquestionably they can help, if you believe. And I know, I have seen, I have heard, they have related to me, they have books, they have a special person, a sort of officer. It is true. Besides and anyway, if you don't believe, then you are doomed when a certain time comes, so say the prophecies; whereas, if you do, then they can help even in great sickness. I know people who have seen or who have spoken with others who have seen. And healing is even the least that they tell. Theirs is truly a God all-powerful. He has worked a hundred wonders." So a priest is sent for, or an exorcist; illness is healed; the household after that counts as Christian, it is baptized; and through instruction it comes to accept the first consequences: that all other cults are false and wicked, all seeming gods, the same.[177]

---

[172] Roland Allen, *Missionary Methods: St. Paul's or Ours*, Fifth Edition (London: World Dominion Press, 1969), pp. 4-12.

[173] Ramsey MacMullen, *Christianizing*, pp. 36-40.

[174] Origen, *Against Celsus* III.55, ANF, IV, 486.

[175] Hinson, *Evangelization*, p. 38.

[176] MacMullen, *Christianizing*, pp. 37-39.

[177] Ibid., pp. 40-42.

Persons who wanted to inquire further into the Christian message found the church anxious and ready to present Jesus as the answer to every noble human quest. The Scriptures were the primary basis of dialogue with prospective converts. Jews were shown how they pointed to Jesus as the Messiah. Persons given to philosophy were challenged to discover from the writings God's incarnate son, the source of all truth.

Training in Righteousness. Only persons expressing a sincere desire to become Christians were admitted to the catechumenate. The aim of this stage was preparation for baptism through moral transformation and indoctrination. Entrance into the divine kingdom required a life that had ceased to sin and an understanding of the precepts and responsibilities of membership in the family of God. In essence this stage consisted of ethical and mental training in the prerequisites for participation in the new covenant of God.[178]

Catechumens received ongoing instruction in proper behavior. The Scriptures were used to stress the contrast between the society of God and the world. Documents such as *The Two Ways* were also used to clarify the major moral differences.[179] Guidebooks on Christian behavior like Clement of Alexandria's *Instructor* gave even more specific directions for proper conduct.[180] Sermons at the gatherings, written homilies and circulated treatises served to continually reinforce the Christian standard of separation from the world.

The method of inculcating the catechumens was to nurse them gently into the belief that they could achieve new life as offered by the church. An elaborate process developed. Every catechumen received close personal supervision from a sponsor who daily gave advice, instruction and encouragement. Sponsors served as spiritual umbilical cords in that they provided a direct link between the unborn child of God and the body of Christ.[181]

Catechumens were prompted to seek birth into the church through a careful process of limited participation. At the agape feasts they could see the impact of Christian fellowship but were forcefully reminded of their own outside status by eating a different bread and drinking from a different cup. During Sunday gatherings they sat with the church for the reading of the

---

[178] Hinson, *Evangelization*, pp. 76-77.

[179] Gonazlez, *Christian Thought*, pp. 66-70.

[180] Clement was typical of many Christian writers of the second and third centuries. Believers were expected to be "above reproach" in all areas of life. Attention was given to appearance as well as conduct. Clement of Alexandria, *Instructor* Books II and III, ANF, II, 237-298.

[181] Dix, *Apostolic Traditions*, p. 31.

Scriptures, sermons, hymns, and prayers but were ejected prior to the celebration of the Eucharist.[182]

During the period of the catechumenate Holy Spirit was understood to already be at work within the individual. The Spirit was exorcising evil spirits that lingered on and in the flesh.[183] This was done in conjunction with the individual's progressive reception of the Word of God and took place through the laying on of hands and prayer by the saints, as persons purified and empowered by the Spirit.[184] In this process the Holy Spirit was thought to quicken the mind to understand the Scriptures and major doctrines of the church. Further, the Spirit was at work in the individual shedding light on the ways of righteousness and enabling the learner to conform to the standards of God's image. The Spirit was beginning to create within the hearer a consciousness of God and his holiness.

The Spirit was also seen to take a direct involvement in the individual's moral transformation. Through the gift of prophecy operating in a prophetic teacher or other charismatic believers personal shortcomings were revealed and specific steps toward righteous living were identified. A not uncommon phenomenon was the giving of personal instruction by the Spirit with a special focus on conduct in the home.[185] In short the Spirit worked through the prophet-teachers to give specific instructions to the catechumens on how the most private aspects of their lives required change before they could know God.

Acts of Enfoldment. In the events surrounding baptism the individual was enfolded into the family of God and was understood to receive the Holy Spirit as a personal internal presence. Within the process the Spirit was understood to become the immediate instructor of divine truth. Thus, the primary objective, specifically associated with baptism, was illumination and a secondary objective, specifically associated with the unction, was ordination for ministry within the church.

Baptism was engulfed in a period of intense study. Candidates were expected to make a pledge of faith based upon the essential doctrines of the church. The covenant they were about to enter required absolute commitment. Hence, the learners were drilled in the *Rule of Faith* and its rational foundations in the Scriptures. With the passage of time memorization

---

182 Ibid., pp. 28-30.

183 The church's reliance upon frequent exorcisms reflected an expanding belief in demons as prevalent evil forces which attached themselves to the flesh. Demons were especially associated with sickness. Cyprian, *Epistles* LXXV.15, ANF, V, 402.

184 Dix, *Apostolic Tradition*, p. 30.

185 Ibid., pp. 61-62.

of creedal forms took on increasing significance but understanding remained the primary concern throughout the ante-Nicene period.[186]

The sacraments provided key object lessons which illustrated the major doctrines of the church. Before, during, and after their enactment the learners were encouraged to ask questions concerning their meaning. Conversely, the officiants asked probing questions of the recipients in order to assure their level of understanding and commitment. In the end however it was through the Holy Spirit acting in the sacramental acts of incorporation themselves that the knowledge of God was attained.[187]

Union and communion with God, and the resulting knowledge of him, were experientially effectuated in baptism. In that event the individual by the direct work of the Holy Spirit died to the old self, became a new creation, was cleansed of all past sins, and was caused to know God. Following the Johannine imagery the Spirit became the internal witness of things said by and about Jesus. And from the Pauline imagery the Spirit began to dwell in the believer as a source of new life and covenant with God.

The illumination which the Spirit brought was rooted in the mental comprehension of the gospel but transcended a mere understanding of doctrine or the Scriptures. It was the product of a personal encounter with God, one in which the individual was transformed in deepest character. To be illumined was to be apprehended by God in a manner which brought union with him. Thus, human study was considered preparatory for but ancillary to direct divine instruction by the Spirit.[188]

The mystical, existential nature of illumination placed it beyond the limits of objective description. While the rituals surrounding baptism became highly routinized, the benefits remained dependent upon individual faith and response. Nevertheless, direct contact with the divine in the person of the Holy Spirit with its resulting transforming knowledge was considered elemental to true baptism.[189]

Reception of the Spirit through an anointing with oil following baptism signified a second dimension of the Spirit's perceived relationship with believers as learners. Performed in the presence of the gathered church, this event signaled the individual's entrance into the charismatic community, the community marked, defined, and controlled by the Holy Spirit. Here the Spirit brought the believer into the realm of the ongoing revelation of Jesus Christ. Empowered by the heavenly unction, the believer was ordained to share in the life of the kingdom and qualified to receive and dispense gifts

---

[186] Origen, *Against Celsus* III.51, ANF, IV, 484- 485.

[187] Dix, *Apostolic Tradition*, p. 62.

[188] Consider Cyprian's description of his baptism cited above, pp. 116-117.

[189] See the discussion on pedagogical objectives above, Chapter 3, pp. 74-78.

from God within the church. The Holy Spirit was envisioned as a comforter-coach, guiding persons into service for God especially in the form of inspired speech.[190]

Tutelage of the Spirit. After their salubrious incorporation into the body of Christ, believers were understood to live under the careful tutelage of the Holy Spirit. The objective of this period was to carry them on unto perfection as members of God's new creation. Spiritual persons nourished their knowledge of God through a diet of the Scriptures supplemented by prophecies and heroic testimonies and reinforced by the sacramental rituals of the church.[191]

The principal content of study for the baptized believer was the Scriptures. With the special guidance of the Holy Spirit the true and deep meanings of the ancient writings were thought to come to life. The process included all of the avenues of instruction open to the catechumens plus those associated with the restricted ceremonies. Through personal study, private meditation and corporate worship the Holy Spirit was perceived to be working within the believer to provide deeper understanding of God's written revelation.[192]

The Spirit was also perceived to bring immediate revelations from God to those persons who had received the Spirit as a holy unction. As the Holy Spirit mingled with the believer's spirit he was able to convey the innermost thoughts of the individual to God. In this manner the Spirit interceded for the saints. Conversely, the Spirit was able to bring the thoughts of God into the innermost dimensions of the believer. The Spirit within could make those thoughts known by bringing them forth in visions, dreams, and prophecies.[193]

As spiritual persons believers were also instructed by the Spirit through corporate experiences. Prophetic speech activity seemed to have a special place in the closed celebration of the Eucharist.[194] And at least for the first century Christians the believers were understood to be able to discern the source of a spirit which gave a message in the church. Hence, believers shared an interdependent relationship in the experiences of ongoing revelations.[195]

Conclusions. The methods of instruction perceived by the early church to be used by the Holy Spirit varied according to the level of a person's

---

[190] See the discussion on environment for learning, above, Chapter 3, pp. 78-86.

[191] See above, Chapter 3, pp. 82-86.

[192] Novatian, *Treatise Concerning the Trinity* XXIX, ANF, V, 640-641.

[193] Irenaeus, *Against Heresies* III.241, ANF, I, 458.

[194] Tertullian, *Against* Praxses II, ANF, III, 600.

[195] Ash argued that the test of true prophecy early shifted from group discernment by the Spirit to objective criteria. James L. Ash, Jr., "The Decline of Ecstatic Prophecy in the Early Church," p. 233.

spiritual development. At every stage of Christian growth the Scriptures as words spoken by the Holy Spirit retained the dominant place in the content of instruction. They were publicly read and presented in tracts, treatises, and sermons as words from God. However, at each level of Christian formation the sacred writings were used by the Spirit in a different manner. For those outside the church they pointed to the person of Jesus Christ as the answer to every noble human quest. The catechumens experienced the Scriptures as a guidebook on how to please a righteous God. Those being enfolded into the church were instructed from the Scriptures on the wondrous "mysteries" of how God provided salvation through Jesus in the church. Those considered to be spiritual persons were thought to have entered into the realm of personal instruction by the Spirit whereby they had access to the full meaning of the written revelations.

The church served as guardian of divine revelation. The Scriptures, creeds, doctrines, and traditions were carefully preserved. Together they formed an authoritative basis for conduct, ritual, and belief. Elements of these various contents were carefully woven into the corporate experiences of the church. Catechumens and believers alike were continually reminded that the words came from the Spirit and the ceremonies in which they were used were directed by the Spirit.

At each stage the church itself as the society of the Spirit existed as a form of content for instruction by the Spirit. The method was to progressively expose individuals to life in God's kingdom. Persons outside the church were enticed by the contrasts of the church with earthly kingdoms especially through the elements of the miraculous attributed to the divine Spirit. Catechumens were permitted to experience in a limited fashion life in the kingdom of the Spirit. Through the enfolding process individuals were carefully made participants in the church's corporate life. As spiritual persons believers spoke of experiencing the Spirit working both from within and through the church to make their knowledge of God full. To be a member of the church was to share in the life and knowledge of God. It was to have union with him.

The Spirit was also perceived to use prophetic revelations as a means of instruction on every level. Persons outside the church were confronted with the existence of revelations from the Spirit as a sign that God was speaking through the church. Catechumens were often the objects of these messages as they came through members of the church and gave specific guidance in personal conduct as well as encouragement. The process of enfolding was thought to prepare persons to participate fully in the Spirit's ongoing ministry within the church especially speech activity. Hence, spiritual persons had the Spirit within to discern true prophecy and to give revelations. In every situation the Spirit's instruction through prophecy was considered the authoritative voice of God.

The Holy Spirit was understood to be a personal force acting on, in, and through individuals to prepare them for final union with God. He drove away evil spirits that would taint and thereby condemn the creature. He healed the human mind in order that it could comprehend the truths necessary to turn to God. His presence sanctified the entire being in preparation for union with God. He brought the glorious presence of God into the individual's whole being thereby causing each to see and know God. He served as an internal guide, coach, and trainer who helped the believer conform in character to the image of Christ and serve God in faithfulness.

CONCLUSIONS

The early church viewed people as creatures in need of redemption unto God. Jesus Christ was the provisionary gift from God whereby redemption was to be obtained. Through him God was calling forth a new order of creation. As in the original creation the Holy Spirit was the creative power of God working to bring forth new order. The role of the Spirit was to cleanse sinners and recreate them in new life. The new order was to be one in which God ruled supreme. Therefore, the Spirit worked within believers to create a certain knowledge of God and his righteousness. The Spirit guaranteed knowledge of the covenant of the kingdom and the ability to live accordingly. The new order was a messianic kingdom ruled by a charismatic Messiah, the resurrected Jesus. But in fulfillment of prophecy it was also a charismatic community, one which received an anointing from the Messiah and participated in his reign. The Holy Spirit was the anointing which Jesus received and therefore was the gift of anointing which he dispensed to his church in order that he might rule in, through and by it.

Christian formation was viewed as a process governed by the Holy Spirit. The process pivoted around the experiences of enfolding into the church; cleansing, new life, and illumination at baptism, and empowerment and ordination for service at the anointing with oil. But the transformation associated with the rites of initiation was preceded by a period of careful preparation under the supervision of the Spirit.

Christian formation involved every dimension of human life. The flesh, soul, spirit, and heart were each in need of renewal. The mind was especially in need of changing. Thus, reason was appealed to throughout the process. Yet reason was not the dominant element or catalyst for development. Genuine knowledge of God was a reasonable possibility, but it was not achieved through mental processes. Rather, it was received through a direct encounter with God.

Preparation for encounter with God and life in the kingdom of God focused upon issues of volition, morality and understanding. In general they followed that sequence. Nonbelievers were challenged to seek life from Jesus. They were expected to demonstrate a sincere desire to at least know more about him, to choose to seek a better way of life from him. Thus, the first step in Christian formation was to willfully respond to an invitation by a Spirit controlled church to know God.

The catechumenate focused on morality. Persons seeking to know God were expected to cease all sinful behavior. Self-control, mastery of the flesh, upright conduct, and purity of motive were prerequisites for cleansing from past sins and for new life in the Spirit. The pattern of the ante-Nicene church was to insist that persons act like Christians before they received in baptism the knowledge of God. Because of their continuous association with the church catechumens were recipients of the Spirit's assistance in this quest. It was the Spirit who penetrated their being with the powerful gospel. The internalized Word of God worked from within to help the individual in their consciousness of and motivation toward righteousness. The Holy Spirit further drove away evil spirits which attempted to attach themselves to the learner and inhibit moral progress.

The period of intense preparation immediately preceding baptism focused on understanding. Candidates were expected to understand the rule of faith and the creed they would confess. Special attention was given to the covenantal demands of the gospel. Understanding did not produce the knowledge of God. Rather, it defined the terms under which God could be known and the requirements for life in his kingdom.

In baptism, the Holy Spirit was thought to bring knowledge of God through encounter with him. It was then that the Spirit began to dwell in the believer and function as an internal witness to the revelation of Jesus. The mysteries of life in Christ began to be unfolded.

As a result of receiving the Spirit believers were equipped to participate in the corporate life of the kingdom of God. The unction of the Spirit guided persons into service for God especially equipping them to be spokespersons for Christ.

Following the pivotal experiences of enfoldment, the Spirit was perceived to operate in the pattern of the Johannine Paraclete. The internalized teacher began the task of leading the believer into all truth. The mysteries of life in the church were explained (with the help of the bishop). Because their minds were healed believers were able to understand more fully the Scriptures and other inspired content. But, most emphatically, the Spirit was now the immediate source of Christian knowledge. To have the Holy Spirit dwell within was to live in union and communion with God.

Chapter 5

CONCLUSIONS AND IMPLICATIONS:
TOWARD A PARADIGM OF CHRISTIAN EDUCATION

The ultimate objective of this dissertation is to construct a paradigm of Christian education based upon early Christianity's perception of the pedagogy of the Holy Spirit. Chapters two, three, and four provided a descriptive analysis of ante-Nicene understandings of the role of the Holy Spirit in the educational functions of the church. The purpose of this chapter is to draw some conclusions from that study by way of comparison with the paradigms of Lewis Sherrill,[1] Roy Zuck[2] and Rachel Henderlite[3] reviewed in chapter one[4] and to then construct a paradigm for Christian formation.

COMPARATIVE ANALYSIS

Within the literature of early Christianity, the portrait of the Holy Spirit as an agent of Christian pedagogy varied radically from the paradigms of Christian education proposed by Zuck and Henderlite and significantly from the paradigm deduced from Sherrill's work. Disparity between their systems and the pedagogical image of the Spirit in the ancient literature provided a framework from which to draw some general conclusions for this study.

---

[1] Lewis Sherrill, *The Rise of Christian Education* (New York: Macmillan Company, 1944). The paradigm used for comparison was one deduced from Sherrill's treatment of primitive Christian education. His personal paradigm was presented in a later work, The Gift of Power (New York: Macmillan Company, 1955).

[2] Roy B. Zuck, *The Holy Spirit in Your Teaching* (Glen Ellen, Illinois: Scripture Press, 1963). Reviewed above, pp. 13-16.

[3] Rachel Henderlite, *The Holy Spirit in Christian Education* (Philadelphia: Westminster Press, 1964). Reviewed above, pp. 16-19.

[4] For a summary of their paradigms see above, pp. 19-22.

A PERSONAL PRESENCE

The early Christians understood the Holy Spirit to be a divine, personal presence who acted in their midst to direct the church in its ministry of teaching. Sherrill recognized the interpersonal nature of the primitive church's experience of the Spirit as teacher. He correctly identified the Spirit's approach of teaching in and through the church as an extension of the mission of Jesus, that is, the Spirit was another Paraclete. He further recognized the Spirit's method of teaching through inspired teachers and his interaction with all the members of the community. But Sherrill erred on two major points.

One error in Sherrill's history was his confinement of the Spirit's personal interaction with the church to a brief period ending early in the second century. The literature revealed that prophetic speech activity and other overt manifestations attributed to the Spirit continued throughout the ante-Nicene period. Sherrill simply failed to recognize the historical-theological significance of the Spirit's presence for the early church.

A second error in Sherrill's treatment was his overestimate of the Spirit's manic control of the teaching process. His description of the primitive Christian gatherings implied all instruction was dependent upon inspired speech with little or no room for natural human interaction. He portrayed creedal confessions as antithetical to the Spirit's presence. However, the church's obsession with the traditions of the apostles, coupled with the New Testament emphasis on teachers and teaching and the early rise of bishops as guardians of the faith indicated that there was no period during which normal human efforts in teaching were devalued by the church.

Both Zuck and Henderlite failed to recognize the place of personal manifestations of the Spirit in the corporate life of the church. Zuck allowed for inspiration only in the writing of the Scriptures. To him supernatural demonstrations by the Spirit ended with the apostles. The Spirit's involvement in teaching and learning in the church was limited to an enhancement of natural laws.

Henderlite was true to her neo-orthodox theology and focused on issues of faith and response to the Gospel. She did not address the possibility of overt manifestations by a personal Spirit. Her experience in the church apparently led her to conclude that the Holy Spirit operated in a covert fashion. His presence could be known only by the results achieved, that is, personal conformity to the essential moral nature of Christ.

Thus, Zuck and Henderlite each made orthodox statements concerning the person of the Holy Spirit and recognized the Spirit's prescribed function of governing the church, but they failed to consider the possibility of personal encounter with the Spirit as the Spirit of power, prophecy, and the new age.

The early church experienced the Spirit as the power of God breaking into the world. The Spirit was a forceful presence overcoming the powers of darkness. Demons were cast out by the Spirit. Sickness was healed. Miracles were performed. Prophecies were given, and every Christian personally knew the Spirit as the power of God to break the bonds of sin.

The church also knew the Spirit as the source of prophecy. Luke picked up on the Old Testament prophecies concerning the return of prophecy during the messianic age. The birth narratives of Jesus as well as the Lukan record of the expansion of the church (Acts) gave prominence to the role of the Spirit in the return of prophetic activity. The ante-Nicene writers not only attested to the continuance of prophecy, they placed special significance on it as a sign Christians were indeed the chosen people of God.

The overt manifestations by the Spirit of power and prophecy contributed to the church's belief that the eschatological end time had arrived. But it was the Spirit's work in the personal transformation of individuals which provided the overwhelming sense that they had entered into a new age. Experiences of regeneration, sanctification and illumination were described in detail as works of the Spirit which provided certain assurance of life in the presence of God.

It was not until the fourth century that Christianity clearly articulated its Trinitarian theology. The reason for the hesitancy may be attributed to several factors, including a fear of polytheism and the priority given to clarifying Christology.[5] But it cannot be said that the early church did not know who the Spirit was. They knew him as the divine personal presence of God who did what Jesus would do. According to the pattern of early Christianity, Christian education requires the personal presence of the Holy Spirit characterized by prophecy, healings, exorcisms, and other objective manifestations.

ENVIRONMENT FOR LEARNING

For the early Christians it was the presence of the Holy Spirit which defined the church as an environment for learning. The *ekklesia* was understood to be called and constituted by the Holy Spirit for the Spirit was God's power to create the eschatological Israel. The kingdom of God was actualized because the Spirit was making the Lordship of Jesus a reality. The Spirit was the life giving and unifying force in the body of Christ making it

---

[5] Kenneth Scott Latourette, *A History of Christianity*, Vol. I, Beginnings to 1500 (New York: Harper and Row, 1975), p. 151.

more than an assembly of individuals. The church was the habitation of God, a society marked by his presence.

Sherrill recognized the pneumatic character of primitive Christian gatherings as the primary factor in establishing an environment for learning but he failed to fully consider the character of the church as a contrast-society governed by the Spirit. The environment of the church was not limited to its gatherings. Members carried it into every dimension of life.

Zuck gave little place for the Spirit in the environment for learning. The Spirit's role was to help the teacher select an environment which made best use of the natural laws of learning.

Henderlite recognized the importance of the corporate life of the church as an environment for learning. She called for a consciousness of the Spirit's ability to teach through all that the church does. But, once again, she failed to recognize the dynamics of a Spirit-led community.

According to the ante-Nicene writings the environment in which Christian education took place was that of the church living under the sovereign direction of the Holy Spirit. The church was to be a messianic community governed by the charismatic messiah and serving as a light to the nations of God's righteousness. In this it was called to be a contrast-society, a kingdom marked by the character and presence of God and therefore the only reasonable alternative to existing social orders.

The early Christians projected the church as a society which placed a premium on people and relationships. They described themselves as an intimate family, a family which radically redefined the existing social order by treating all persons as equals. The church existed as a fellowship of love which went to great lengths to care for its needy members.

Participation in the church required entering into close personal relationships. Sponsors provided catechumens ongoing oversight for their moral and spiritual development. There were daily gatherings in homes with frequent meal functions. The motivation for these gatherings was an experiential bond of love. The *koinonia* of the Spirit created familial ties which superseded natural understanding.

Christian gatherings were paradoxically characterized by both ordered control and spontaneous participation. The concern of Paul for decency and order was evident throughout the ante-Nicene period. The primacy of the bishop as guardian of the faith and traditions included the careful preservation of rituals. Descriptions of the Sunday worship services from various regions of the empire revealed a strong uniformity in order and practices.

The implication was that the gatherings provided both a sense of security and spontaneous participation. The uniformity of rituals and doctrines coupled with stress upon moral conduct contributed to an environment of rigid control. Participation in the kingdom of God required conformity to set standards but also provided an overwhelming sense of belonging and security.

Gatherings also invited the spontaneous participation of all members. Individuals contributed the elements of the love feasts and Eucharist as well as offerings for the needy. The sharing of the kiss of peace provided an outlet for communicating the internal blessings of God as did periods of impromptu songs and prayers. Further, every member was a potential channel for the charismatic gifts of the Spirit.

In summation, the environment in which Christian instruction took place was a social-spiritual environment. Stress was placed upon personal dignity, individual participation, moral conformity, familial relationships, rituals and traditions, corporate unity and charismatic activity all of which contributed to a powerful consciousness of belonging to the family of God.

CONTENT OF INSTRUCTION

During the ante-Nicene period the church had a variety of sources for authoritative content. The Scriptures, oral traditions from the apostles, creeds and hymns, the rule of faith and ongoing prophecy and prophetic activity by the church were the primary sources. The qualifying factor was that they were breathed by the Holy Spirit and that the Spirit's presence continued in them. They were words (or messages) being spoken by the Spirit.

Sherrill, Zuck and Henderlite each failed to grasp the broad spectrum of revelational content. Sherrill recognized the use of the Hebrew Scriptures and apostolic epistles during primitive Christianity but essentially understood the content of instruction to be Spirit inspired interpretation of these. He inadvertently relegated the use of oral and written traditions to the period beginning in the second century. His treatment of the creeds as incipient in the faith but antithetical to the Spirit distorts their evolution from earliest sources and their close association with the Spirit.

Zuck's emphasis on using strictly the Scriptures as transmissive content was foreign to early Christian thought. The roots of Zuck's approach lay in his understanding of revelation, inspiration, and illumination. The early church did not make fine distinctions between revelation and inspiration. In general they represented two dimensions of the same events. Revelation focused on God as the source of his own self-disclosure. Inspiration focused on the Spirit as the means of God's self-disclosure. While early Christians recognized a special character in the inspiration of the Scriptures, they understood the Spirit to speak authoritatively through many other sources. The uniqueness of the Scriptures primarily was not in the Spirit's movement upon its human authors but rather in the unique role they played in pointing to Jesus Christ. As such, the stress was upon the Spirit's continued breathing through the Scriptures to unveil God's self-disclosure in Jesus.

On the other hand, Henderlite erred in making inspiration a secondary doctrine in origin and function. The view that the Scriptures were inspired as a sovereign act of the Spirit was not a late addition to the faith as she contended. Rather, it was rooted in the Hebrew understanding of the Scriptures and was accepted by Jesus and the apostles.

Zuck and Henderlite differed from the early church's use of the term "illumination." Both authors tied illumination to the Scriptures. For them it was essentially a Spirit induced experience of heightened understanding of the written revelations. Early Christianity understood illumination to be the result of direct personal encounter with God. Generally associated with the rite of baptism, the experience was understood to be the impact of immediate communion with God. Illumination was not considered a heightened understanding of the Scriptures. It was rather knowledge which flowed from the glorious personhood of God directly into the regenerated human being. The experience began at baptism and through the indwelling Spirit continued throughout the life of the faithful. Because of this enlightenment believers experienced a heightened understanding of the Scriptures which served as an essential element in their continued spiritual growth. But in contrast to Zuck and Henderlite the early believers emphasized the knowledge of God as being the key to understanding the Bible, not vice versa.

OBJECTIVES

The pedagogical objectives associated with the Holy Spirit by Christians of the first three centuries were rooted in the church's concept of divine mission. The foundational mission of the church was to extend the mission of Jesus by being the spiritual Israel which existed as a sign from God for the nations. The ultimate mission of the church was to achieve union with God which was attainable in the church but was also yet to be fully realized.

There were three pedagogical objectives closely associated with the Spirit. First, the Spirit sought to prepare persons for union with God through the training of their characters in moral discipline. Second, the Spirit sought to prepare persons for union with God through the perfecting of their faith. Third, the Spirit aimed at union with God through the salubrious incorporation of persons into the body of Christ where union with God was first actualized. These objectives differed significantly from the ones proposed by Sherrill, Zuck, and Henderlite.

Sherrill projected a goal of personal liberty and autonomy under the sovereignty of a personal God. He viewed the church as aiming at the building of a kingdom in which each person was an equal personality living under the guidance of the Spirit by faith in the living Jesus Christ. The problem with this goal, from the perspective of early Christianity, was that it failed to adequately deal with the questions of sin and redemption. Because of sin there could be no freedom under the sovereignty of God without union with him. Early Christians were more concerned with salvation and deliverance than autonomy and personal fulfillment.

Zuck portrayed the Spirit as working to make the Bible relevant to the life-needs of the learner. By focusing on understanding and application this goal stopped far short of the early Christian experience of the Spirit. The early church was not content with discovering a better way of living. It aimed for the ultimate, to have new and eternal life through communion with God.

Henderlite understood the Spirit's objective to be the moral transformation of the individual through a direct confrontation with the person of Jesus Christ. Early Christians would have fully agreed with her except that she stopped short of the Spirit's ultimate goal. Conformity to Christ through moral transformation was for them the means of union with God rather than an end in itself.

The pedagogical objectives of the early church addressed the basic human need of transformation through the redemptive work of Jesus. They were rooted in the church's identity and sense of mission as the eschatological community of God. Through the active presence of the Holy Spirit it was possible to encounter God, in his glorious righteousness. All of the educational objectives of the church were toward the preparation of persons to encounter the all-consuming God and to live before him.

ROLE OF THE LEARNER

For early Christianity the learner was an individual who had been marred by sin and existed at a recognizable stage of response to God's offer of redemption through Jesus Christ. The role of the learner was carefully prescribed by the level of learning that had been achieved. Persons outside the church were called upon to repent and seek the truth in Jesus. Catechumens were expected to demonstrate personal moral discipline and to otherwise prepare themselves for the demands of living in covenant with Jesus. Persons presenting themselves for baptism were expected to understand the creedal confession they would make and to express unwavering faith in the transforming power of God. Persons being incorporated into the church were called upon immediately after baptism to open themselves to the Holy Spirit and commit themselves to the life and ministry of the church. Having received the Spirit and entered the church believers were expected to pursue perfection in the faith.

Sherrill's view of the learner during primitive Christianity was compatible with the early Christian perception of believers as spiritual persons pursuing perfection. He portrayed the learner as an active participant in the community gatherings. Through the indwelling Spirit each person was potentially a teacher and a learner.

Zuck virtually ignored the role of the learner. For him the learner was a person with needs who was basically a recipient in the process. The learner's function was to listen and respond in faith. The early Christians challenged persons at every level of learning to actively respond, question, and participate in shaping their own growth. Persons outside the church were encouraged to dialogue with believers. Catechumens were held accountable for their progress and believers were called upon to be contributing members of the church as a learning community.

Henderlite stressed the learner's autonomy under the sovereignty of God. For her the role of the learner was to contemplate and choose. Learners were to be challenged through hearing gospel stories, and they were expected to internally wrestle with the Spirit until their choice was evident. Early Christianity differed in that questions of volition were essentially to be settled prior to entering the catechumenate. Members of the church had already established their resolve to follow the leading of the Spirit.

Early Christianity carefully defined the role of learners according their stage of response to the redemptive provisions of Jesus. In general learners were expected to conform to the standards of God so that they might know him and live under his dominion. Preparation for encounter with God required a desire to know him, genuine inquiry into the means of knowing him, personal resolve to conform to his image as demonstrated by the cessation of sin, and faith. Life in the presence of God required ongoing faith and communion with him through participation in the church.

ROLE OF THE HUMAN TEACHER

Early Christianity recognized two types of teachers, pastor-teachers and prophet-teachers. Both types were understood to function under the supervision of the Holy Spirit. Pastor-teachers served the primary functions of preserving and transmitting the sacred traditions of the church. These teachers were watchmen over the Body of Christ protecting it from error in practice or faith. The role of pastor-teachers was to preside over Christian gatherings and rituals, to serve as a resource person, and to supervise the corporate life of the church.

Prophet-teachers served the single function of speaking in the Spirit. They were persons who had received the gift of prophecy and devoted themselves to being a channel through which the Spirit could publicly speak. Everyone who had received the Spirit was potentially a prophet-teacher.

For the period of primitive Christianity Sherrill described all human teachers as endowed instruments operating under the direct supervision of the Spirit. Anyone in communion with the Spirit could be directed to serve that role. In essence he accurately described the prophet-teachers who ministered throughout the early centuries. But Sherrill erred in that he considered pastor-teachers antithetical replacements for prophet- teachers. Both types existed simultaneously as complementary teachers in the early church.

Zuck presented the human teacher as the primary figure in the learning process. The teacher must be a believer who has experienced the illumination of the Scriptures by the Spirit. Only persons endowed by the Spirit with the gift or ability to teach should be allowed to teach. The gift of teaching comes to the individual with the Spirit's indwelling at conversion but is in reality only the enhancement or addition of natural abilities. Finally, teachers must know and utilize the God-given laws of teaching and learning.

Early Christians would have agreed with Zuck that teachers must be believers who are knowledgeable of the Scriptures and have a gift of teaching. The similarities ended there. For the early church the gift of teaching was associated with the direct intervention of the Spirit rather than the enhancement of natural abilities. The gift was never associated with conversion. Pastor- teachers received their gift through the laying on of hands at their ordination to a teaching rank of ministry. A special presence of the Spirit was understood to come to rest upon them. Prophet-teachers received the gift of teaching as the Spirit descended upon them at Christian gatherings.

Henderlite understood the human teacher to be someone who had by faith chosen to obey the Spirit's leading into that service. The teacher served two primary functions. First, the teacher presented the data of the Christian faith to the learner. Second, the teacher confronted each person with the necessity of decision while leaving the individual free to decide as he or she was able.

In general, early Christianity would have accepted Henderlite's description of the human teacher as a presenter of data but would not identify with the invariable emphasis in decision making. A call for rational response to the gospel was incipient in the Christian message but it was not an all-encompassing function of the teacher. For believers the teacher's presentation was a means of communion with God, a communion which was transforming of their entire being. Thus, Henderlite failed to recognize the supervising presence of the Spirit and the possibility of direct knowledge by encounter.

METHODS OF INSTRUCTION

The methods of instruction associated with the Holy Spirit in the life of the early church varied according to the learners level of development, the nature of the gathering, and the content being presented. The Spirit was understood to permeate the church so that all that was said and done in and through the church was considered a means of communion with God. The Spirit's indwelling of the believer and the believer's reception of the Spirit further formed the basis of immediate instruction by the Spirit. The paradigms for instruction taken from the works of Sherrill, Zuck, and Henderlite failed to recognize the breadth of the Spirit's methods of instruction.

Sherrill correctly recognized the overt methods of the prophet speaking forth the word of the Lord. Zuck was also correct in his observation that the Spirit worked through the natural laws of teaching and learning. And Henderlite correctly emphasized the function of all the events in the life of the church as methods of instruction by the Spirit. However, an accurate picture from the perspective of early Christian literature would require a composite of all three views with the addition of other methods.

One set of methods omitted by all three authors was the set incorporated into the processes of evangelism. The presence of the miraculous, especially healings and exorcisms, in the church's confrontation with evil in the world, was perhaps the most effective method of communicating the gospel to nonbelievers.

Another set of methods ignored by Sherrill, Zuck and Henderlite were those associated with the catechumen's training in moral discipline. Controlled participation in the life of the church, close inspection by sponsors and elders, and public censure all conflict with modern Western values and do not fit well into paradigms which overly stress the autonomy of the individual.

The methods connected with the believer's salubrious incorporation into the Body of Christ were similarly avoided. A direct illuminating and transforming encounter with God was perceivable in Sherrill's paradigm but implicitly absent from those of Zuck and Henderlite. Thus, both of the latter writers precluded the possibility of ongoing revelations and restricted the methods of Christian education to those associated with the rational process of presentation, followed by reflection, followed by decision and action.

A PARADIGM OF CHRISTIAN EDUCATION

The question remains, what would Christian education look like today if it took seriously the early Christian perception of the pedagogy of the Holy Spirit? Obviously, it would be impossible to reenact the system of Christian education followed by the ante-Nicene church. That system was dynamic and contained many variables as it interacted with a changing world and church. The learning objectives, the roles of teachers and learners, the environment for learning, the methods of instruction and even the content of instruction all underwent varying degrees of change as the church adjusted itself to face new challenges. But the essential elements of early Christian education were consistent throughout the period and offer the foundations for an alternative paradigm for contemporary Christian education.

TEACHERS

Early Christian tradition provided a pattern for the utilization of multiple types of teachers in the church. The Holy Spirit served both as the superintendent of teachers and as a teacher. Three other sets of teachers were identifiable and served specialized functions within the paradigm. Pastor-teachers and prophet-teachers had prescribed community functions and were carefully regulated by tradition. Sponsors, although not classified as teachers by the early church, served as a type of informal teacher with less definitive responsibilities. Contemporary Christian education should include the four types of teachers.

The Holy Spirit. The essential element in the paradigm is the actualization of the personal presence of the Holy Spirit as governor of all learning in the church and as teacher. However, since the Spirit is Lord of the church, his function cannot be prescribed. It can only be described based upon the sources which are accepted as authoritative, in this case early Christian tradition. From that perspective, it is the Spirit who prescribes the functions of the church.

Descriptively, the Holy Spirit should be known as teacher in at least five dimensions of the individual and corporate life of the church. First, the Spirit should be encountered as the transforming power of God who prepares persons to know God. In this capacity the Spirit works on and within the individual to create a heightened sense of reality and self-consciousness. The role of the Spirit is to introduce the individual to the unseen God by creating an awareness of the presence of God. This is externally accomplished by manifestations of the Spirit such as exorcisms, healings, and the moral transformation of others. Internally, the Spirit heightens the individual's ability to confront such manifestations as the initial basis for a new self-definition as a creature in need of God.

Secondly, the Spirit should be encountered as the source of written revelation from God. The chief pattern of teaching utilized by the Spirit is to speak through the Scriptures. Through them the Spirit is known and simultaneously makes known the things of God.

Third, the Spirit should be known as the internal presence of God who serves as a source of communion between the individual and God. In that capacity the Spirit makes God (and the standards of his righteousness) an inescapable reality which provides impetus and direction in life.

Fourth, the Spirit should be known as a trainer and equipper for service. As a teacher the Spirit should be experienced as the provider of all that is needed to function in the kingdom of God. Hence, individuals should know the Spirit as the life and power of God flowing through them.

Fifth, the Spirit should be known to individuals as the voice of God speaking through the church. The Spirit's dynamic presence in the rituals, activities, and relationships of the church would also provide a means of instruction. The tradition suggests the Spirit should also teach by inspiring human teachers to proclaim messages from God.

Human Teachers. There should be three types of human teachers in the church: sponsor-teachers, pastor-teachers, and prophet-teachers. Sponsor-teachers should serve the function of a coach and guide. They should help form the deep interpersonal bonds between the learner and the church. Their role would be to daily oversee the individual's spiritual growth, provide personal testimonies for encouragement, remind of truths established in the church, and provide correction when mistakes are made. Essentially the sponsor-teacher gives one-on-one supervision of the development of the disciplined life of the kingdom of God.

Pastor-teachers should serve two primary functions. First, they should give oversight to the spiritual life of the church as it gathers. Second, they should carefully preserve and communicate the established traditions of the church. Essentially pastor-teachers should oversee the corporate discipline of the body of Christ. As such they are sponsor-teachers for groups of people. It is their responsibility to see that all things are done in harmony with God's revealed plan for his kingdom. By preserving the established doctrines, faith and practice of the apostles they would assure unity within the local assembly and with the church catholic.

Several ranks of pastor-teachers could exist, each with differing duties and authorities. One rank of teachers could be assigned the pastoral oversight of small clusters of believers. Another rank might be assigned the oversight of joint gatherings of clusters. However, the ministry of pastor-teachers should be defined in terms of relationships and responsibilities. That is, pastor-teachers should exist only as they give oversight and guidance to a designated representation of the body of Christ to which they have been joined.

Prophet-teachers should serve the primary function of being the immediate voice of God to the church. Through them the church is demonstrably reminded of the presence of the Holy Spirit as teacher and Lord. They draw their authority to speak directly from God, but are subject to the judgment of the church as to their authenticity. Corporate confirmation, moral behavior, and harmony with the Spirit of the Scriptures are the only basis for the evaluation of prophet-teachers.

The selection and monitoring of all human teachers in the church should be considered the priority of the Spirit. Sponsor-teachers should come forth voluntarily out of the ranks of the laity as all persons who have received the Spirit are qualified to communicate in the Spirit with others. However, the reception of the Spirit can only follow the development of spiritual discipline so that sponsor-teachers must be persons who have been properly and fully incorporated into the life of the church.

Pastor-teachers must undergo a more careful process of identification. Since their responsibilities are corporate, their ministries are dependent upon recognition by the church. And since their responsibilities require advanced knowledge of the Scriptures, and doctrines and practices of the church, it is the church's responsibility to assure they have that knowledge. Fundamentally, however, pastor-teachers receive their place in the church because the indwelling Spirit has led them to that place and the church has recognized that the Spirit has called and equipped them for the role. At that juncture the church must join with them in seeking a special gift from the Spirit which will enable them to fulfill their calling.

In summation, all human teachers are to be viewed as extensions of the teaching ministry of the Holy Spirit. Human teachers are dependent upon the reception of the Spirit to function properly. Pastor-teachers and prophet-teachers require a special call from God and special qualifying gifts from him. The defining principle for all teachers should be their relationship to God and the church.

OBJECTIVES

The objectives of Christian education according to the paradigm of the Holy Spirit must transcend the natural realm of human existence and aim at knowledge by encounter with God. Specifically, the aims of Christian education must break out of the strict confinement of rationalism. Cognition and reflection are not, in and of themselves, adequate means of achieving full redemption unto God and therefore should not be the sole baggage in which pedagogical objectives are cloaked.

According to the early pattern of pedagogy by the Holy Spirit the critical goal in Christian education is for the individual to receive illumination directly from God through the redemptive acts of regeneration and sanctification. The premise is that God can be known through personal encounter. However, there are prerequisites for knowing God which call forth a series of secondary objectives.

One prerequisite for illumination is conformity in conduct to the demands of God's righteousness. In order to see God, know him, and live, the individual must demonstrate the resolve to participate in his life. Therefore, church education must aim at helping the learner develop personal spiritual discipline. A supportive aim is for the learner to gain knowledge of the standards of conduct required by God. The church must set before its constituency a pattern of living which is conducive to life in the kingdom of God.

Another prerequisite for illumination is an informed faith in Jesus. Knowledge of God is available only through the eternal Word of God and the redemption provided in him. Thus, church education must aim at the learner gaining a basic understanding of the history of God's salvation acts as they culminate in the life, death, resurrection, ascension and promised return of Jesus. It is essential that every person seeking the knowledge of God understand the basic story of God's redemptive acts in Christ. However, cognitive understanding is only one factor in the development of faith. Experiences of the presence of God in the community of faith are also required. Hence, the essential objective is for the learner to be exposed to the rudiments of the gospel accompanied by tangible evidences of its power.

Having led the individual into a personal encounter with God, the focus of Christian education must shift to the maintaining of the familial relationship with him. Church education must aim for the incorporation of the individual into the body of Christ as family of God. Specifically, the church must lead persons into shared experiences and relationships through which the Spirit operates. Christian education must also aim at the cultivation of personal communion with God. Individuals must be led into a life of communion through the Scriptures, prayer and meditation which allow the Holy Spirit to function as the indwelling teacher.

In conclusion, Christian education must aim for learning which encompasses the totality of human existence with a view toward the ultimate goal of union with God. There must be behavioral, cognitive, volitional, and spiritual objectives which reflect the process of redemption.

THE LEARNER

In order to follow a paradigm of Christian education built upon early Christian traditions of the Spirit, the church must assume a biblical understanding of the essential nature of human beings. Learners are creatures of God who need redemption of their whole personhood unto God. Before conversion, they are sinners who retain something of the image of God, but are subject to the judgment of God. At the same time they are objects of God's love and they are capable of knowing God through the work of the Spirit in their life.

Learners should be educated according to their level of attainment in the grace of God. Persons outside the church must be viewed as objects of God's love in need of discovering the truth about Jesus. Persons seeking to know God must be viewed as needing deliverance from sin and the forces of evil. They are candidates who must demonstrate their desire to know God, but they are also unborn children of the church who must be tenderly cared for. Persons who have come to know God must be treated as full members of his household who have equal access to him, but need the life of the church to bolster their faith.

CONTENT

The content of instruction in Christian education must find its origins in God. The church must teach what he has said and is saying through the Holy Spirit. The Scriptures must take the central place in all instruction but the church must also identify other avenues through which God is speaking.

The centrality of the Scriptures is based upon their eternal connection with Jesus Christ as the Word of God to humanity. They are the primary revelation from and about Jesus. They are not only a gift from God which bears the authoritative mark of inspiration, that is words from God, they are the Word of God. Therefore, relationship with God through Jesus Christ cannot be separated from communion with God through Scriptures.

The Bible should thus be used in two fashions. For those who do not know God, it is a textbook about God and his redemptive actions in Jesus Christ. For those who have come to know God, the Bible is a source of immediate communion with him. The early Christian usage of Scriptures suggests, with a couple of notable exceptions, believers did not consider themselves to receive a hidden or alternative understanding of the Bible.[6]

---

[6] Two noted exceptions were the views held by Clement of Alexandria and Origen. Both men made use of allegorical interpretation of the Scriptures. However, it should be noted that their quest for a spiritual meaning of the Scriptures was rooted in a firm belief in the inspiration

They were aided by the Spirit to better understand passages which had seemed aloof. But the essential difference in the believer's study of the Scriptures were affective. The Spirit working both within the believer and through the Bible caused the Word of God to have its intended effect on the individual. Therefore, while the Scriptures always retain their historic objective character, the primary use of the Bible among believers should be as a means of immediate communion with God. It should be read and studied toward that end.

Other forms of content must also be used in Christian education. God should be perceived as speaking through the doctrines and practices of the church. The gospel must authoritatively be presented in oral form. Established standards for Christian behavior must be carefully studied and applied. The fundamental standard for determining Christian content is whether it has been breathed by the Holy Spirit. That which has been breathed by the Spirit can be known from two perspectives. The Spirit working within believers will create an internal witness of its validity. And that which is breathed by the Spirit will conform to the Word of God revealed in Christ and through the Scriptures.

METHODS OF INSTRUCTION

The pedagogy of the Holy Spirit mandates methods of instruction appropriate for life in the Kingdom of God. All instruction should bear the markings of the Spirit's presence. And all that is said and done in the church which is attributed to the Spirit should be considered a means of communion with God.

The methods of instruction should also be appropriate for the stage of spiritual formation in which the learner lives. The unconverted require methods of confrontation with love. The proclamation of the gospel to them should be in the power and demonstration of the Spirit. Those seeking salvation require the methods of a gentle coach and sponsor. The presentation of the gospel to them must be tied to the life and practices of the church. They must share in the learning experiences of the believers, that is, hearing the Scriptures read and expounded upon by pastor-teachers, learning through the worship of God and hearing prophecies which are relevant to their daily lives. The chief method of instruction with the church should be participation in corporate life with the Spirit.

---

of every word in them. See, Justo L. Gonzalez, *A History of Christian Thought, Vol. I, From the Beginnings to the Council of Chalcedon* (Nashville: Abingdon, 1970), pp. 199-204.

ENVIRONMENT FOR FORMATION

Perhaps the most critical element in the pedagogy of the Holy Spirit is the environment which is needed for Christian formation. The environment for learning must be that of the kingdom of God on earth. The social-spiritual environment of the church as the household of God is foundational to both the method and content of instruction, for it is the life of the Spirit breathing in and through the church which communicates life to individuals. Therefore, the church must be a society in which God may be encountered through relationships of love and acceptance, through a sense of moral purity, and through prophetic manifestations in speech and actions.

One essential element of this paradigm of pedagogy is the continual manifestations of the charismatic gifts. Through these the realization of the sovereign presence of the Spirit is enhanced and the Spirit retains the role of teacher.

CONCLUSIONS

The pedagogy of the Holy Spirit calls forth an approach to Christian education that takes seriously the historical doctrines, practices and experiences of the church. It requires fresh awareness that the church is to be the temple of the Spirit, that the Spirit is to be known in powerful manifestations, that the church has been called to be God's contrast society on earth, and that membership in the family of God requires discipline and transforming encounters with God. The pedagogy of the Holy Spirit is a pedagogy which actualizes redemption unto God through the Spirit's work in and through individuals.

BIBLIOGRAPHY

Ackroyd, P. R. and C. F. Evans, eds. *The Cambridge History of the Bible*, Vol. I, *From the Beginnings to Jerome*. Cambridge: Cambridge University Press, 1970.

Adams, John Wesley. "The Teaching Role in the New Testament: Its Nature and Scope as a Function of the Developing Church." Ph.D. Dissertation, Baylor University, 1976.

Allen, Roland. *Missionary Methods: St. Paul's or Ours*. Fifth Edition London: World Dominion Press, 1969.

Altamer, Bethold. *Patrology*, trans. by Hilda C. Graef. New York: Herder and Herder, 1960.

Arndt, W. F. and Gingrich F. W., ed. and trans. *A Greek-English Lexicon of the New Testament and other Early Christian Literature*. Chicago: University Press, 1957.

Arnold, Eberhard. *The Early Christians: A Source Book on the Witness of the Early Church*. Grand Rapids: Baker Book House, 1979.

Aron, Robert. *The Jewish Jesus*. Trans. Angnes H. Forsyth. Maryknoll: Orbis Books, 1971.

Arrington, French L. *Paul's Aeon Theology in 1 Corinthians*. Washington, D.C.: University Press of America, 1977.

Ash, James L. "Decline of Ecstatic Prophecy in the Early Church." *Journal of Theological Studies* 37 (1976), 227-252.

Aune, David Edward. *The Cultic Setting of Realized Eschatology in Early Christianity*. London: E. J. Brill, 1972.

_____. *Prophecy in Early Christianity and the Ancient Mediterranean World*. Grand Rapids, Michigan: William B. Eerdmans, 1983.

Barclay, William. *Train Up a Child: Educational Ideals in the Ancient World*. Grand Rapids, Michigan: William B. Eerdmans, 1983.

Barnett, Maurice. *The Living Flame*. London: The Epworth Press, 1953.

Barrett, Charles Kingsley. *The Gospel According to St. John: An Introduction with Commentary and Notes*. London: S.P.C.K, 1960.

————. *The Holy Spirit and the Gospel Tradition*. London: S.P.C.K., 1966.

Barth, Karl. *Church Dogmatics* Vol. IV. *The Doctrine of Reconciliation*. Edinburgh: T & T Clark, 1974.

Bauer, Johannes B., ed. *Bauer Encyclopedia of Biblical Theology*. London: Sheed and Ward, 1970.

Bauer, Walter, William F. Arndt, and F. Wilbur Gingrich. *A Greek-English Lexicon of the New Testament and Other Early Christian Literature*. 4th ed. Chicago: University of Chicago Press, 1957.

Baumgarter, Friedrich. "*Pneuma*." *Theological Dictionary of the New Testament*, Vol, II. Ed. Gerhard Kittel. Trans. by Geoffrey W. Bromiley. Grand Rapids: Wm. B. Eerdmans, 1964.

Beasley-Murray, G. R. "Jesus and the Spirit." *Melanges Bibliques*. Ed. Albert Descamps and Andre de Halleux. Gembloux Dugulot, 1970.

Benjamins, Harry S. "Pneuma in John and Paul: A Comparative Study of the Term with Particular Reference to the Holy Spirit." *Biblical Theological Bulletin* 6 (1976), 27-48.

Benson, Clarence H. *A Popular History of Christian Education*. Chicago: Moody Press, 1943.

Berkhof, Hendrikus. *The Doctrine of the Holy Spirit*. Atlanta: John Knox Press, 1977.

Berkhof, L. *Systematic Theology*. Grand Rapids: Wm. B. Eerdmans, 1969.

Berkouwer, G. C. *Man the Image of God*. Trans. by James F. Davidson. Grand Rapids: Wm. B. Eerdmans, 1976.

Blackmore, W. B. "Holy Spirit as Publics and as Charismatic Institutions." *Encounter* 26 (1975), 161-180.

Boring, M. Eugene. "Influence of Christian Prophecy on the Johannine Portrayal of the Paraclete and Jesus." *New Testament Studies* 25 (1978), 113-123.

Brauman, Georg. "Advocate, Paraclete, Helper." *New International Dictionary of New Testament Theology*, Vol. I. Ed. Colin Brown. Grand Rapids: Zondervan Publishing House, 1975.

Bromiley, Geoffrey W. "Anthropology," *The International Standard Bible Encyclopedia*, Vol. I, Grand Rapids: Wm. B. Eerdmans, 1979.

_____. *The International Standard Bible Encyclopedia*. Grand Rapids: Wm. B. Eerdmans Publishing Co., 1979.

Brown, Colin, ed. *The New Testament Dictionary of New Testament Theology*. Grand Rapids: Zondervan Publishing House, 1975.

Brown, Francis, S. R. Driver, and Charles A. Briggs, eds. *A Hebrew and English Lexicon of the Old Testament*. Oxford: Claredon Press, 1962.

Brown, Raymond E. *The Gospel According to John*. Garden City, New York: Doubleday, 1970.

_____. "Diverse Views of the Spirit in the New Testament." *Worship* 57 (1943), 225-236.

_____. *The Anchor Bible: The Gospel According to John* (xiii-xxi). Garden City, New York: Doubleday & Company, Inc., 1970.

_____. "The Kerygma of the Gospel According to John." *Interpretation* 21 (1967), 391-392.

_____. "The Paraclete in the Fourth Gospel." *New Testament Studies*, 13 (1967), 113-132.

Bruce, Frederick F. *The New Testament Development of Old Testament Themes*. Grand Rapids: Wm. B. Eerdmans Publishing Company, 1977.

_____. *The Spreading Flame: The Rise and Progress of Christianity from its First Beginnings to the Conversion of the English*. Grand Rapids: Wm. B. Eerdmans Publishing Co., 1979.

Bultmann, Rudolph. "*Ginosko*." *Theological Dictionary of the New Testament*, Vol. I. Ed. Gerhard Kittel. Trans. by Geoffrey W. Bromiley. Grand Rapids: Wm. B. Eerdmans, 1964.

Burgess, Stanley M. *The Spirit and the Church: Antiquity*. Peabody, MA: Hendrickson Publishers, 1984.

Burgess, Harold William. *An Invitation to Religious Education*. Birmingham, Alabama: Religious Education Press, 1975.

Burns, J. Patout and Gerald M. Fagin. *Message of the Fathers of the Church: The Holy Spirit*. Wilmington Delaware: Michael Glazier, Inc., 1984.

Campbell, T. C. "The Doctrine of the Holy Spirit in the Theology of Athanasis." *Scottish Journal of Theology* 27 (1974), 408-440.

Carson, Don A. "The Function of the Paraclete in John 16:7-11." *Journal of Biblical Literature* 98 (1979), 547-566.

Coe, George Albert. *A Social Theory of Religious Education.* New York: Charles Scribner's Sons, 1917.

Coenan, Lothar. "Church." *New International Dictionary of New Testament Theology*, Vol. I. Ed. Colin Brown. Grand Rapids: Zondervan Publishing House, 1975.

Collins, William Emmett. "The Beginnings of Christian Education." Ph.D. dissertation, Marguette University, 1973.

Congar, Yves. *I Believe in the Holy Spirit.* Trans. by David Smith. New York: Seabury Press, 1983.

Cully, Iris V. *The Dynamics of Christian Education.* Philadelphia: Westminster Press, 1958.

Cully, Kendig. *The Search for a Christian Education Since 1940.* Philadelphia: Westminster Press, 1965.

Culpepper, R. Alan. *Anatomy of the Fourth Gospel: A Study in Literary Design.* Philadelphia: Fortress Press, 1983.

_____. *The Johannine School: An Evaluation of Johannine School Hypothesis Based on the Investigation of the Nature of Ancient Schools.* Missoula, Montana: Scholars Press, 1985.

Danielou, Jean. *Gospel Message and Hellenistic Culture.* Trans., edited and postscript by John Austin Baker. Philadelphia: Westminster Press, 1973.

_____. *The Theology of Jewish Christianity.* Trans. by John A. Baker. Philadelphia: The Westminster Press, 1977.

Davies, J. G. "The Primary Meaning of *Paracletos*." *Journal of Theological Studies* 4 (1953), 35-38.

Dix, Gregory. *The Shape of Liturgy.* London: Dacie Press, 1975.

_____, ed. and trans. *The Treatise on the Apostolic Tradition of St. Hippolytus of Rome.* London: S.P.C.K., 1937.

Dodd, C. H. *The Interpretation of the Fourth Gospel.* Cambridge: University Press, 1968.

Draggs, George D. "Holy Spirit and Tradition: The Writings of St. Athanasuis." *Sobornost* 1 (1979), 51-72.

Dugmore, Clifford W. *The Influence of the Synagogue Upon the Divine Office.* Westminster: The Faith Press, 1964.

Dujarier, Michel. *A History of the Catechumenate: The First Six Centuries.* Trans. by Edward J. Haash. New York: Sadlier, 1979.

Dunn, James D. G. *Baptism in the Holy Spirit.* Philadelphia: Westminster Press, 1970.

_____. *Jesus and the Spirit: A Study of the Religious and Charismatic Experience of Jesus and the First Christians as Reflected in the New Testament.* Philadelphia: The Westminster Press, 1975.

_____. "Prophetic I - Sayings and the Jesus Tradition, the Importance of Testing Prophetic Utterances Within Early Christianity." *New Testament Studies* 24 (1978), 175-198.

_____. "Spirit, Holy Spirit." *New International Dictionary of New Testament Theology,* Vol. III. Ed. Colin Brown. Grand Rapids: Zondervan Publishing House, 1975.

Easton, Burton Scott, ed. and trans. *The Apostolic Tradition of Hippolytus.* Cambridge: Cambridge University Press, 1935.

Eavey, C. B. *History of Christian Education.* Chicago: Moody Press, 1964.

Edwards, O. C. and John H. Westerhoff, eds. *A Faithful Church: Issues in the History of Catechesis.* Wilton, Connecticut: Moorehouse-Barlow, 1980.

Ehrhardt, A. *The Apostolic Succession in the First Two Centuries of the Church.* London: Lutterworth Press, 1953.

Elliott, Harrison S. *Can Religious Education Be Christian?* New York: Macmillan Company, 1940.

Eno, Robert B. "Authority and Conflict in the Early Church." *English Theology* 7 (1976) 1, 41-60.

Ervin, Howard M. *Conversion-Initiation and the Baptism in the Holy Spirit: An Engaging Critique of James D. G. Dunn's "Baptism in the Holy Spirit."* Peabody, Massachusetts: Hendrickson Publishers, 1984.

_____. "Hermeneutics: A Pentecostal Option." *Pneuma* 3 (1981), 43-55.

Ferguson, John. *Clement of Alexandria.* New York: Twayne Publishers, Inc., 1974.

Flew, Robert Newton. *Jesus and his Church: A Study of the Idea of the Ecclesia in the New Testament.* London: The Epworth Press, 1951.

Franck, Eskill. *Revelation Taught: The Paraclete in the Gospel of John.* Chicago: C.W.K., 1985.

Gangel, Kenneth O. and Warren S. Benson. *Christian Education: Its History and Philosophy.* Chicago: Moody Press, 1983.

Gillespie, Thowas W. "Pattern of Prophetic Speech in First Corinthians." *Journal of Biblical Literature* 97 (1978), 74-95.

Gonzalez, Justo L. *A History of Christian Thought,* Vol. 1, *From the Beginnings to the Council of Chalecdon in A.D. 415.* Nashville: Abingdon Press, 1970.

Graham, Holt H. "Gospel According to St. Mark." *Anglican Theology Review: Supplemental Series* 7 (1976), 43-55.

Grayston, Kenneth. "A Problem of Translation: the Meaning of Parakaleo, Paraklesis in the New Testament." *Scripture Bulletin,* 11 (1979), 27-31.

Grimes, Howard. "Theological Foundations for Christian Education." *An Introduction to Christian Education.* Ed. Marvin J. Taylor. Nashville: Abingdon Press, 1966.

Grassi, Joseph A. *Jesus as Teacher: A New Testament Guide to Learning the Way.* Winona, Minnesota: St. Mary's, 1978.

Groome, Thomas H. *Christian Religious Education: Sharing Our Story and Vision.* San Francisco: Harper & Row, 1980.

Guhrt, Joachim. "Covenant." *New International Dictionary of New Testament Theology,* Vol. I. Ed. Colin Brown. Grand Rapids: Zondervan Publishing House, 1975.

Guthrie, Donald. *New Testament Introduction.* Illinois: InterVarsity Press, 1970.

Harnack, Adolf. *The Mission and Expansion of Christianity in the First Three Centuries,* trans. and ed. by James Moffatt. New York: G. P. Putnam's Sons, 1908.

Hay, Lewis S. "Galatians 5:13-26." *Interpretation* 33 (1979), 67-72.

Haykin, Michael A. G. "The Spirit of God: The Exegesis of 1 Corinthians 2:10-12 by Origen and Athanasius." *Scottish Journal of Theology* 35 (1982), 513-528.

Hawthorne, Gerald F., ed. *Current Issues in Biblical and atristic Interpretation.* Grand Rapids, Michigan: William B. Eerdmans, 1975.

Henderlite, Rachel. *The Holy Spirit in Christian Education.* Philadelphia: Westminster Press, 1964.

Higgins, A.J.B., ed. *New Testament Essays*. Manchester, England: The University Press of the University of Manchester, 1959.

Hinson, E. Glenn. *The Evangelization of the Roman Empire: Identity and Adaptability*. Macon, Georgia: Mercer University Press, 1981.

Horne, Herman Harrell. *Jesus the Master Teacher*. New York: Association Press, 1925.

_____. *The Philosophy of Christian Education*. New York: Fleming H. Revell, 1937.

Howe, Allan Henry. "The Teaching Jesus Figure in the Gospel of Mark: A Redaction-Critical Study in Markan Christology." Ph.D. dissertation, Northwestern University, 1978.

Hunter, Harold. "Tongues Speech: A Patristic Analysis." *Journal of the Evangelical Theological Society*, 23 (1980), 125-137.

Jacob, Edmond "Psyche." *Theological Dictionary of the New Testament*, Vol. I. Ed. Gerhard Kittel. Trans. by Geoffrey W. Bromiley. Grand Rapids: Wm. B. Eerdmans, 1964.

Jeremias, Joachim. *Jesus' Promise to the Nations*. Trans. By S. H. Hooke. London: SCM Press, 1958.

_____. *New Testament Theology*. New York: Scribner, 1971.

Jewett, P. K. "Holy Spirit." *Zondervan Pictoral Encyclopedia of the Bible*. Ed. Merrill C. Tenney. Grand Rapids: Zondervan Publishing House, 1976.

Johnston, George. "The Doctrine of the Holy Spirit in the New Testament." *Scottish Journal of Theology* 1 (1948), 47-55; 233-240.

_____. "The Prophetic Task of the Church." *Bulletin of the American Association of Theological Schools* (1962), 146-156.

_____. "'Spirit' and 'Holy Spirit' in the Qumram Literature." *New Testament Sidelights*, ed. H. K. McArthur. Hartford, Connecticut, 1960.

_____. *The Spirit-Paraclete in the Gospel of John*. Cambridge: University Press, 1970.

_____. "The Spirit-Paraclete in the Gospel of John." *Perspective* 9 (1968), 29-37.

Jones, Tom B. *The Silver-Platial Age*. Sandoval, New Mexico: Coronado Press, 1962.

Jungmann, Josef A. *The Early Liturgy*. Notre Dame, Indiana: University of Notre Dame Press, 1977.

Kalamaras, Archimandrite Meleties. *Didymus the Blind and the Holy Spirit*. Rigopoulos, Thessalonike, 1973.

Kamlah, Eberhard. "Spirit, Holy Spirit." *The International Dictionary of New Testament Theology*, Vol. III. Ed. Colin Brown. Grand Rapids: Zondervan Publishing House, 1975.

Kee, Howard Clark. *Christian Origins in a Sociological Perspective*. Philadelphia: Westminster Press, 1980.

Kelber, Werner H. *The Oral and Written Gospel: The Hermeneutics of Speaking and Writing in the Synoptic Tradition, Mark, Paul and Q*. Philadelphia: Fortress Press, 1983.

Kittel, Gerhard, ed. *Theological Dictionary of the New Testament*. Trans. Geoffrey W. Bromiley. Grand Rapids: Wm. B. Eerdmans Publishing Company, 1964.

Klappert, Bertold. "King, Kingdom." *New International Dictionary of New Testament Theology*, Vol. II. Ed. Colin Brown. Grand Rapids: Zondervan Publishing House, 1975.

Kleinknecht, Herman. "*Pneuma*." *Theological Dictionary of the New Testament*, Vol. II. Ed. Gerhard Kittel. Trans. Geoffrey W. Bromiley. Grand Rapids: Wm. B. Eerdmans, 1964.

Koch, Robert. "Spirit." *Bauer Encyclopedia of Biblical Theology*, Vol. III. Ed. Johannes B. Bauer. London: Sheed and Ward, 1970.

Kuhn, Harold B. "The Nature of Man." *The Zondervan Pictoral Encyclopedia of the Bible*, Vol. IV. Ed. Merrill C. Tenney. Grand Rapids: Zondervan Publishing House, 1976.

Kydd, A. N. *Charismatic Gifts in the Early Church: An Exploration into the Gifts of the Spirit During the First Three Centuries of the Christian Church*. Peabody, MA: Hendrickson Publishers, Inc., 1984.

Lampe, Geoffry W.H. *God as Spirit*. Oxford: Oxford University Press, 1977.

_____, ed. *The Cambridge History of the Bible* Vol 2. *The West From the Fathers to Reformation*. Cambridge: Cambridge University Press, 1969.

_____. *The Seal of the Spirit: A Study in the Doctrine of Baptism and Confirmation in the New Testament and the Fathers*. London: S.P.C.K., 1967.

Latourette, Kenneth Scott. *A History of Christianity* Vol. I, *Beginnings to 1500*. New York: Harper & Row, 1975.

LeBar, Lois E. *Education That is Christian*. Old Tappan, New Jersey: Revell, 1958.

Lee, James Michael. *The Flow of Religious Instruction*. Birmingham, Alabama: Religious Education Press, 1973.

_____. *The Shape of Religious Instruction*. Birmingham, Alabama: Religious Education Press, 1971.

_____. "To Change Fundamental Theory and Practice." *Modern Masters of Religious Education*. Ed. Marlene Mayr. Birmingham, Alabama: Religious Education Press, 1983.

_____. "The Authentic Source of Religious Instruction." *Religious Education and Theology*. Ed. Norma H. Thompson. Birmingham, Alabama: Religious Education Press, 1982.

Lightfoot, J. B. The Apostolic Fathers. Grand Rapids: Baker Book House, 1980.

Little, Sarah. "Theology and Religious Education." *Foundations for Christian Education in an Era of Change*. Ed. Marvin J. Taylor. Nashville: Abingdon Press, 1976.

Lohfink, Gerhard. *Jesus and Community: The Social Dimension of Christian Faith*. Philadelphia: Fortress Press, 1984.

MacMullen, Ramsay. *Christianizing the Roman Empire (A.D. 100-400)*. London: Yale University Press, 1984.

Magness, Lee. "Teaching and Learning in the Gospels: The Biblical Basis of Christian Education." *Religious Education Journal* 70 (1975), 629-635.

Manschreck, Clyde L. *A History of Christianity From Persecution to Uncertainity*. Englewood Cliffs, New Jersey: Prentice-Hall, Inc., 1974.

Makrakis, Apostolos. *Divine and Sacred Catechism: As Taught by the Holy Spirit and its Official Instruments from the Day of the Pentecost Until the Last Ecumenica Synod*. Chicago: Hellenic Christian Educational Society, 1946.

Mayr, Marlene, ed. *Modern Masters of Religious Education*. Birmingham, Alabama: Religious Education Press, 1983.

Meyer, Paul. "Holy Spirit in the Pauline Letters: A Contextual Exploration." *Interpretation* 33 (1979), 3-18.

Miller, Randolph Crump. *The Clue to Christian Education.* New York: Charles Scribner & Son, 1950.

_____. "The Holy Spirit in Christian Education." *Religious Education Journal* 57 (1964), 178-184; 237-238.

_____. "Theology in the Background." *Religious Education and Theology.* Ed. Norma H. Thompson. Birmingham, Alabama: Religious Education Press, 1982.

Minear, Paul S. *Images of the Church in the New Testament.* Philadelphia: The Westminster Press, 1960.

_____. *To Heal and to Reveal the Prophetic Vocation According to Luke.* New York: Seabury Press, 1976.

Mal, Hans J. *Identity and the Sacred.* New York: The Free Press, 1976.

Moltmann, Jurgen. *The Church in the Power of the Spirit.* New York: Harper & Row, 1975.

Moody, Dale. *Spirit of the Living God: The Biblical Concepts Interpreted in Context.* Philadelphia: Westminster Press, 1968.

Moule, Charles F.D. *The Holy Spirit.* Grand Rapids: Wm. B. Eerdmans, 1978.

Moule, H.C.G. *Person and Work of the Holy Spirit.* Grand Rapids, Michigan: Kregal Publications, 1977. [Reprint of 1890 ed. pub. by Hodder and Stoughton, London, under title *Vini Creator.*]

Muirhead, Jan A. *Education in the New Testament.* Monographs in Christian Education No. 2. New York: Association Press, 1965.

Munro, Winsome. "Authority and Subjection in Early Christian 'Paideia' with Particular Reference to the Pauline Corpus and 1 Peter." Ed.D. dissertation Columbia University, 1974.

Nock, Arthur Darby. *Early Gentile Christianity and Its Hellenistic Background.* New York: Harper & Row, 1964.

Opsahl, Paul D., ed. *The Holy Spirit in the Life of the Church.* Minneapolis: Augsbury Publishing House, 1978.

Pannenberg, Wolfhart, Avery Dulles and Carl E. Braaten. *Spirit, Faith, and Church.* Philadelphia: Westminster Press, 1970.

Papadopoulos, S. G. "Anthanasius of Alexandria on the Holy Spirit According to the Letters of Serapion." *Ekklesiastikos Pharos* 53 (1971), 33-70.

_____. *Fathers, Growth of the Church, Holy Spirit*. Athens, 1970.

Parmetier, M. "St. Gregory of Nyssa's Doctrine of the Holy Spirit." *Ekklesiastikoc Pharos* 58 (1976), 41-100; 387-444; 59 (1977), 323-429.

Pelikan, Jaroslav. *Development of Christian Doctrine: Some Historical Prolegomena*. London: Yale University Press, 1969.

Pittenger, Norman. *The Holy Spirit*. Philadelphia: The Pilgrim Press, 1974.

Procksch, Otto. *"'agios."* *Theological Dictionary of the New Testament*, Vol. I. Ed. Gerhard Kittel. Trans. by Geoffrey W. Bromiley. Grand Rapids: Wm. B. Eerdmans, 1964.

Quasten, Johannes, and Joseph C. Plumpe, eds. *Ancient Christian Writers*. Westminster, Maryland: The Newman Bookshop, 1946.

Roberts, Alexander, and James Donaldson, eds. *The Ante-Nicene Fathers*, 10 Vols. Grand Rapids: William B. Eerdmans, 1956.

Rood, Wayne R. *Understanding Christian Education*. Nashville: Abingdon Press, 1970.

Schattenman, Johannes. *"Koinonia"*. *Theological Dictionary of the New Testament*, Vol. I. Ed. Gerhard Kittel. Trans. Geoffrey W. Bromiley. Grand Rapids: Wm. B. Eerdmans, 1964.

Schmidt, Karl L. *"ekklesia."* *Theological Dictionary of the New Testament*, Vol. III. Ed. Gerhard Kittel. Trans. Geoffrey W. Bromiley. Grand Rapids: Wm. B. Eerdmans, 1964.

Schrage, Wolfgana. *"Synagoge."* *Theological Dictionary of the New Testament*, Vol. VII. Ed. Gerhards Kittel. Trans. Geoffrey W. Bromiley. Grand Rapids: Wm. B. Eerdmans, 1964.

Schweizer, Eduard. *The Church as the Body of Christ*. Richmond, Virginia: John Knox Press, 1964.

_____. *"Pneuma."* *Theological Dictionary of the New Testament*, Vol. II. Ed. Gerhard Kittel. Trans. Geoffrey W. Bromiley. Grand Rapids: Wm. B. Eerdmans, 1964.

_____. *The Holy Spirit*, trans. by Reginald H. Fuller and Ilse Fuller. Philadelphia: Fortress Press, 1980.

Seebass, Horst. "Holy." *New International Dictionary of New Testament Theology*, Vol. II. Ed. Colin Brown. Grand Rapids: Zondervan Publishing House, 1975.

Shapland, C.R.B., trans. and ed. *The Letters of the Anthanasius Concerning the Holy Spirit*. London, 1957.

Sherrill, Lewis Joseph. *The Gift of Power*. New York: Macmillan Company, 1955.

_____. *The Rise of Christian Education*. New York: Macmillan, 1944.

Sjoberg, Erik. "*Pneuma*." *Theological Dictionary of the New Testament*, Vol. II. Ed. Gerhard Kittel. Trans. Geoffrey W. Bromiley. Grand Rapids: Wm B. Eerdmans, 1964.

Smart, James. *The Teaching Ministry of the Church: An Examination of the Basic Principles of Christian Education*. Philadelphia: Westminster Press, 1958.

Smith, D. Moody. "Johannine Christianity: Some Reflections on its Character and Delineation." *New Testament Studies* 21 (1975), 222-248.

Smith, H. Sheldon. *Faith and Nurture*. New York: Charles Scribner's Sons, 1941.

Smith, William A. *Ancient Education*. New York: Philosophical Library, 1955.

Stam, John E. "Charismatic Theology in the Apostolic Tradition of Hippolytus." *Current Issues in Biblical and Patristic Interpretation*. ed. Hawthorne. Grand Rapids, Michigan: Wm. B. Eerdmans, 1975.

_____. *Episcopacy in the Apostolic Tradition*. Basel: Friedrich Reinhardt Kommissionsverlag, 1969.

Stephanou, Eusebius A. "Charismata in the Early Church Fathers." *Greek Orthodox Theology Review* 21 (1976), 125-146.

Stephens, Peter. "The Gifts of the Spirit in the Church," *The Holy Spirit*. Ed. Dow Kirkpatrick. Nashville, Tennessee: Tidings, 1974.

Stronstad, Roger. "The Influence of the Old Testament on the Charismatic Theology of St. Luke." *Pneuma* 2 (1980), 32-50.

_____. *The Charismatic Theology of St. Luke*. Peabody, Massachusetts: Hendrickson Publishers, 1984.

Swete, Henry Barclay. *The Holy Spirit in the Ancient Church: A Study of Christian Teaching in the Age of the Fathers*. London: Macmillan & Company, 1912. [Reprinted Grand Rapids, Michigan: Baker Book House, 1966.]

Taylor, Marvin J., ed. *An Introduction to Christian Education*. Nashville: Abingdon Press, 1966.

_____, ed. *Foundations for Christian Education in an Era of Change*. Nashville: Abingdon Press, 1976.

Tenney, Merrill C., ed. *The Zondervan Pictorial Encyclopedia of the Bible*. Grand Rapids: Zondervan Publishing House, 1976.

Thompson, Norma N., ed. *Religious Education and Theology*. Birmingham, Alabama: Religious Education Press, 1982.

Turner, M. Max B. "Jesus and the Spirit in Lucan Perspective." *Tyndale Bulletin* 32 (1981), 3-42.

_____. "The Significance of Receiving the Spirit in Luke-Acts: A Survey of Modern Scholarship." *Trinity* 2 (1981), 131-158.

Ulich, Robert. *A History of Religious Education*. New York: New York University, 1968.

Van Dusen, Henry P. *Spirit, Son and Father: Christian Faith in the Light of the Holy Spirit*. New York: Charles Scribner's Sons, 1958.

von Campenhausen, Hans. *Ecclesiastical Authority and Spiritual Power in the Church of the First Three Centuries*. Trans. by J. A. Baker. London: Adam & Charles Black, 1969.

_____. *The Fathers of the Greek Church*. Trans. by Stanley Godman. New York: Pantheon Books, 1958.

_____. *Men Who Shaped the Western Church*. Trans. by Manfred Hoffman. New York: Harper & Row, 1964.

von Meding, Wichmann. "Temple." *New International Dictionary of New Testament Theology*, Vol. III. Ed. Colin Brown. Grand Rapids: Zondervan Publishing House, 1975.

Vorlander, Herwart. "*Anthropos*." *New International Dictionary of New Testament Theology*, Vol. I. Ed. Colin Brown. Grand Rapids: Zondervan Publishing House, 1975.

Wegenast, Klaus. "Teach." *New International Dictionary of New Testament Theology*, Vol. III. Ed. Colin Brown. Grand Rapids: Zondervan Publishing House, 1975.

Wibbing, Siegfried. "Body." *New International Dictionary of New Testament Theology*, Vol. I. Ed. Colin Brown. Grand Rapids: Zondervan Publishing House, 1975.

Wilkinson, John. *Egeria's Travels*. London: S.P.C.K., 1971.

Wilson, Carl W. *With Christ in the School of Disciple Building.* Grand Rapids: Zondervan, 1976.

Wilson, Clifford A. *Jesus the Master Teacher.* Grand Rapids: Baker, 1974.

Worley, Robert C. *Preaching and Teaching in the Earliest Church.* Philadelphia: Westminster, 1967.

Yates, J.E. *The Spirit and the Kingdom.* London: S.P.C.K., 1963.

Zuck, Roy B. *Spiritual Power in Your Teaching.* Chicago: Moody Press, 1972. [Original title *The Holy Spirit in Your Teaching.* Chicago: Scripture Press, 1963.]

EPILOG

Much has transpired in the twenty-five years since this dissertation was written. During that span of time I have spent my professional life divided between the parish and the academy. While I was still writing the dissertation, I began teaching part-time at the Church of God School of Theology (now the Pentecostal Theological Seminary); in 1995 I joined the faculty full-time. Since 1989, I have also served as the founding pastor of the New Covenant Church of God in Cleveland, Tennessee. These dual roles have been most fulfilling and complementary. However, the combined responsibilities have interfered with plans to revise this work for publication.

With the advent of on-demand printing it is now possible to release this volume without revisions to the original content. Clearly, the exegetical and theological references are dated; there has been a proliferation of scholarly works on the Holy Spirit during this interim. Pentecostal scholars have especially begun to address pneumatology including its Biblical foundations. Little has been added to Patristic treatments of the Spirit.

In the field of practical theology some attention has been given to contemporary charismatic/Pentecostal themes, but very little has been written on the role of the Holy Spirit in Christian discipleship. One exception would be Carol Lackey Hess's 1990 doctoral dissertation at Princeton Theological Seminary, *Educating in the Spirit*, and an article in Religious Education Journal drawn from the dissertation. However, Hess did not consider early Christian perceptions of the Holy Spirit (i.e., what the Scriptures or even church tradition say) in her constructive, practical theology.

It is my desire to update and expand the scope of this work. For now, I trust this dated and stylistically limited edition will be of some benefit to students of discipleship, patristics, and pneumatology.

Jackie David Johns
Cleveland, Tennessee
June, 2012

Cover Art

The cover art is an early Christian depiction of Pentecost. It was painted by a Syriac-Maronite monk named Rabbula during the 6th century as an illustration within an illuminated collection of the four Gospels. This *Rabbula Gospel Book* is one of the finest Byzantine works produced in Asia, and one of the earliest extant Christian manuscripts. The *Gospel* was completed and signed by Rabbula in 586 at the Monastery of St. John of Zagba, which is thought to have been in the region between Antioch and Apamea. Nothing else is known about Rabbula.

Note the scene is adorned by a large blue vault which represents the realms of heavenly glory. Above the arch are verdant trees which symbolize the garden of paradise. The Spirit of the Living God, depicted as a dove, descends from the heavens and enters earthly realms positioned directly over Mary who is speaking with the Apostles. Tongues of fire, another symbol of the Spirit, crown Mary and each of the Apostles.

Printed in Great Britain
by Amazon

56214363R00101